ANCIENTS AN

General Editor: Phiroze Vasunia, Professo

How can antiquity illuminate critical issues in the modern world? How does the ancient world help us address contemporary problems and issues? In what ways do modern insights and theories shed new light on the interpretation of ancient texts, monuments, artefacts and cultures? The central aim of this exciting new series is to show how antiquity is relevant to life today. The series also points towards the ways in which the modern and ancient worlds are mutually connected and interrelated. Lively, engaging, and historically informed, *Ancients and Moderns* examines key ideas and practices in context. It shows how societies and cultures have been shaped by ideas and debates that recur. With a strong appeal to students and teachers in a variety of disciplines, including classics and ancient history, each book is written for non-specialists in a clear and accessible manner.

THE ART OF THE BODY: ANTIQUITY AND ITS LEGACY • MICHAEL SQUIRE

DEATH: ANTIQUITY AND ITS LEGACY • MARIO ERASMO

DRAMA: ANTIQUITY AND ITS LEGACY • DAVID ROSENBLOOM

GENDER: ANTIQUITY AND ITS LEGACY • BROOKE HOLMES

LUCK, FATE AND FORTUNE: ANTIQUITY AND ITS LEGACY • ESTHER EIDINOW

MEDICINE: ANTIQUITY AND ITS LEGACY • CAROLINE PETIT

POLITICS: ANTIQUITY AND ITS LEGACY • KOSTAS VLASSOPOULOS

RACE: ANTIQUITY AND ITS LEGACY • DENISE EILEEN McCOSKEY

RELIGION: ANTIQUITY AND ITS LEGACY • JÖRG RÜPKE

SCIENCE: ANTIQUITY AND ITS LEGACY • PHILIPPA LANG

SEX: ANTIQUITY AND ITS LEGACY • DANIEL ORRELLS

SLAVERY: ANTIQUITY AND ITS LEGACY • PAGE DUBOIS

WAR: ANTIQUITY AND ITS LEGACY • ALFRED S. BRADFORD

ISBN: 978-1-84885-200-6 • www.ancientsandmoderns.com

'It may seem that physical sex has no history. (The human race does it, and needs to do it, and has always done it.) But actually there is a real need to consider how the very conceptualization of sex itself has changed, with its different boundaries, constructions and anxieties. Daniel Orrells' intelligent, coherent and intellectually exciting book offers just such a consideration. He takes the somewhat stagnant debate about ancient sexuality in a wholly new and profitable direction, and in so doing gives the field a real shake-up. Orrells is an excellent scholar and writes with wit and verve. In placing the history of the sexual act alongside the ideology of the body, of the person and of agency, his important – but never self-important – book has the potential to break out to a very wide readership.'

Simon Goldhill, Professor of Greek Literature and Culture,
University of Cambridge

'This is a spectacular book – learned, provocative, witty, highly readable and tightly argued. Daniel Orrells complicates and complements the arguments of Michel Foucault's *History of Sexuality*, showing that the sexual lives of the Greeks and Romans, however different from our own, are nonetheless central to modern notions of sexuality, sexual identity, and gender expression. Starting in the Renaissance, Orrells demonstrates that the reception of ancient Greek and Roman literature played a key role in the development of the psychoanalytic understanding of sexuality; that classical scholars, poets, and eventually nineteenth-century sexologists turned to "the classics" for vocabularies and methods of knowing about sex, and of thinking about sex as a form of knowing. This book is immensely informative and delightful to read, presenting complex debates in lucid, playful prose.'

Kirk Ormand, Professor of Classics, Oberlin College, author of
Controlling Desires: Sexuality in Ancient Greece and Rome

DANIEL ORRELLS is Reader in Classics and Ancient History at the University of Warwick. He is author of *Classical Culture and Modern Masculinity* (2011), co-editor of *African Athena: New Agendas* (2011), and author of a number of essays and articles on classical antiquity in modern intellectual history.

ANCIENTS AND MODERNS

SEX
ANTIQVITY AND ITS LEGACY

DANIEL ORRELLS

Published in 2015 by
I.B.Tauris & Co. Ltd
London • New York
www.ibtauris.com

ISBN: (HB): 978 1 84885 519 9
ISBN: (PB): 978 1 84885 520 5
eISBN: 978 0 85773 950 6

A full CIP record for this book is available from the British Library

Typeset in Garamond Pro by Ellipsis Digital Limited, Glasgow

CONTENTS

ACKNOWLEDGEMENTS

I would like to begin by thanking the two anonymous readers and Phiroze Vasunia, Series Editor, who all ploughed through and fastidiously critiqued an earlier draft of this book, liberally offering their knowledge for my consideration. Audiences at Cambridge, Durham, Oxford and London, and UC Davis and UC Irvine have provided me with further food for thought. These readers and listeners have, I hope, transformed and improved my work. I greatly appreciate the professionalism of Alex Wright and his team at I.B.Tauris. Denise Cowle has been a highly efficient and attentive copy-editor. This book could not have been written without the generosity and intelligence of good friends and interlocutors. Katie Fleming, Annelise Friesenbruch and Miriam Leonard have all been there through the process. I must likewise cite dear companions, Tasha Marhia and Amanda Tidman, as well as Tessa Roynon and Carl Hall, and Alistair Johnston, James Mack and Ben Winyard: thanks for keeping me buoyant, bright and breezy. Thank you also Jayne and Brian Orrells for all your love and support, and Kate Orrells for moving to a new sunnier world, right by Preston Park! To Rohan McCooty: 'Sagt es niemand, nur den Weisen, weil die Menge gleich verhöhnet'. Finally, I would like to record my gratitude to and appreciation of Aude Doody, whose warmth and wisdom in life *and* Latin literature have brought this book to its completion.

The context for much of my writing of this book was Berlin, Germany. I was kindly supported financially by an Alexander von Humboldt

Foundation Fellowship, under which scheme I was welcomed to the Winckelmann Institut under the auspices of Professor Luca Giuliani. I was also generously granted research leave by the University of Warwick.

FOREWORD

Ancients and Moderns comes to fruition at a propitious moment: 'reception studies' is flourishing, and the scholarship that has arisen around it is lively, rigorous, and historically informed; it makes us rethink our own understanding of the relationship between past and present. *Ancients and Moderns* aims to communicate to students and general readers the depth, energy, and excitement of the best work in the field. It seeks to engage, provoke, and stimulate, and to show how, for large parts of the world, Greco-Roman antiquity continues to be relevant to debates in culture, politics, and society.

The series does not merely accept notions such as 'reception' or 'tradition' without question; rather, it treats these concepts as contested categories and calls into question the illusion of an unmediated approach to the ancient world. We have encouraged our authors to take intellectual risks in the development of their ideas. By challenging the assumption of a direct line of continuity between antiquity and modernity, these books explore how discussions in such areas as gender, politics, race, sex, and slavery occur within particular contexts and histories; they demonstrate that no culture is monolithic, that claims to ownership of the past are never pure, and that East and West are often connected together in ways that continue to surprise and disturb many. Thus, *Ancients and Moderns* is intended to stir up debates about and within reception studies and to complicate some of the standard narratives about the 'legacy' of Greece and Rome.

All the books in *Ancients and Moderns* illustrate that *how* we think about the past bears a necessary relation to *who* we are in the present. At the same time, the series also seeks to persuade scholars of antiquity that their own pursuit is inextricably connected to what many generations have thought, said, and done about the ancient world.

Phiroze Vasunia

INTRODUCTION

Classical antiquity and the history of sexuality

Michel Foucault's *Histoire de la sexualité* has not only been at the centre of debates in classical scholarship for almost 30 years, but has also ensured that the study of the ancient world has become central to the study of gender history and the history of sexuality more generally. His *Histoire* has ensured that understanding ancient sexual norms and transgressions has become a profoundly important project for understanding *today's* rights and wrongs of sexual behaviour. And yet, because Foucault and some of those historians who have followed him have been so eager to emphasise the ruptures and discontinuities in the history of sexuality (the historically constructed nature of our experiences of desire and passion), the reception of Foucault's work has often become a battle between those 'constructivists' who have supported and qualified his work and those others, called 'essentialists', who have continually debated whether we can historicise sexual desire. *Sex: Antiquity and its Legacy* does not propose to intervene in these debates directly. Rather than try to suggest that ancient and modern sexualities are somehow fundamentally the same, or somehow fundamentally different, this book contends that the reception of classical antiquity was at the heart of the nineteenth- and early twentieth-century systematisation and taxonomisation of sexuality; a cultural landscape which we still inhabit today. This book will argue that sexology and psychoanalysis emerged out of a longer history of modern writings since the Renaissance, which turned back to the ancient world to understand the nature of sexual desire. Rather than attempt a history of 'real-life' sexual practices and behaviours, this book will argue that the emergence of scientific discourses in the nineteenth century, which sought to turn sexual desire into an object of knowledge, came from a history of writings interested in what it might mean to know about sex.

Between 1976 and 1984, Michel Foucault, the French historian, philosopher and political activist, published a trilogy of books called *Histoire de la sexualité*, which ensured that modern sexuality could not be understood without thinking about ancient Greek and Roman societies. In the first volume, *La Volonté de savoir* (translated as *The Will to Knowledge*), Foucault argued that the history of sexuality should not be viewed in terms of a pattern of a period of expressive liberalism succeeded by an era of repression, which eventually bubbled over into another period of sexual permissiveness. While many historians writing prior to Foucault in the 1960s drew up this morphology, Foucault himself was very critical of this model, which he called the 'repressive hypothesis'.[1] Such historiography, Foucault saw, was often a product of the 'sexual revolution' of the 1960s: freedom of sexual expression led to historians writing more openly and frequently about sex, with the presumption that the historical moment in which they were writing was more liberated than the Victorian age that had preceded them. Many counter-cultural movements of the 1960s had stressed that political emancipation was best embodied in sexual liberation: if one knew the truth about one's sexuality, if one was freed from old-fashioned, prudish mores and constraints, one could, it was argued, be more truly oneself.[2] But knowing yourself (be it through organised women's groups which sought to talk positively and openly about female sexual pleasure, or the ritual of coming out as a gay person in the context of a homophobic community) did not always seem so revolutionary to Foucault. Rather, the will to know one's sexuality in the 1960s was actually the latest chapter in a longer history of knowing about sexual desires and pleasures, which Foucault dated back to the mid- to late-Victorian period. Just as other historians sought to distinguish the 1960s from the repressive nineteenth century, so

Foucault perceived a fundamental historical continuity: the sexual revolution had emerged out of that previous period. The diverse clusters of sexualities which affirmed themselves from the 1960s through the 1980s were identities that had already more or less been demarcated and described by certain nineteenth-century legal and medical texts. As Foucault argued in *The Will to Knowledge*, the Victorian period was not one that cast a curtain over the subject of sexuality. Certain nineteenth-century states across Western Europe did bring in legislation against same-sex sexual practices, and nineteenth-century churches certainly were very influential over the sexual behaviours of their congregations. And yet, this historical period, Foucuault argued, witnessed an explosive proliferation of debate about sexuality. The nineteenth century, it seemed, couldn't stop discussing sex. Indeed, Foucault went further than that: the nineteenth century *invented* the notion that one had a sexuality – that in a sense one simply *is* one's sexual preference. The idea that the sex of the person with whom one has sex should determine the identity category that one inhabits is an idea, Foucault thought, that originated at this time. And for Foucault, the invention of the category of the 'homosexual' most clearly evidenced this historical process. These are the words in which Foucault famously put it:

> As defined by the ancient civil of canonical codes, sodomy was a category of forbidden acts; their perpetrator was nothing more than the juridical subject of them. The nineteenth-century homosexual became a personage, a past, a case history, a childhood. [. . .] [His sexuality] was everywhere present in him: at the root of all his actions because it was their insidious and indefinitely active principle; written immodestly on his face and body because it was a secret that always gave itself away. [. . .] [T]he psychological, psychiatric, medical category of homosexuality was constituted from the moment it was characterized – [Carl Otto] Westphal's famous article of 1870 on 'contrary sexual sensations' can stand as its date of birth – less by a type of sexual relations than by a certain quality of sexual sensibility, a certain way of inverting the masculine and the feminine in oneself.

> Homosexuality appeared as one of the forms of sexuality when it was transposed from the practice of sodomy onto a kind of interior androgyny, a hermaphroditism of the soul. The sodomite had been a temporary aberration; the homosexual was now a species'.[3]

Now, Foucault seems to be saying here that the homosexual as such came into existence in the year 1870 CE . . . a remarkably strange claim to make, since it seems obvious that certain men and women have always enjoyed sexual relations with their own sex. But Foucault was not actually making such a case. Rather, he argued for a 'veritable discursive explosion' in the discussion of sex, using a specifically authorised vocabulary that codified where one could talk about it and with whom. He suggested that this desire to talk about sex emerged from the ritualised confession of the Roman Catholic Church, which called for its followers to admit to their sinful desires and actions. At the same time, civil and canonical codes drawn up by state rulers outlined strict guidelines around sexual practices inside and outside marriage: adultery was particularly heavily punished in medieval and early-modern societies as wealthy and powerful families sought to maintain their hold over feudal structures. By the start of the eighteenth century, the control that religious authorities had over the discourse about sexual pleasure was being eroded, while there was an emergence of 'a political, economic, and technical incitement to talk about sex'.[4]

Foucault relates how a whole range of new intellectual disciplines became organised, with self-appointed experts who might be able to speak both moralistically and rationally about sex. It was in the eighteenth century that governments came to see their 'subjects' or 'people' rather as a 'population', whose birth and death rates, marriages, and mental and physical health needed careful management and surveillance. While older church and civil codes legislated on the married couple and how it should procreate for the good of the community, now, by the mid-nineteenth century, civil servants, lawyers, criminologists and medical doctors sought to classify and taxonomise the 'sexual perverts' and 'deviants' who put at risk the health of society. The disciplines of biology, psychology, sociology, anthropology and criminology became institutionalised within universities, which then fed into government policy. As Foucault put it,

> all those minor perverts whom nineteenth-century psychiatrists entomologized by giving them strange baptismal names became scientific 'objects of knowledge': there were Krafft-Ebing's zoophiles and zooerasts, Rohleder's auto-monosexualists; and later mixoscopophiles, gynecomasts, presbyophiles, sexo-aesthetic inverts, and dyspareunist women.[5]

For many nineteenth-century experts, it seemed, everyone had to have a knowable sexuality, in order to be known. It was not simply the Church who named the subject, but medicine and law that gave the population their 'strange baptismal names'. So, then, zoophiles and zooerasts were people who enjoyed sex with animals; auto-monosexualists could only have sex with themselves (that is, masturbate); mixoscopophiles liked watching other people having sex; gynecomasts were men whose perverse pleasures were signalised by their overly developed breasts; presbyophiles had sex with old(er) people; sexo-aesthetic inverts were stimulated by dressing in the clothes of the opposite sex; and dyspareunist women found sexual intercourse painful. And this (as we shall soon see) was only a selection of the terms that were used to categorise the population.

But, most importantly, as Foucault had outlined (in the paragraph quoted above), one's sexuality 'was everywhere present in' the subject, 'at the root of all his actions' because it was the 'insidious and indefinitely active principle' that shaped his personality – who she or he was. Foucault highlighted the publication of a late nineteenth-century pornographic, possibly autobiographical, book called *My Secret Life*, which detailed in comprehensive and explicit detail the sex life of a Victorian gentleman.[6] Whereas previous historians had argued that the very act of writing such a book demonstrated Victorian hypocrisy, Foucault saw this and other late-Victorian pornography as a product of the medico-legal obsession with the elaborate discourse of sex in the nineteenth century. And so Foucault's statement that, from

1870, 'the homosexual was now a species' should make more sense: under older 'civil and canonical codes', non-procreative forms of sex outside marriage were punishable as sins and infringements of legislation: the man who committed 'sodomy' (which covered various sorts of sexual acts in English law), was someone who had succumbed to a sin and had thereby committed a crime which demanded punishment, whereas the 'homosexual' was someone whose sexuality explained everything about his self.[7]

In the second and third volumes of *Histoire de la sexualité*, Foucault went on to analyse the sexual norms and transgressions of ancient Greece and Rome. Turning away from a 'history of the desiring subject', Foucault focused on a history of the ancient discourses on sexual appetites, practices and norms.[8] In this way, he sought to demonstrate how different ancient society was from the modern discourse of taxonomisation. Greeks, Foucault argued, did not categorise people according to the person with whom they had sex (homo-, hetero- or bisexual). Instead, an ancient Greek man was defined according to how well or how badly he could control his appetites: 'what differentiates men from one another [. . .] is not so much the type of objects towards which they are oriented, nor the mode of sexual practice they prefer; above all, it is the intensity of that practice'.[9] Foucault examined a series of classical Greek texts which underlined how pleasure could be made useful for Greek society more broadly. Foucault's Romans, on the other hand, were interested in how sexual desires could be integrated into a more general regimen for the care of the self, in the face of an increasingly despotic imperial world which left many bereft of their social and political powers.[10] While classical societies did often have strict norms and transgressions regarding sex, these did not revolve around classifying male subjects around a particular sexuality. One particular concern that ancient male writers continually evinced in Foucault's account was a concern with phallic penetration: sex was acceptable for a man (regardless of the sex of the partner) as long as he was the penetrating partner.[11]

The second and third volumes of *Histoire de la sexualité*, unsurprisingly, were widely read by classicists. Many were excited by his interpretations of texts, and applied his readings to other works he had not included. Other classicists were more critical and perceived serious gaps in Foucault's knowledge: when he talked about *sexualité* it seemed that he only mostly ever meant men's sexuality. He did not attempt to excavate anything about the actual feelings and behaviours of women, slaves and children. Of course, disinterring such emotions and actions from texts written almost entirely by male authors would have been extremely difficult, and yet Foucault did not engage, for example, with the corpora, albeit fragmented, left by Sappho and Sulpicia.[12] Furthermore, Foucault's history dealt heavily in prescription, protocol and procedure. Foucault rarely considered how ancient writers satirised or questioned the rules and regulations their societies organised around sexual pleasure. Foucault's ancients emerged as an earnest, philosophical bunch.[13] One of the most heated debates among classicists to have emerged from Foucault's work was between David Halperin and Amy Richlin. Halperin's work on the socially constructed nature of sexuality was greatly influenced by Foucault. In the face of criticism, Halperin sought to clarify Foucault's sometimes difficult prose and oblique interpretations of texts, teaching classicists much about ancient Greek male sexuality while doing so. At the same time, Richlin found Foucault's Greeks problematic, and the Romans especially so, because Foucault had not recognised at all the ancient persecution suffered by men who had sex with other men. Foucault, so well known for his political activism through the 1960s and 1970s had, it seemed, forgotten to think about the homophobia and discrimination gay men were forced to endure in ancient times, along with the subcultures they might have cemented in order to cope. Rather than arguing for the historical and constructed nature of sexuality, Richlin contended that classicists should be identifying the homophobic prejudices that supported Roman society, just as other feminist classicists were, at the same time, revealing the misogyny at the heart of ancient patriarchal structures. Halperin's and Richlin's debate challenged classicists to think very hard about ancient notions of social and sexual hierarchy, subculture and equality.[14] Most recently, James Davidson has joined the field to question Foucault's construction of ancient paranoia about phallic penetration, to argue that 'Greek love' between males was not simply pederastic, but could operate between two adult male partners.[15] The work of these classicists has provoked scholars to think seriously about a very wide range of ancient media beyond the canon – erotic and pornographic texts, images and objects – which had often been deemed subliterary and insignificant: the debates around ancient sex witnessed some of the most sustained reflection about what ancient literature might teach us about social history.

Sex: Antiquity and its Legacy does not seek to add to these discussions about Foucault's descriptions of ancient sexual discourses. Instead, this book re-examines Foucault's account of the invention of sexuality in the nineteenth century. In particular, it argues for the centrality of ancient texts for those modern discursive descriptions of the sexual. That is not to say, though, that *Sex: Antiquity and its Legacy* will argue against Foucault that there is a basic historical continuity between ancient and modern ideas about sexuality – that nineteenth-century medicine was applying ancient notions in a modern context. The reader will have have noticed that the strange-looking words – the 'baptismal names' – that Foucault had found in the pages of nineteenth-century medical texts all have Greek or Latin roots. Of course, the languages of different sciences had, by the end of the nineteenth century, used the classical languages for several centuries, yet this book does not seek to itemise the etymological roots of the modern scientific language of sex. Rather, *Sex: Antiquity and its Legacy* examines how the late nineteenth- and early twentieth-century sciences of sexual desire, sexology and psychoanalysis emerged out of a long history of thinking about what it means to know about desire by turning to ancient texts. This book, then, is not a history of the classical tradition, a history of how ancient notions of sex influenced, impacted and set the contours for modern ideas on the subject. Rather, it contends for the centrality of classical reception studies for the history of modern sexuality more generally: this book examines how the appropriation of certain classical texts facilitated and helped to authorise the modern medical systematisation of sexuality.

Sex: Antiquity and Its Legacy hinges on the publication of a very important book. In 1886, a highly respected Austro-German psychiatrist called Richard von Krafft-Ebing published a forensic reference book for other psychiatrists, doctors and legal professionals, in which he assembled numerous case studies of sexual pathology. He called his work *Psychopathia Sexualis: eine klinisch-forensische Studie*, and it was a marked success: it had gone through numerous editions and translations by the beginning of the twentieth century and became one of the most widely read and quoted texts of sexology in the nineteenth and early twentieth centuries. Its significance was such that it mapped out many of the categories of sexual identity with which we still live today, as Krafft-Ebing standardised and popularised terms such as homosexual, fetish, sadist and masochist.[16] While the Latin of the title advertised the learned nature of the book, much of the content of the book itself was also in Latin. As Krafft-Ebing wrote, 'in order that unqualified persons should not become readers', he 'saw himself compelled to choose a title understood only by the learned, and also, where possible, to express himself in *terminis technicis*'.[17] Of course, Latin was the standard language of expert expression in medicine and the natural sciences, in that Latin, along with Greek, provided the basis for so much technical terminology. But precisely how did Latin come to provide the technical terms for sex in Krafft-Ebing's magisterial tome? How did Latin become the authoritative language of the science of sex? What role did the sexual vocabulary of ancient Rome play in the development of nineteenth-century sexology? These are the questions that the first half of the book addresses.

If we take a glance at Krafft-Ebing's bibliography in *Psychopathia Sexualis*, we get the beginnings of an answer. Along with other sexologicial and criminological works, Krafft-Ebing *only* lists a book called *Geschichte der Lustseuche, erster Theil: die Lustseuche im Alterthume* by a physician called Julius Rosenbaum, and *Darstellungen aus der Sittengeschichte Roms* by Ludwig Friedländer. Alongside an important nineteenth-century history of ancient Rome, then, the only book Krafft-Ebing consults, is one called (in English) *The History of the Plague of Lust, Part One: The Plague of Lust in Antiquity*. While the history of sexology has, since Foucault, received much scholarly attention, the importance of classical antiquity for the development of sexology has received no detailed examination. *Sex: Antiquity and its Legacy* uncovers a history of ancient, Renaissance, early-modern and modern Latin texts that made it possible for Krafft-Ebing to write in Latin in order to write about sex, at the end of the nineteenth century. This book traces out a history of Latin texts about sex which enabled the science of sex to seem and sound authoritative by speaking in Latin.

To delve further into these issues, this book begins in the Italian Renaissance when the poetry of Catullus was exercising the finest philological minds. It was the sexual nature of some of his poems that interested many of his readers. As Chapter I will examine, a certain poem particularly intrigued his readers: Poem 16, as we now number it, in Catullus' poetry book threatens to 'fuck' two of his readers 'in the ass and in the mouth' because they 'think that [his] verses are a bit soft'. Nevertheless, Catullus claims, 'it is proper for a pious poet to be chaste himself', but he continues, 'it is not at all necessary for his little verses to be'. Catullus' aggressive defence of his poetry was a paradoxical gesture: just as his poetry supposedly reflected his sexually transgressive behaviour in the eyes of two of his readers, so he threatens to 'fuck' these two readers 'in the ass and the mouth' if they cannot see that his words do not reflect his actions. Catullus' rape of these readers' mouths reflects Catullus control over their mouths, over what they say. His threat of anal and oral penile insertion demonstrates his desire for authority over language, the authority to say whatever he wants in his poetry.

Catullus' poem reflects a very Roman concern about the impenetrability of the body of the free-born adult male Roman citizen. To participate in a sexual act for such a subject was simply to assert his authority, position and status in society. The Roman man penetrated but was not to be penetrated – the meaning behind the aspersion about Catullus' softness in Poem 16. The activeness of the Roman man, or the *vir*, was to be contrasted with the passivity of women, slaves and boys. For a man to take the passive role in sex was to unman himself. To have sex as a *vir* meant exercising one's masculine power and authority.[18] Seeing sex as a discourse on male power appeared especially interesting to a young Italian poet looking for patronage from the Medicis. In the 1420s, Antonio Beccadelli circulated copies of his *libellus* of sexually explicit Latin epigrams written in the style of Catullus and Martial, under the Catullan defence that what a poet writes in his poetry does not reflect who he really is. A flurry of debate and consternation among Italian humanists ensued. Chapter I of this book looks at Beccadelli's *The Hermaphrodite* and its reception among contemporary readers in order to uncover what it meant to write about sex in Latin during the Italian Renaissance. Who had the authority to use the sexual language of Catullus and Martial? Indeed, could the Roman discourse of male sexual power be used authoritatively by the Renaissance poet, and to what effect? What did it say about the poet and what he wanted? What could such Latin tell about the poet's sexual desires?

In Chapter II, we turn to the longer-term impact of the sexual Renaissance Latin epigram. Later in the fifteenth century, the famous humanist scholar Marsilio Ficino set about translating all of Plato's dialogues, including the *Symposium* in its entirety for the first time into Latin, and produced his own sympotic commentary on the *Symposium*, entitled *De Amore*. But, despite Ficino's attempts, other humanists still thought the classics were a highly dangerous source of information. In particular, many worried about the possibility that women might read and misinterpret the ancient texts. Such was the concern by the early-modern period when, in Western Europe, certain male and female intellectuals began to question the masculinism of classical humanism. The poetry and philosophy of female figures such as the courtesan Tullia d'Aragona and other women able to write Latin was seen as especially problematic in the male-dominated world of European humanism.

Chapter II examines the response to such female voices in the form of the *Satyra Sotadica*, published in the early 1660s by Nicolas Chorier, an eminent French lawyer and historian, in which a classically educated woman Tullia (her name a clear allusion to Tullia d'Aragona), teaches her younger cousin, Octavia, the arts of sex. In this dialogue, written in Latin, the two cousins quote and re-work famous moments in male-authored, golden-age Roman poetry and turn the classical canon into a riotously erotic cornucopia. Just as male humanists were so worried about women's (in)abilities to read Latin and Greek, so Chorier turned these concerns into a pornographic pleasure-fest for his educated, Latinate male readership. At the same time, Chorier was also responding to contemporary debates, also conducted for the most part in neo-Latin prose, about the mechanics of the body. Seventeenth-century science had become very interested in understanding the desires that drove human action and endeavour. These secularising discussions, which turned back to Lucretius' mantra that Venus was behind everything, offered Chorier the opportunity to suggest that it was an understanding of the *sexual* body that should be at the centre of these inquiries. As in Chapter I, the *Satyra Sotadica* confronted its readers with the question of how Latin confers authority to speak and know about sex. Whereas Beccadelli's book circulated among male Italian humanists, the *Satyra Sotadica* fantasised (anxiously) about what would happen if women had command over Latin.

Chapter III examines how Beccadelli's and Chorier's literary works become the basis for a scholarly work on ancient sexual practices which, in turn, provided a technical vocabulary for the study of venereal disease and sexology in the nineteenth century. We focus on the moment when, in 1824, Beccadelli's *Hermaphrodite* was republished and furnished with an in-depth essay in Latin, appended to the edition by a philologist called Friedrich Karl Forsberg, explaining the meaning of the sexual references in Beccadelli's poetry. Forsberg's edition emerged at a time when ancient sexual mores and behaviours were attracting wide interest, with the remarkable discoveries of numerous bizarrely constructed phallic images and artefacts at Pompeii and Herculaneum in the middle of the eighteenth century which had produced a market in collecting ancient erotica and curiosa. Many of these objects also found their way into large museums in European cities, only to find themselves, however, cordoned off away from the public, kept hidden in a private cabinet. By the end of the eighteenth century, literary collections of priapic and obscene epigrams were also appearing, which included a not altogether satisfactory selection of Beccadelli's poetry. The siphoning off of these ancient phallic artefacts, along with gentlemanly enthusiasm for collecting phallica – which was also reflected in the collections of priapic poetry in print – provided a corpus of texts and objects that would provide classicists with a discrete, distinct object of study. One of the first, earnest studies into ancient sexuality in the nineteenth century was, then, Forberg's essay that supplemented his edition of Beccadelli's poetry book. But Forberg's essay was itself a collection: it comprised essentially an anthology of ancient texts, many of which were epigrams, larded with citations from the *Satyra Sotadica* proving his explanations of Latin terms for various sexual acts.

Forberg seemed keen on writing a scholarly work at a time when classical studies (or *Altertumswissenschaft*) was becoming institutionalised and professionalised in German universities and beyond, and he used Latin as an authorititative language in order to taxonomise ancient sexual behaviour. At the same time, Forberg characterised himself as the god Priapus as he realised that many readers would have been amused and even titillated by his work. One of his closest contemporary readers did not seem interested, however, in Forberg's ironic side. Julius Rosenbaum, a physician from Halle, used Forberg's essay to write an even longer, more compendious work on the ancient 'plague of lust', as he called it, back to which could be traced the origins of modern venereal disease. The sexual terms – which peppered Catullus and Martial's epigrams and were taken up by Beccadelli, along with the racy Latin discourses about sex in Chorier's *Satyra Sotadica*, all analysed minutely by the philologist Forberg – were Latin terms which became the technical terminology that organised Rosenbaum's book which, in turn, provided the vocabulary of expertise for Krafft-Ebing's *Psychopathia Sexualis* in 1886, as Chapter III traces out. Forberg's compilation of a sexual lexicon ended up as Krafft-Ebing's authoritative compendium of Latinate sexual pathology. Catullus' poem had wittily asked its readers to think about what it means to use sexual language in Latin commandingly, whereas Krafft-Ebing, it seemed, was able to use such language with authority at the end of the nineteenth century thanks to the professionalisation of classical studies and the medicalisation of ancient Rome's sexual vocabulary.

In Forberg's essay and Rosenbaum's book, the Latin and the Greek languages were mined for their riches so that the former could list sexual acts enjoyed by the ancients and the latter could expound on the nasty conditions that resulted from participating in those sexual acts. With Krafft-Ebing, however, the sexual vocabulary of ancient Roman culture became subsumed into a discourse on sexuality: these Latin terms became the signifying acts of underlying identities. For Krafft-Ebing, one's internal sexual identity affected every aspect of one's life. And what should count as sexual activity could be expressed in Latin, since Latin, in *Psychopathia Sexualis*, came to be the literal expression of what sex could be. Beccadelli's epigrams questioned their readers as to how one might write about sex in Latin with authority, whereas Chorier's *Satyra Sotadica* worried and fantasised about what could be said and known about sex if women had command over Latin. Finally, it seemed with Krafft-Ebing, on the other hand, that Latin had become a truly scientific language for talking about sex thanks to the efforts of classical philology and the study of venereal disease earlier in the nineteenth century. At last, sex could be known, and Latin could be used as an instrument of control by the doctor over the populace as he authoritatively categorised the sexual identities of the modern world.

But, as Simon Goldhill puts it, 'sexual knowing, above all, finds it hard to escape the work of fantasy and memory, the confusion of desire, and the seduction of retold narratives'.[19] Knowing sex is not simply knowing 'the facts of life'. 'There is no zero-degree language of sexuality', Goldhill continues. 'There is no literalness from which euphemism is a divagation, no register of usage that is not marked precisely as a register'.[20] Whereas some of Krafft-Ebing's readers felt that he had given them a name and uncovered the truth of sex, others certainly did not. And it was the supposed literalness of Krafft-Ebing's Latin that troubled one of his closest readers at the end of the nineteenth century. I mentioned that Krafft-Ebing's book was the hinge upon which this book turned, and this is where it turns in its second half: Chapter IV focuses on the Oxford-educated classicist, Renaissance scholar and man of letters John Addington Symonds, who not only was one of Krafft-Ebing's most learned contemporary readers, but also countered Krafft-Ebing's supposedly scientific Latinate knowledge by turning to the authority of ancient Greek history and literature. As we will see, Krafft-Ebing not only relied on the Latin language, but he also saw his own times, at the *fin de siècle*, as reflected in the history of the decadent and debauched Roman Empire. John Addington Symonds, on the other hand, sought to resist Krafft-Ebing's pathologisation of the homosexual, in particular, by trying to write a history of Greek love which provided a counter-example to Krafft-Ebing's sick perverts. Symonds earnestly sought to make a real contribution to scientific research on sex in the nineteenth century by turning to ancient Greek literature. But Symonds was writing at a time of intense debate about how history should be written. The nineteenth-century was intensely self-conscious about its place in history.[21] In particular, what did it mean for Symonds as a homosexual, wondered Symonds, to write a history of same-sex desire? Did his sexual desires make him more authoritative and knowledgeable about this subject? Symonds doubted it: while the Greeks might have offered a noble image of love between men in the face of nineteenth-century pathologisation, Symonds was cynical about the possibilities of reliving Greek love in the modern age. As his history of Greek love was to explore, the ancient Athenians themselves looked back in wonder at Achilles and Patroclus.

Just as Symonds sought to use the latest historical research to write about Greek love, he was also aware that knowing about his sexuality was also fantasising about the Greeks. Turning back to classical antiquity did not guarantee that one could – literally – know about one's sexual desires in the present. Ancient Greek, then, did not provide some sort of secret code for all nineteenth-century homosexuals to communicate with one another without fear of blackmail or prosecution.[22] Rather, Symonds was writing at a time when numerous different theories about sexual desire between males were circulating, along with several different appropriations of ancient Greece in order to defend those erotic relations. But, if it was difficult enough for a wealthy, socially privileged Oxford-educated man such as Symonds to know about Greek love, then the situation for women at the end of the nineteenth century might be seen as even trickier, as Chapter V examines: it was only at the end of the nineteenth century and into the beginning of the twentieth, that women were beginning to surmount man-made hurdles that excluded them from university education. And so a history of love between Greek or even between Roman women, a kind of equivalent to Symonds' work, never appeared. Instead, the ancient image of the tribad, the woman with an enlarged clitoris who enjoyed rubbing and penetrating other women, dominated medical accounts of sex between women in the nineteenth century. While Symonds thought that an educational ethos informed male Greek pederasty, he did not allow ancient Greek women the same privilege and authority. Sex between women signified decadence and degeneration, the tribad a corrupt imitation of a real man. This stereotype became so widespread in *fin-de-siècle* descriptions of women who were attracted to other women that it even influenced classicists who were investigating the writing of a newly discovered ancient Greek poet, Herodas, an Alexandrian writer of the third century BCE. Walter Headlam, a Cambridge don, got the chance to work on the papyrus that had recently been brought back from British-occupied Egypt. The subject matter of Herodas' poems was risqué, the sixth poem especially so, being a dramatic little dialogue between two women in search of a dildo. As this chapter examines, Headlam picked up on the innuendoes about sexual rubbing in the poem, which led him to see Herodas' ladies as two tribads. Just as ancient descriptions of the tribad framed nineteenth-century discourse on sex between two women, so this discourse, in turn, influenced how a Cambridge classicist would read female same-sex sexuality in Hellenistic Greek literature of the third century BCE, even though the tribad does not appear in ancient literature before the second century CE.

Against the figure of the tribad, nineteenth-century classicists consciously constructed an image of a pure and chaste schoolmistress, Sappho. Symonds' scholarship also depicted Sappho as a virtuous and unblemished woman, and his adaptations of her poetry were very widely read. Just when women who were sexually attracted to other women were seen as degenerate imitators of real men, so male writers at the end of the nineteenth century, like Symonds, enjoyed appropriating Sappho's love poetry addressed to other women in order to voice their own desires. It was in this context that two women, writing as a man, wrote their own Sappho-inspired poetry. Chapter V concludes by looking at two poems by 'Michael Field', the pen name of two women, Katherine Bradley and Edith Cooper, who were aunt and niece and also lovers. The voice of 'Michael Field' sought to counter the negative nineteenth-century images of intense affection between women and disconnect female same-sex sexuality from the phallic stereotypes that were circulating at the *fin de siècle*.

Sappho's poetry only existed – and still only exists – in frustratingly tattered fragments, a situation that has encouraged poets since antiquity to fill in the gaps however they see fit. The result has been that numerous Sapphos have been invented and written. Bradley and Cooper used Sappho's fragments as points of departure to write their own full poems and so imagined an ancient Lesbos where Sappho might have lived. In this way their poetry provided them with an alternative space of fantasy away from contemporary scientific discourse. Krafft-Ebing's *Psychopathia Sexualis*, on the other hand, consisted of a collection of narratives provided by the public describing their sex lives. The truth of the historical autobiography was crucial to Krafft-Ebing's enterprise. And just as he was interested in individual histories, so he also saw the historical moment, in which he lived, as a decadent and luxorious ancient Rome about to plunge into savagery and barbarism. Classical historical scholarship on imperial Rome profoundly informed Krafft-Ebing's research into sexual pathology. Chapter VI, however, examines how classical myth became central to the science of Freudian psychoanalysis from the end of the nineteenth century onwards. In contrast to Krafft-Ebing's historical biographies, Freud became very interested in what he called the 'prehistory' of the psyche, that is the period before conscious memory, a time when children supposedly played out the fates of Oedipus and Narcissus in their heads, fantastical fates which would have a formative impact on their sexualities into adulthood.

This final chapter thus brings together the issues explored in *Sex: Antiquity and its Legacy*. The first half of this book traces out how the literary language of ancient Rome, via the Renaissance and early-modern Latin tradition, becomes co-opted for the uses of sexual science in the nineteenth century. The relationship between literary and scientific discourse profoundly informed Freud's development of psychoanalysis: the stories of Greek myth provided the truth of our sexual identities. But even if Freud did not, like Krafft-Ebing, rely on nineteenth-century historical scholarship about the decadence of ancient Rome, his theorisation of sexuality can also be traced back to the late eighteenth-century fascination with the phallic artefacts that emerged in Herculaneum and Pompeii. Richard Payne Knight, an English collector of antiquities, became very interested in these finds and, in the 1780s, published a book that argued that these phallic objects were actually remnants of an original religious worship of the phallus, which represented early man's enlightened veneration of the logic of the natural world. Payne Knight depicted modern man's ancestors as philosophical individuals who offered worship to a deity that combined male and female attributes in celebration of nature's generativity. Images of hermaphrodites also populated the writings of late eighteenth-century German writers, who argued that androgyny, a mixing of the two sexes, was a symbol of ideal beauty. As Chapter VI examines, Freud inherited this intellectual history. Freud argued that the child's early bond with his or her mother was so strong that he or she never truly forgets it. The young child felt completely satisfied with its mother. However, when boys and girls discover that some beings have penises and others, like their mother, do not, they are inducted into the Oedipus complex, which turns them away from desiring their mothers to looking for another partner in their adult lives. While the final chapter will explain Freud's Oedipus in more detail, it suffices to say here that this all-satisfying figure for the young child's imagination was a phallic mother, a woman with a penis, a woman who lacked nothing. Beccadelli's *Hermaphrodite*, Chorier's *Satyra Sotadica*, the collections of phallic objects, the anthologies of priapic epigrams, the collection that was Forberg's book and the anthology of autobiographies of sex lives in Krafft-Ebing's book all sought to bring together all forms of sex for the interest and pleasure of their readers. Freud, on the other hand, theorised the phallic mother, who was supposed to embody the possibility of all desire.

Chapter VI thus attends to another central strand of this book, that is, the question of the relationship between men's and women's authority in the domain of sexual pleasure and desire. Freudian psychoanalysis was designed to heal subjects suffering from mental affliction. Freud argued that a sexual aetiology, a problem in moving on from the phallic mother – that is, a problem in dealing with the Oedipus complex – was behind much mental illness. But did Freud's cure really work? Even if ancient mythology had been commandeered into the services of psychoanalysis, at the end of his career Freud remained concerned about the authority that ancient myth might have *over* us: however hard Freud might have tried, he also suggested that we might never stop being Oedipus or that we might never stop desiring the phallic mother. So profound was this desire that it might always control how the adult relates to and desires another. It might have seemed that classical antiquity had been requisitioned for the purposes of modern sexual health, and yet Freud could not help feeling he was fighting a losing battle *against* the authority of the phallic mother.

Deep in the psyche, then, lay the truth of sexuality which had to be excavated by the analyst, a secret at once so hidden that even the patient did not know it and yet deeply formative of the patient's very identity. Just as the ancient world was seen to have been so profoundly influential on the modern world, so the antiquity of Freudian childhood constituted who the adult would become. For Foucault, it was exactly the operation of extracting this inner truth from the patient through psychoanalysis that would produce the twentieth- and twenty-first-century understanding of sexuality as an internal identity and orientation that affects every aspect of one's life:

> Thus sex gradually became an object of great suspicion; the general and disquieting meaning that pervades our conduct and our existence, in spite of ourselves; [. . .] the fragment of darkness that we each carry within us; a general signification, a universal secret, an omnipresent cause, a fear that never ends.[23]

Foucault's prose deliciously depicts the sense of a sexuality as the truth of identity deep within the human subject. The analogy between modernity and antiquity on the one hand, and adult and child sexuality on the other, provided a foundational logic and language for Freud. *Sex: Antiquity and its Legacy* uncovers the history of the reception of those Latin and Greek texts, which provided modern sexual pathology and psychoanalysis with a vocabulary to produce a certain type of human subject; a subject whose truth is its sexuality. This book thus argues for the centrality of classical reception in the study of the history of modern sexuality in the West. Without further ado, then, let us turn to our story, and back to the Italian Renaissance, where we need to begin.

CHAPTER I

SEX, LATIN AND RENAISSANCE HUMANISM: 'A PRECIOUS STONE IN A PILE OF DUNG'

Between 1425 and 1426, a young and hopeful law student produced a couple of books of seemingly obscene and dirty poetry, which he entitled *The Hermaphrodite*. The man in question, Antonio Beccadelli (1394–1471), originally from Palermo, Sicily, penned his verses with the aim of attracting the patronage of Cosimo de' Medici. Copies were made and the nature of the poetry quickly ensured its rapid dissemination through humanist circles. Despite Beccadelli's explicit allusions to classical writers – the Roman poets Catullus and Martial in particular (to whom we will return) – and despite some clever jokes (as we shall soon see), Beccadelli's attempts seriously backfired. The sexually explicit contents of the book jarred awkwardly with other humanists' fulminations against illicit sexual desires, and the door to the de' Medici court remained firmly closed. Friends of Beccadelli's jumped in to help; eventually various recommendations paid off and he was appointed court poet to Duke Filippo Maria Visconti on 10 December 1429. By late 1434 he had entered the service of King Alfonso V of Aragon and Naples as counsellor and confidant. At last, in Palermo at Alfonso's court, Beccadelli flourished, presiding over a grand group of scholars. In 1455 he wrote a book about Alfonso's deeds, as would befit any court poet, and he also founded the Academia Neapolitana, which continues to this day.[1]

Back in the late 1420s, however, the youthful Beccadelli was gaining notoriety for his lewd book. Bernadino da Siena, a well-known Franciscan preacher, staged public burnings of the work in Milan, Bologna and Ferrara. Beccadelli was burned twice in effigy. One humanist said that he was a 'pimp for boys', and the Pope, Eugenius IV (Pope 1431–47) apparently threatened any reader of *The Hermaphrodite* with excommunication. The anecdote about Cardinal Cesarini (1398–1444) is also worth remembering. One day, he found his secretary reading it. The priest tried to hide it but the cardinal confronted him, making him destroy it. But he also remarked, 'If you had known how to respond, perhaps you wouldn't have had to tear it up. What you should have answered me was that you were searching for a precious stone in a pile of dung'.[2] The cardinal's witticism reflected how it was not clear to Italian humanists how one was to respond to ancient representations of sex and desire. It was not until 1559 that an Index of Forbidden Books was established by Pope Paul IV. And the difficulty of knowing how to read Greek and Latin texts was also reflected in a 1563 decree of the Council of Trent (the sixteenth-century council of the Roman Catholic Church) which stated:

> Books which professedly deal with, narrate or teach things lascivious or obscene are absolutely prohibited, since not only the matter of faith but also that of morals, which are usually easily corrupted through the reading of books, must be taken into consideration, and those who possess them are to be severely punished by the bishops. Ancient books written by the heathens may by reason of their elegance and quality of style be permitted, but by no means read to children.[3]

Precisely what might be learnt from reading sex in classical Latin verse was open to debate in the 1400s, a debate provoked partly by Beccadelli's book. If Cesarini's secretary had known what to say about the book, then there would have been no problem reading it. So how did *The Hermaphrodite* pose such tricky questions about what it meant for a humanist to know about sex?

The difficulty of reading epigrams

Cardinal Cesarini's witticism reveals the complicated intellectual environment in which *The Hermaphrodite* was written in the first half of the fifteenth century. The classical canon was still far from set, as new works were still being discovered in libraries around the Mediterranean world. And the discovery of Catullus in the early 1300s and his reception in the 1400s reflected the difficulties facing Renaissance humanist scholars and writers: only one manuscript had survived into the Renaissance period, making the text difficult to get hold of. Furthermore, the text itself was notoriously corrupt; meters were confused and poems were run together, and the point of the poem was often lost. As Julia Haig Gaisser has shown, Catullus was *very* hard to read.[4] On top of these problems, Catullus' short poems seemed full of obscenity. What was a humanist to make of such writing? One of the issues that reflected the Renaissance response to Catullus was how to interpret Lesbia's sparrow in Poem 2, where Catullus describes Lesbia's affectionate relationship with her pet *passer*. The poet Giovanni Gioviano Pontano (1429–1503), a friend of Beccadelli, wrote a poem 'Ad pueros de columba' (in 1457) which evoked Catullus' kissing-poems, running allusions to Martial 11.6 into it, which had interpreted the sparrow as not a bird but a penis. A deluge of poems about sparrows, doves and kisses followed. And, in 1489, Angelo Poliziano, the Florentine classical scholar and poet, famously argued in his *Miscellanea*, a collection of short essays on classical texts, that 'that sparrow of Catullus [. . .] allegorically conceals a certain more obscene meaning which I cannot explain with my modesty intact'. Poliziano then quoted Martial 11.6: 'Give me kisses, but Catullan ones. / And if they be as many as he said, / I will give you Catullus's sparrow'.[5] The question as to whether there was a penis in his text was not simply an amusing intellectual skirmish but an issue of real scholarly debate well into the sixteenth century. Catullus' text focused his Renaissance readers' attention on the relationship between the poet's words and the poet's body.

When Renaissance writers and scholars wanted to justify their interest in the obscenity of Catullus, they were able to turn to Catullus' own rationalisation for rude verse, which questioned the very relationship between the poet's sexual self – his own feelings – and the language he used in his poetry:

> For it is proper for a pious poet to be chaste
> himself, but it is not at all necessary for his little verses to be
> (16.5–6).

And yet the poem (Catullus 16) from which these lines come, shows that Catullus' argument was hardly straightforward:

> I will fuck your ass [*pedicabo*] and I will fuck your mouth
> [*irrumabo*]
> Aurelius you pussyhole and Furius you fairy
> you who think because my verses
> are a bit soft that I have no shame.
> For it is proper for a pious poet to be chaste
> himself, but it is not at all necessary for his little verses to be.
> Actually these have wit and charm
> And if they are a little soft and a bit shameless
> and can make someone tingle a bit
> – I don't mean in boys, but in those hairy old men,
> who can't get it up.
> You, who of my many thousands of kisses
> have read, do you think I'm less of a man?
> I will fuck your ass and I will fuck your mouth.

The relationship between the Catullan text and Catullus' own sex life comes under ironic scrutiny. The aggressive invective that opens this poem spotlights the power of the poet's voice to represent, by violating his addressee's mouth. As William Fitzgerald has pointed out, 'the mouth in Roman culture was the most important site of purity or contamination:

eating, speaking, and kissing – the latter as much a social as a sexual activity – all required a pure mouth, but above all speaking, for the Roman's word was sacred'.[6] The verb that Catullus uses, *irrumare*, means 'to put the penis into the mouth' (as opposed to *pedicare*, meaning 'to put the penis in the ass'). The act of *irrumatio*, Fitzgerald says, 'becomes a figure for the poet's power to assign his own meanings to those who, perforce, are silent while he speaks'.[7] Catullus' verbal threat reflects the Roman conceptualisation of sex as a relationship of power and authority, whereby the free-born adult male asserts his position and status over those inferior to him.[8]

But, at the same time, Catullus' poetic voice was also self-ironising and self-questioning, as his claim to authority over the language he uses is undercut by his own authorititative language. The poem is suspended in paradox: Catullus states that his readers should distinguish between the man and his poem, in a poem where he threatens to rape anally and orally free-born Roman men. As Daniel Selden has put it, 'if the poet is actually virtuous and chaste, he will never carry out the rape, and, if he carries out the rape, he substantiates the claims against his morals'.[9] Just as Aurelius and Furius had apparently questioned Catullus' masculinity, so Catullus' response has us wonder how disgusting or how pleasurable these acts of *irrumatio* and *pedicatio* actually are for Catullus. Catullus' poem blurs disgust with lust, repulsion with seduction. Is this the language of obscene punishment or a cover for sexual pleasure? And we, the readers, are left wondering how ironically knowing we are to imagine Catullus was in using this language. How confidently assertive, cleverly self-mocking or transparently insecure is Catullus to seem here? With how much authority does Catullus use the words *pedicabo* and *irrumabo*?

Beccadelli's *The Hermaphrodite* emerged at this intellectually turbulent time when not just getting a grasp on Catullus' meaning was difficult, but also simply getting hold of Catullus' text. As Beccadelli put it:

> I'm on fire [*ardeo*], my dear Galeazzo, to find wanton Catullus
> So I can gratify my mistress.
> The lusty lass loves to read the tender poets,

And she prefers your verses, learned Catullus,
And just now she sweetly asked me for them with many a prayer,
Thinking that her favorite poet was perhaps in my house.
'I don't have the book,' I said, 'my light, my nymph.
But I'll make sure I do. Perhaps you'll get the work.'
She insists and asks me for the friendly book constantly,
And treats me to dire threats.
Wherefore, by all the gods, dear friend
(may Cytherea be just as kind to your prayers)
I beg you again and again: find this book for me
So that I can make myself more pleasing to my goddess (*Hermaphrodite* 2.23)[10]

Renaissance readers' desire to get hold of Catullus' scarce and corrupt text became focused on the issue of understanding Catullus' bodily desires behind the words he put on the page. In Beccadelli's poem, the desire for the text – the desire to get hold of his text – becomes the desire to get beyond the text in order to have sex with his girlfriend. And yet, it is impossible to have sex without Catullus' text, implies Beccadelli: he 'burns' (*ardeo*) for Catullus just as much as his mistress.

If knowing how to have sex meant knowing how to read Catullus, then this meant knowing about the language of sex, pleasure and desire. The opening poem of *The Hermaphrodite* reiterated Catullus' defence of obscene poetry (1.1.5–8), alerting his reader's attention to his command over the Latin language. But, as Catullus had blurred the line between giving offence and giving pleasure, between seduction and violation, so *The Hermaphrodite* was to please *and* displease in equal measure, as its poems confronted its readers with the question of what they were to make of the sexual vocabulary of the Latin language. As he explained the title of the book:

Our book has at the same time a cunt [*cunnus*] and a cock [*mentula*]
so how very fitting [*conveniens*] a name it has! (1.3.3–4)

The *conveniens nomen* is not just suitable but obscenely alludes to the act of sexual coition itself: *cunnus* and *mentula* coming together. This text isn't simply about sex – it is sex! Beccadelli continues:

> But if you call it 'Ass' [*podicem*] because it sings with its ass,
> it will still have a not unfitting [*non inconveniens*] name (1.3.5–6).

The Hermaphrodite will offend any reader *and* please any sort of desire. It will seduce and insult in equal measure. As a *mentula*, it will assault; as a *cunnus* or *podex*, it will provide pleasure. At the end of his book, Beccadelli sends his 'little book' straight into the whorehouse where 'futues et futuere', where it will fuck and be fucked (2.37.32), exemplifying the ambivalent and even belligerent relationship that this book will have with its readers: some will be turned on by it (*The Hermaphrodite* as *cunnus* and *podex*), whereas others will feel assaulted by its invective mood (*The Hermaphrodite* as *mentula*). Beccadelli's book confronts the reader with the possibilities of their responses to its poetry, asking them to think about how they react to its language: offended and assaulted, tickled and pleasured? Just as Catullus had both loved and hated ('Odi et amo . . .' 85.1), so *The Hermaphrodite* blurred the line – questioned the difference – between sex and violence, beauty and the grotesque, the licit and the illicit. Beccadelli might have been worried about the 'thousand Catos [. . .] a thousand who only like serious reading' (2.35.3–4), but he knew that these critics were 'rigid' ('censore . . . rigido'), both lusty *and* disgusted. Beccadelli asked of his humanist readers what was to be made of the language of sex in Latin.

The difficulty of getting hold of both Catullus' manuscript as well as the meaning of his text was reflected in the type of poetry he was seen to have written. Catullus' short poems were compared by his Renaissance readers with Martial's epigrams, which were already more widely circulated and read during the fourteenth and fifteenth centuries. But epigrammatic poetry was characteristically slight, ephemeral and fragile. Martial had himself often worried about the possible loss of his poetry and complained about plagiarism of his verses. He was concerned that a poem could belong to anyone who recites it (1.52), or he hears other poets pretending that they are 'vomiting snake venom' under his name (7.12). Martial's poems were desirable commodities, but also vulnerable entities. As Rimell has put it:

> Epigrams are eminently recyclable, of course, not only because of the genre's 'low', 'throwaway' status, but also because a book of epigrams is so patently fragments and repetitive: who would notice if a poem was missing from a collection, if another author paraphrased one of them, or pinched some lines from different poems and put them together to make a new one?[11]

Just as Beccadelli sought the manuscript of Catullus, as we have just seen, in another poem (1.41), he begged a friend for his 'extremely scarce' copy of Martial ('perrara epigrammata'). The scarcity of classical manuscripts during the fifteenth century is reflected in yet another poem by Beccadelli (2.29) in which he asked a pawnbroker to take a manuscript of the plays of Plautus. As the name suggests, the 'epigram' was originally a monument but, with Martial, it was also a gossipy fragment just as much as a memorial of remembrance. As Rimell has explained, the Roman epigram had become, with Martial,

> simultaneously speech and writing, conversation and text, as humble occasional poetry that is at the same time monumental, a guarantor of fame and immortality; it is both free and closeted, autonomous and dependent, chaste and obscene, both spectacular and repressed, raucous and silent.[12]

The point of the fragile epigram was hard to grasp, as it delighted in paradox and oxymoron. And Martial's ludic voice became a model for Beccadelli, whose language blurred the line between sexy and repulsive, beautiful and ugly, desire and hate. There are, for example, several poems seemingly in praise of a woman called Alda. In one (1.18) we read:

Venus and the Graces have chosen their home in Alda's eyes.
And in her lips Cupid himself smiles.
She doesn't piss [*mingit*], but if she did piss [*meiit*], she pisses
[*mingit*] balsam,
She doesn't shit [*cacat*], but if Alda did shit [*cacat*], she shits
[*cacat*] violets.

The opening couplet sounds like traditional praise, but the closing pair of lines makes an obscene mess: how many times can you write 'piss' and 'shit' in a poem praising a woman? Are we meant to imagine that shit can smell like violets – is Alda *that* lovely? To say that Alda makes it hard to distinguish between flowers and faeces is ambivalent praise indeed.

In another poem to Alda (2.3), Beccadelli's praise is again paradoxical:

If you had a bow and quiver, Alda, you would be Diana.
If you had a torch in your hand, Alda, you would be Venus.
Take up the lyre and the plectrum: you will become, as it were
a very Apollo.
If you had the horn and thyrsus, you would be Bacchus.
If you didn't have these things and did have my cock in your
cunt,
You would be more beautiful, Alda, than the gods or goddesses.

Alda looks both chaste and sexy, like Diana *and* Venus – both Madonna and whore. She can look like a singer of songs and an intoxicated reveller, Apollo *and* Bacchus. Alda can be any deity she wants. High-brow, classicising verse (it sounds like Ovid's Sappho's admiration of Phaon in *Heroides* 15), *and* low-brow, obscene, hyper-aggressive chat-up line: just as Alda constantly changes, so does what Beccadelli wants – can any desire satisfy him?

If Alda can metamorphose from one deity to another, so Beccadelli can constantly change position, so that we don't know what we're reading or how to feel. Several epigrams are addressed to a woman he calls Ursa

('She-bear'). The derogatory name reflects the misogynistic use to which it is put: Beccadelli complains that Ursa likes to be on top during sex (1.5); her clitoris is as big as her nose (1.8). In book 2, we read a suite of poems about this woman. In the first, (2.7), Beccadelli addresses his friend Giovanni Aurispa about Ursa's huge and endlessly voracious *vulva* (2.7). The insatiability of desire was, of course, a theme in Catullus when he loses count of his kisses with Lesbia. Ursa's vulva looks back to Martial, who had caricatured the grotesquely ravenous Lydia, whose vagina was so loose that it was like 'an old shoe wet through in muddy water' (11.16.4). Martial had concluded: 'I'm said to have fucked her in a pond. I don't know about that: I think I fucked the pond' (11–12). Beccadelli went one step further again when he worried that he might 'be shipwrecked in her cunt for sure' (2.7.6). Then in 2.8, Beccadelli impersonates Aurispa's reply in highly misogynistic terms, which show profound disgust for the female body: 'her smelly *vulva* will put you off' (2.8.6), in terms that will remind us of Alda:

> It smells so that if someone compared her groin to shit
> A great sewer would be violets and sweet roses (2.8.9–10).

But in the very next poem, addressed to Ursa who is weeping, Beccadelli exclaims his profound love for her and denies having written any poems 'except ones that praise' her (2.9.13). And then, in the next poem again (2.10), Beccadelli abuses Ursa in terms even more hellishly cruel and misogynistic than before, as he complains of his 'Tartarean penalties', having to endure Ursa's abhorrent body. What are we to think of Beccadelli here? Did his Renaissance readers laugh with or at him? When he says that he has only written poems 'quae te laudent' ('which praise you', 2.9.13), does he end up suggesting that his disgust for Ursa is concealing his lust?

In another poem (1.15), faeces taste like honey: Beccadelli recounts a story to explain why 'once someone bends males over / he can't give up the misdeed once he's begun' (1.15.23–4). He asks us 'why nearly every animal veils with a tail its unmentionable members' except for bears (5–6). Once upon a time, he explains, there was a bear that was starving hungry. He often saw honeycombs ('favos') but thought they were turds ('merdas'), and so he didn't eat them at first. 'But driven by hunger, he soon stopped, nibbled' and 'tasted the honey, and didn't just eat, he devoured' it. The 'Argus-eyed' farmer soon noticed and 'grabbed hold of the tail of the mighty bear and pulled'. But the bear refused to let go and the farmer pulled so hard that the tail tore away. 'So', Beccadelli wickedly jokes at the end of the story, 'once someone bends males over / he can't give up the misdeed once he's begun'. The bear that mistakes honey for turds is like the man for whom bending over men is sweet like honey. Beccadelli mixes the sweet with the stale, the tasty with the repellent, the fragrant with the foul. Beccadelli's paradoxical epigrammatic book blurs the line between the desirable and the abhorrent.

The beautiful is mixed with the grotesque in other ways. Just as the epigram-as-inscription had been a significant part of Martial's aesthetic, so Beccadelli also included epigrams in remembrance of women. But Martial's poetry was pervaded by the imagery of disease, death and the decadence of Roman imperial culture.[13] Analogously, *The Hermaphrodite* was written while Beccadelli was living in Siena when, in 1424, the plague hit the town killing many inhabitants, a handful of whom are memorialised in Beccadelli's book. And so, even as Beccadelli tries to arrest the mutability of life in plague-ridden Siena, the epitaphs to these girls ring very strange. In one, Orietta, 'the most beautiful and moral girl' is described as one who 'in her beauty and virtues she was like the very inhabitants of heaven, a great glory to her city Siena' (1.24.3–4). But the epitaph closes ambiguously: 'I am sure [. . .] that this girl will throw down Jupiter from his high throne' (9–10). Is Beccadelli suggesting that Orietta is the sort of saint that we should be worshipping rather than those old pagan gods? Or is he implying that her ascent into heaven will arouse Jupiter's notorious erotic interest? The next poem is also an epitaph, this time to Orietta's sister Battista, who also died in the plague. She is praised as a beautiful musician and dancer, but then is ominously compared: 'She pleased everyone with her song more than Philomela' (1.25.5). Of course, Philomela, the daughter of Pandion, was changed into a nightingale after being raped by her brother-in-law, Tereus, who also cut out her tongue. The epigram is haunted by an image of censorship and rape: Battista's music has been silenced by death, just as Philomela had also been quieted. Beccadelli's epitaphic epigrams certainly don't straightforwardly, lovingly immortalise their young subjects. And just as Orietta and Battista were cut off before their prime (Battista is a 'virguncula', a little virgin), in another poem Beccadelli exploits these epigrammatic tensions with ephemerality and longevity, bodily temporality and poetic immortality. In 2.6, the young man Philopappa ('daddy-lover') is ablaze for the old man Sterconus (whose name sounds like *stercus*, 'shit'). Beccadelli's book is populated by girls who died before they could love and gerontophiles who love men way past their prime. To explain such a strange love affair, Beccadelli again turns to the world of fable:

> The fox asked the ass why he ate dung.
> 'Because I remember', he said 'when the dung was grass'.
> That's what I think you [Philopappa] would say to anyone who might ask:
> You love him so much because he was of a tender age – once (2.6.27–30).

Yet again, we see Beccadelli producing a concoction which mixes lust with disgust in confusing tasty food with the waste that should be left behind.

Beccadelli's Latin continually blurs the line between turn-on and turn-off in scenes that might make for pleasurable reading and might repel. Beccadelli questioned his readers as to what they were to make of his Latin poems. Indeed, the idea that there was a correct and authoritative way of reading Latin was addressed in several of the epigrams featuring Mattia Lupi (most likely a fictitious persona), the pederastic schoolteacher, as Beccadelli suggests that the very figure who was supposed to teach his pupil to read Latin properly was also the figure who was having the most sex. See, for instance, this two-line epigram (2.16):

Mattia Lupi has three students in his private school
and one of the three is his houseboy

Tris habet archana Mathias Lupius aula
discipulos: unus de tribus est famulus

The school of Mattia, the *grammaticus* (a grammar teacher for boys), comprises merely three pupils, one of whom is a young male servant, who is paying for lessons with his physical labours. The phrase 'archana aula' – a private school in Renaissance Latin – is also drolly made use of in an unfinished epic poem about the Greek hero Achilles, called *The Achilleid* by the Roman poet Statius. In this poem Achilles' mother, Thetis, hides her son; appalled that he is fated to die young in the Trojan War, she hopes that when the Greeks muster their forces they would not find Achilles. On the island of Scyros, Achilles the boy was dressed as a girl until the cunning hero Ulysses comes looking through the 'arcana aula', the 'secret chambers' of the maidens of the island (*Achilleid* 1.750), eventually finding Achilles who is also fated to help the Greeks win the war. Beccadelli makes witty use of the change in meaning of the word *aula* from classical to Renaissance Latin, as his learned reference to Statius (in the Renaissance a popular read alongside Virgil) suggests that his private 'schoolroom' is like the secret 'chamber' containing boys dressed as girls. This acerbic joke about the relationship between classical pedagogy and pederasty sophisticatedly alludes to a joke about the Latin. Just as Mattia the teacher confuses learning the classics with sex, so Beccadelli's own poem makes a clever joke about the sexualisation of the Latin language: you would only get the joke if you, the reader, knew what *aula*, schoolroom, used to mean in classical Latin. Or rather, you would only get the joke if you had learnt Latin, suggesting that you might too have been taught by a Mattia Lupi, thereby implicating you, the reader, in the joke. Beccadelli confronts his reader with the question of whether they should be appalled by his text or amused by its cleverness. Indeed, who has the authority to decide how to read Beccadelli's Latin, when the reader is left wondering about what they had learnt when they were learning to read Latin? Beccadelli asks his readers to think about what it means to learn Latin and have a command over the language: does it mean that one should be able to read and write it correctly, or that one can re-write and re-read classical Latin to see the sexual double entendres in the text? Is there a difference between these alternatives? Just as Statius got his readers thinking about the relationship between the girlish boy Achilles, who would become the hero of the *Iliad*, so Beccadelli wonders how the pederastic schoolroom makes the Renaissance man.[14]

How to read Beccadelli?

Beccadelli, then, repeatedly presents himself as the knowing ironist, as a poet who knows how to play with the Latin language. He presents himself as a man who is in command: he uses his knowledge of Latin to describe and objectify women; he subjects the sexual desires of others to his authoritative gaze. We are to see and laugh at Alda through his eyes; Battista, who died in the plague in Siena, can no longer sing like Philomela and, like Philomela, is forced to be silent. Beccadelli is the Latin epigrammatist who claims to have the authority to use Latin howsoever he wants, because it bears no relation to who he really is, as Catullus had done before him (*Hermaphrodite* 1.1.5–8). At the same time, however, Beccadelli's text shows an awareness of the irony Catullus had shown in Poem 16, when he claimed to be in charge of the reception of the Latin he wrote. And so, Beccadelli is also the man who doesn't have full control over the Latin he speaks: his cruel words about Ursa, written for his friend Aurispa, had been carried off by someone else ('refert', 2.9.16), so that Ursa got report of them. And he is also the man who cannot get hold of the Catullan text in order to pleasure his 'domina', a 'mistress', to whom Beccadelli is enthralled and who, it seems, had already herself read Catullus, 'her favourite poet' (2.23.6).

The Hermaphrodite, as the text itself predicted, was controversial and polarised opinion. Letters and poems circulated between humanists and were later published extolling *and* lambasting its contents. Beccadelli's opening poem rehearsed Catullus' ironic defence for writing obscene poetry.

And this is an argument to which Beccadelli returns again and again during the controversial reception of his *libellus*.[15] In one letter, Poggio Bracciolini of Florence, Beccadelli's friend and fellow humanist, responded to the defence, replying that he agrees with Beccadelli's argument.[16] But he then asks Beccadelli to think about imitating 'the serious poets rather than the frivolous; the upright rather than the sexual [. . .] Let our words match our lives [*Conveniant verba moribus nostris*]'. And yet, in the very next sentence he says: 'I am not one of those who think that they can deduce a man's life from his verses'. In one single paragraph, then, Poggio concurs with Beccadelli's defence, then contradicts him, only then to say that he would never be so inept as to match a man's poems with his morals. Poggio's letter shows how difficult it was to know how to respond to Beccadelli's text; a text which, as we have seen, blurs the beautiful and the grotesque, the clever and the appalling.

Many of Beccadelli's Renaissance readers seemed to be highly critical of *The Hermaphrodite*, but these critics couldn't help but use Beccadelli's own language in their efforts to censor him. In one anonymous poem circulated in 1429 that was called *The Prostitutes of Pavia write to Milan in praise of Antonio Panormita* (Beccadelli's nickname signifying his family's origins in Palermo), the poet makes use of classical Latin's elaborate vocabulary of phallic penetration in order to itemise the obscenity in *The Hermaphrodite*:

> Nor does he just fuck pussies [*futuit*] or take prick
> in the cunt, he also mouth-fucks [*irrumat*] soft-males.
> He butt-fucks [*paedicat*] boys so well that no piles
> grow in their assholes (lines 11–14)[17]

The Hermaphrodite was, then, seen as a book that anthologised sexual possibilities, just as Beccadelli had intended. In 1432, Pier Candido Decembrio, another well-known humanist working in Florence, wrote a mock – and mocking – epitaph for Beccadelli, in which he couldn't help using as much bad language as possible:

I produced bilge water in Latin poems.
Cunts and balls, penises, assholes, and butts,
shit and crap, singing all this foully from my mouth
(lines 20–2)[18]

Around the same time, another poet, Porcellio Pandoni, circulated verses advertising his own works, a publicity campaign that aimed to ostracise Beccadelli from the arena of respectable Latinity:

Hasten hither noble boys and chaste girls.
This is no page marked by a Sicilian hand.
Prick and cunt, there are none [*Mentula, cunnus abest*]. Ursa does not lie on top of Priapus.
No one buttfucks [*paedicat nemo*], Alda does not wiggle her flanks.
There is no asshole [*nullus podex*], no member gets erect here [*nullum . . . inguen*]
no woman shits Assyrian flowers [*nulla femina*].
You may read these poems, Cosimo; these poems are suitable for Cosimo.[19]

The repeated negatives and emphasis on absence obviously and very clearly mark up the presence of sexual obscenity in Porcellio's poem. The reader is left wondering whether they can tell the difference between authoritative censoriousness and manipulating irony. How knowing are we to imagine Porcellio to have been? When could the language of sex be used in Latin so that it is 'suitable for Cosimo' de' Medici, the very patron Beccadelli was courting when he was writing *The Hermaphrodite*?[20]

Beccadelli had predicted that his poetry book would be read by a thousand Catos: rigid censors, both sexually aroused and disgusted. *The Hermaphrodite* was designed to stimulate and repel. It was a book where faeces, flowers and honey mix, a book where beautiful young virgins turn Jupiter on in heaven and remind us of rape victims in Ovid. It makes fun of pederastic schoolmasters in Latin that implicates us readers in the joke. Beccadelli confronted his readers with the difficulties of reading and writing the language of sex in Latin with authority. While his scholarly contemporaries were working hard to secure readings of Catullus, so Beccadelli underlined the complexities of controlling the meaning of ancient epigram, and of regulating how they were to be read and what was to be learnt from them. Catullus 16 offered an ironic comment about how the poet might not be able to regulate the reception of the language he used in his poetry. Catullus' poem wittily questioned how the Roman conceptualisation of sex as masculine power conferred authority on the Roman poetic voice. If the state of the manuscript of Catullus made him literally difficult to understand, then his poetry was itself already thinking about the complexities of how it was to be received. Beccadelli's voice emerged at this turbulent time in Renaissance humanism as it provoked his humanist readers to think hard about the proprieties of reading and writing about sex in Latin.

CHAPTER II

THE *SATYRA SOTADICA* AND THE EROTICS OF LATINITY

Beccadelli's *The Hermaphrodite* emerged in a world inhabited mainly by male scholars. The book was written to garner the attention of a male patron; it became the subject of letters between male humanists; male poets responded to its circulation; and male readers such as Cardinal Cesarini and his secretary discussed it. Moreover, almost every poem in the book focused on what men want (old women, young women, beautiful women, ugly women, old men, boys . . .). *The Hermaphrodite* afforded male Italian humanists an opportunity to dispute and negotiate their intellectual positions in relation to one another. And yet, as we have already seen, the issue of women engaging with Latin emerges at certain moments in the text: Ursa had got report of Beccadelli's nasty verses about her, and Beccadelli's mistress had read and enjoyed Catullus' poetry. We begin the chapter with an overview of how a homosocial world of male humanists sought to harness the erotics of the Platonic dialogue between an older man and his male pupil for the purposes of a philosophical education. The relationship between men's and women's conceptions of love was of particular concern for Renaissance Platonists, who argued that a heavenly, intellectual and chaste love between men was superior to the physical, carnal, sexual love between men and women. Such a position justified the exclusion of women from the all-male domain of humanist, scholarly circles.

It is against this background that we can more closely examine the modern reception of ancient reports that it was a *woman* who had invented the genre of the sex manual. While nothing survives of these intriguing texts, except for possible scraps, we do, however, possess Ovid's *Ars Amatoria* (or *The Arts of Love*), the most famous ancient text on the arts of seduction, in which the author presents himself as an expert on erotics. But Ovid's advice is addressed to men and women, and as a result numerous contradictions emerge in his poem as he tries to instruct both sexes. Ovid, a male author writing in a genre supposedly invented by a woman, ends up portraying a world of mutual suspicion and mistrust as each sex tries to outwit and seduce the other in a quest for their own pleasure. The idea that women had special access to sexual knowledge which competed with men's became a particular concern for Renaissance philosophers, for whom a conceptualisation of Platonic love between males was so fundamental for the construction of the homosocial community of humanist scholars. One striking embodiment of this anxiety was the courtesan, poet and philosopher, Tullia d'Aragona, (*c.*1510–56), who wrote her own version of a Platonic dialogue in Italian, in which she undermined contemporary humanistic interpretations of Platonic love and argued for a place for women in such debates. Tullia's voice aroused sufficient interest and concern that, 100 years after she had died, her namesake starred in a book called the *Satyra Sotadica*, written in the early 1660s by the Frenchman Nicolas Chorier (1612–92). In this dialogue in Latin, Tullia educates her younger cousin, Octavia, about sex before the latter's wedding. Tullia and Octavia turn back to the canon of Roman authors – including Ovid, Virgil and Horace – and read into these classics all sorts of double entendre and sexual innuendo in justification of the pursuit of their sexual pleasures, often at their husbands' expense. The games played between men and women in Ovid's *Ars Amatoria* become a series of violent duels in the *Satyra Sotadica*. In Chapter I, the authority to speak in Latin about sex was a discussion held among male poets and their humanist readers. Now, in Chapter II, we see that the question of who could speak about sex with more authority was also a question about the gendered nature of knowledge in Renaissance Europe. Chorier's *Satyra Sotadica* shows us that men's fantasies and anxieties about women who could read and write Latin reflected men's concerns about the intrusion of women in the all-male space of Renaissance philosophy, built on the bonds of chaste, Platonic love between men.

A man's world?

Even if Beccadelli wanted to get hold of Catullus' text in order to have sex with his girlfriend, the opening word of his poem makes clear that it was Catullus for whom he was burning with desire ('ardeo . . . mollem reperire Catullum', 2.23.1). The world of Renaissance humanism brought men and boys together into often very intimate relationships. Relations between males were a real area of concern for many sixteenth-century humanists, as was reflected in Beccadelli's mockery of the pederastic *grammaticus*.[1] In a letter to his friend Poggio, Beccadelli had defended *The Hermaphrodite* by avowing that 'our Latins have written such things, and that Catullus, Tibullus, Propertius, Juvenal, Martial, and before them Virgil, Ovid, still circulate among us'.[2] Beccadelli identified himself with other male poets. Beccadelli then turned back to an epigram he had found quoted in Aulus Gellius' *Attic Nights* (19.11, which can now also be read in *The Greek Anthology*, 5.78), in which Plato supposedly wrote,

> My soul was on my lips as I was kissing Agathon.
> Wretched soul – it came hoping to cross over to him.

The possibility that knowledge was a product of an erotic relationship – that one learnt from someone whom one loved; that knowledge was best transferred between lovers – posed difficult questions for Beccadelli's readers. Even if his Latinity had caused much consternation about the relationship between sex and scholarship, Beccadelli's placement of Plato with Catullus and other Latin poets was not facetious. Until the standardised translations of Marsilio Ficino (1433–99), along with his commentaries, there was no fully comprehensive rendering into Latin of the Platonic texts. Plato was read in Latin excerpts far more commonly than in Greek in the first half of the fifteenth century, so seeing him through the prism of Roman authors would not have seemed anomalous. Whereas Beccadelli never managed to access the exclusive circle of Cosimo de' Medici, Marsilio Ficino, however, found himself born within it, the son of the personal physician of Cosimo. It is hardly surprising, then, that Ficino was keen to clear up these heated debates by turning to Plato in Greek. But relations between men became an especially tricky issue.

Ficino was working at an exciting time, when Western Europe's engagement with classical culture changed in some significant ways. Whereas the so-called Renaissance of the twelfth century had focused its attention on texts of natural sciences, philosophy and mathematics, Italian Renaissance humanists of the thirteenth century and onwards turned to a broader range of cultural production, including a burgeoning interest in classical sculpture and the visual arts. Textually, this period also saw a new emphasis made on the learning of Greek itself, rather than reading in Latin translation. Among others, it was the works of Plato which became highly prized in this period. As Francesco Petrarch (1304–74) famously put it, 'Plato is praised by greater men, Aristotle by a greater number'. Read in context (this sentence comes from his *On his own Ignorance and That of Many Others* – this title reflecting Petrarch's digestion of the Platonic Socrates' insistence that all he knew was his own ignorance), Petrarch contended, along with other Renaissance intellectuals, that Platonic philosophy came closest to Christian truth.[3]

The issue of male–male desire in ancient Greek culture, however, provided a troubling frame for the Renaissance reception of Plato. In the medieval period, two partial translations of the *Timaeus* and a few poor Latin versions of the *Meno*, *Phaedo* and *Parmenides* were the only Platonic texts available to scholars.[4] A complete manuscript of Plato only arrived from Byzantium in Italy in 1423 (only a year or so before Beccadelli was writing *The Hermaphrodite*). In 1438 a deputation arrived in Florence from Byzantium, including the emperor John VIII Palaeologus, hoping to explore the feasibility of reunifying the Orthodox and Catholic churches. In the retinue was a Platonic scholar, George Gemistos (1355–1452). While in town he gave lectures on Plato to the Florentines. The story goes that the famous and powerful businessman and politician Cosimo de' Medici attended one of these events and was inspired to found an *Academia Platonica* in Florence. The passion for Plato, however, did not blossom unimpeded. Some scholars demonstrated considerable hostility to what seemed like a dangerous new trend in learning and education. One, called George of Trebizond (1395–1486), a scholar from Crete who eventually found his way into the pocket of Pope Nicolas V as his secretary, was a firm supporter of Aristotelianism, and wrote a fulminating attack on Plato and his new followers. The correct interpretation of ancient Greek brought huge material rewards and influential political position. Ancient ideas wielded modern power . . . and dangers: Plato was so perilous for modern male students and their pupils precisely because he encouraged pederasty, alleged George. In contrast to Plato the boy-loving woman-hater, George characterised Aristotle as the perfect father and husband.[5]

Although Platonic scholars responded to defend Socrates and Plato, the association between Greek pedagogy and pederasty stubbornly remained. For Marsilio Ficino, one of the most important and influential scholars and teachers of Plato's texts in Renaissance Europe, whose translations of Plato into Latin became the standard texts, this issue also proved tricky. For the passage in the *Charmides*, when Socrates blushes at the lovely eponymous boy, Ficino could find no higher meaning and simply omitted the passage. In his commentary on his translation, he noted he had

> changed a few things and had even omitted a few things. For things which once sounded harmonious to the pure ears of the Attic Greeks will perhaps sound much less harmonious to cruder ears. Thus a certain Homerian (or rather Platonist) Aristarchus, used to say that whatever things seem less than harmonious should be set down not to Plato but to Chronus [Time].[6]

A contemporary of Ficino, Cardinal Basilios Bessarion (*c.*1403–72) who had come with the delegation to Florence, felt compelled to write a defence of Plato countering George of Trebizond's critique. In 1469 his *In Calumniatorem Platonis* came out, in which he argued that Socrates did not endorse pederasty and that erotic poems supposedly written by Plato were ancient forgeries. Whereas Beccadelli's *The Hermaphrodite* had brought together the beautiful with the grotesque, the admirable with the contemptible, Plato with Catullus, Bessarion argued that Socrates distinguished between two types of love: one physical and the other Platonic, that is spiritual, chaste and devoted to learning and God. Just a few years later in 1474, Ficino also wrote a defence of Platonic love in a treatise he called *De Amore*. This text was to act as a commentary to his translation of the *Symposium* and so also attempted to iron out the controversy surrounding Plato. If *The Hermaphrodite* mixed up the delicious with the disgusting then in Ficino's *De Amore*, on the other hand, a very different sort of fare is served: the work describes a fictional banquet organised by Lorenzo de' Medici. He gathers a group of learned men to conclude their dinner with a recital of Plato's *Symposium* followed up with a discussion of every speech in the dialogue. In Plato's *Symposium*, Pausanias gives the second speech on the subject of love and divides his object of analysis into 'Aphrodite common to the whole city' and 'heavenly Aphrodite'. The former is associated with physical passions, while the latter can only occur between men and is 'free from wantonness' (*Symposium* 180c). In Ficino's banquet, Pausanias' speech assumes real significance for understanding Platonic love. The speech of Pausanias is adapted by the poet and philosopher Guido Cavalcanti, who gives the final oration in Ficino's text, contrasting 'vulgar love' with the 'divine' variety: 'For true love is nothing but a certain urge striving to fly up to the divine beauty, aroused by the sight of bodily beauty; but the adulterous love is a precipitation from sight to touch'.[7]

Despite Ficino's careful attempts to distinguish seeing beauty from touching it, the rediscovery of classical sculpture was about to severely test his thesis. The rediscovery of the Apollo Belvedere around ten years later (*c.*1479) marked a hugely important moment in the history of the Renaissance. It is hard now to imagine the impact of ancient nude statuary on those who first saw it in the fifteenth and sixteenth centuries. Nudity had primarily been associated with pity and compassion – Christ on the cross. Already Donatello's *David* (*c.*1430) had suggested that the naked male form was to be desired rather than pitied. The serene visage and the graceful and noble posture of the Apollo Belvedere, in particular, captivated the imagination of the rich and powerful. Sometime before 1509, it was probably on display in the garden of the Church of San Pietro in Vincoli, and by 1511 it was in pride of place in the Belvedere at the Vatican. An associate of Ficino as a youth, Michelangelo (1475–1564), was especially taken by Greek literature and sculpture. His statue of Bacchus (*c.*1496–8) with a boy peeking out from behind the well-shaped thighs of the god enjoying his grapes was clearly a sensuous work of art. Indeed, the erotic sensuality of Michangelo's own *David* would ensure that the statue was stoned by angry citizens of Florence when it was first put on display in the Piazza della Signoria in 1504.[8]

Battle of the sexes

Although the male physique created by Michelangelo emerged out of a homosocial world of male humanists, it became an important model for a series of highly erotic engravings of sexual postures of men with women that first circulated in the 1520s (a century after Beccadelli's *Hermaphrodite* first appeared). The story goes that when the great artist Raphael died, Giulio Romano (1499–1546) and another disciple were tasked with finishing their master's paintings. In 1523, Romano began work on the decoration of the Sala di Costantino in the Vatican. Allegedly, in a moment of anger at Pope Clement VII for a late payment, Romano drew 16 sexual positions on the walls of the Sala. Although the veracity of this tale cannot be confirmed, it does seem that the well-known engraver Marcantonio Raimondi produced engravings of drawings of sex positions originally done by Romano, which were then printed and circulated, much to the anger of the Pope. Romano fled to Mantua, finding patronage under the anti-papal Duke Federico di Gonzaga. Then, in 1527, Romano's *I Modi* (*Positions*) were published with accompanying sonnets by the satirist Pietro Aretino

(1492–1556). Their distribution was met with both eager curiosity as well as swift condemnation: copies were apparently quickly destroyed. Indeed no copy of this first edition is known to exist and we only have fragments of Raimondi's earlier prints (for instance, at the British Museum and the Bibliothèque Nationale in Paris). Only one early sixteenth-century edition exists (now in a private collection, recently reprinted and edited).[9]

Romano had been inspired by ancient reports about the existence of sex manuals which listed sexual positions for men and women. We no longer possess any such text, and we also have little idea about what these texts might have contained or how they might have been organised. As Holt Parker puts it, 'we are speaking of a vanished literature, known only secondarily and from scraps'.[10] These ancient reports suggest that it was women not men who wrote in this genre. The *Suda* (the Byzantine encyclopaedia compiled in the tenth century CE) records that Astyanassa, Helen's maid, was the founder of this category of writing, producing her *On the Postures for Intercourse* 'which Philaenis and Elephantine later imitated'. These names do not, of course, represent real women. And we only possess one fragment from a work ascribed to a Philaenis, first published by scholars in 1972:

> Frg.1 [col i]: Philaenis of Samos, daughter of Okymenes, wrote these things for those who plan to lead their life with knowledge and not off-handedly [. . .] having worked at it myself [. . .] [col ii] Concerning seductions: So then, the seducer must go unadorned and uncombed so that he does not [appear] to the woman to be on the job [. . .] Frg.3: [. . .] with the thought [. . .] we saying the [. . .] woman is like a goddess [. . .] the ugly one is charming, the older one is like a young girl. Concerning kisses [. . .][11]

As we can see, the reader of this text was to become an expert in saying one thing that really means another. Seduction twisted the meanings of words: a woman is 'really' a goddess; an ugly one is 'really' 'charming', and an older one is 'really' a 'young girl'. Holt Parker has suggested that ancient sex manuals flourished at a time when knowledge-production and -collection became an important concern in the ancient world. Parker has argued that these texts emerged during the Hellenistic period, which demonstrated a continuance of Aristotelian and Peripatetic traditions of analysis and classification. These works, then, could be seen as an erotic response to the Hellenistic culture of encyclopaedism. Sex became the object of a particular sort of knowledge. Indeed 'Philaenis', in the text we have just quoted, underlines the importance of her knowledge for her project. And yet, sexual knowledge is also knowing how to manipulate language and reality so that that reality means whatever you want.

We have, however, no idea whether any ancient sex manual was in fact written by a woman. What is clear, though, is that Romano could not have thought up his *Modi* of men and women without having read Ovid's *Ars Amatoria*, the most famous ancient text on the art of seduction, which was concerned precisely with sexual relations between men and women:

> Let each woman know herself [*nota sibi sit*]; fix your methodology [*modos certos*] according to your body; one shape [*figura*] does not suit all [. . .] There are a thousand modes of love [*mille modi veneris*] (3.771–2, 787).

In this famous passage, Ovid lists the positions (*modi*) differently shaped women should take up, in order to seduce their men. Like 'Philaenis', Ovid emphasises that sex is the object of knowledge ('nota sibi sit'). Indeed, his Latin will shape out in language the contours of women's bodies, his linguistic *figurae* sketching out those lovely, corporeal *figurae*. The composition of Ovid's Latinity reproduces the arrangement of women's bodies. For example,

> The covers, she should press them with her knees, just a little her neck turned back,
> This woman's long flanks need to really be seen all over
>
> [strata premat genibus, paulum cervice reflexa,
> femina per longum conspicienda latus] (3.779–80)

Ovid's text starts us at her knees and we end at her neck, taking in her 'longum latus': the multi-syllabic gerundive 'conspicienda' gives Ovid's reader plenty of time to take in and enjoy the view. Ovid's sexual *figurae* are rhetorical *figurae*, figures of speech: 'the small woman is carried by a horse, but the tallest of brides should never ride on a Hectorean horse' (3.777–78, alluding to *Iliad* 6.397). And Ovid advises: 'Nor should you think it shameful to loosen your hair, like the Phylleian mother [Laodamia], and bend back your neck with your hair flowing' (3.783–84). Small women, but not tall ones, should ride their horse-men, whereas a woman with long hair should do an impression of Laodamia, and let her tresses flow like a torrent of desire. But how should we imagine these lovers who look like Hector and Laodamia? How do we even know what those mythical figures looked like? Just as Ovid's *figurae* seemed to offer an exciting aperture into the *figurae* of erotically entangled bodies, so his rhetorical figures were nothing but that – rhetorical constructions of language. Indeed, Ovid's Latin tantalises his reader's imagination more than it satisfies their desires. Ovid breaks off his list of *figurae* by saying that there are still *mille modi veneris* – 'a thousand sex positions' – more. He leaves us wanting. Before signing off, his very final piece of advice to women is to suggest that she not 'let light into the bedroom through all the windows; it is better if much of your body lies hidden' (3.807–8). Sex is about concealment just as much as revelation, so Ovid's *figurae* tell us. His text teasingly questioned his readers as to what one thought one could know about the subject.

If Ovid was interested in sexual relations between men and women, he was also very concerned about the relationship between men's and women's knowledges of seduction. Victoria Rimell has discussed how 'the *Ars* is a didactic text about self-knowledge and self-image that breeds anxiety, suspicion, and self-doubt, a joke on the rhetoric of knowledge which claims to teach the unteachable'.[12] Books 1 and 2 are addressed to male lovers, but Book 3 speaks to their female counterparts, so that Ovid's advice across the books frequently contradicts itself, making it very hard to get his message. Indeed, as Ovid says of himself: 'I confess, I'm not perfect in this art; what should I do? I fall short of my own advice' (2.547–8). In Book 2, Ovid recommends to the male lover that he should let the woman think she is in charge and let her think he's 'awestruck' ('attonitus', 2.296) by her beauty. Ovid's Latin is reminiscent of Medusa's enemies who are 'numbed by fear' when they see her in Ovid's own *Metamorphoses* (4.802, 'attonitos formidine . . . hostes'). In Book 3, however, Ovid advises women to pretend *not* to have a frightening face (3.553–4), and a woman should be careful *not* to 'twist up her face with a hideous cackle' (3.287). In one book, the male 'lover must pretend to be *attonitus* by his girl's face', and then in the next we find out 'she *really is* a Medusa', as Rimell puts it.[13] Ovid's Latin tells us that seduction is saying one thing but meaning another. Ovidian seduction, in the end, doesn't make much sense. When we get to the point where Ovid describes what should happen in bed, he seems to recommend mutual masturbation to simultaneous orgasm (2.728). And yet, as Rimell has shown, the meeting of the lovers' eyes is reminiscent of the Salmacis–Hermaphroditus story in the *Metamorphoses* (4.347–88), in which Salmacis rapes the beautiful boy. In the *Ars Amatoria*, when man and woman are finally in bed together, the man will see his female lover's eyes 'glint with a flickering brightness, like the sun often reflects from the liquid water' (2.721–2). Ovid's woman looks like Salmacis, whose 'eyes gleamed, like when a mirror held against the sun reflects its shiny, dazzling orb' (*Met.* 4.347–9).[14] It seems that Ovid's male readers have been tricked as the woman, like the predatory Salmacis, is presented as getting the better of him. Ovid's amatory discourse wittily played with the idea that sex for the Roman *vir* was meant to be an assertation and affirmation of his position and status in relation to women, slaves and boys.[15]

The *Ars Amatoria* emphasised the protean nature of desire: 'the wise guy will adapt himself to countless fashions, and like Proteus will one moment be the waves, then a lion, a tree, a shaggy bear' (1.760–2). Ovid's world of sexual pleasure is one in which men and women are constantly competing to outwit one another: Ovid tries to teach other men how to adapt and constantly be on their guard, but he also ironically undercuts his own claim to knowledge when he confesses that he 'is not perfect in this art'. Giulio Romano's visualisation of Ovidian *modi* took place at a time when the contests between men's and women's knowledges became a significant topic of debate for Italian humanists. Already in about 1380, reflecting ancient catalogues of women, Boccaccio had written and circulated his *De Mulieribus Claris*, which inspired other fifteenth-century works listing and describing exemplary, virtuous women. And yet these feminine virtues rarely included wisdom beyond certain 'accomplishments' in activities such as drawing and embroidery, whereas a humanistic education was seen to equip men, on the other hand, for civic and political life. Boccaccio's work, nevertheless, inspired Christine de Pizan (*c.*1364–*c.*1430) – a Venetian court writer for various French dukes and therefore Europe's first professional female writer – to pen *The Book of the City of Ladies* (1405), which used famous women in history to question contemporary misogynistic ideas.[16] Even though, then, Renaissance humanism was dominated by male scholars, a few women *did* manage to acquire a classical education and argued that other women would benefit from such training. Certain women and some men began to argue that educated women would contribute to society more ably. Learned women, it was suggested, could at least make more interesting companions for their husbands and would be better mothers.[17]

The question whether women could also be virtuous like men – the *questione della donna* – could not, however, be ignored. One woman who encroached into this male space was a courtesan, philosopher and poet, Tullia d'Aragona, who intruded into the domain of the Renaissance dialogue.[18] Courtesans were indeed status symbols for the male elite, and their artistic and cultural accomplishments were enjoyed by wealthy and powerful men, including famous humanists, during the Italian Renaissance. Associating with cultured courtesans set rich and influential men apart from the masses and, it has been argued, provided a safer way of having sexual relations with women at a time when syphilis was on the rise in Italy. Courtesans thus helped to solidify and preserve elite male social identity.[19] But the philosophical treatise during the Renaissance was an altogether more male affair. Ficino's dialogue about Plato's *Symposium* featured only male interlocutors, and female speakers were all but marginalised from this genre of writing during the Italian Renaissance.[20] The *Dialogo della Signora Tullia d'Aragona della infinità d'amore* (the *Dialogue on the Infinity of Love by Signora Tullia d'Aragona*), which appeared in 1547, was unprecedented in that it was written by a woman, and a woman, 'Tullia', was cast as the main disputant in a dialogue on the nature of love.[21]

In the *Dialogo*, Tullia critiques Ficino's division of love between a spiritual, intellectual love, and its inferior, carnal opposite, by reformulating Pausanias' opposition. 'Vulgar' or 'dishonourable love' emerges out of a desire to enjoy the body of the object that is loved and to procreate like common animals. Such love does not last and wanes soon after satisfaction. 'Honest' or 'honourable love', on the other hand, is characteristic of noble people, whether rich or poor, and is not generated by desire but by reason. Reflecting Aristophanes' story of divided lovers in Plato's *Symposium*, a lover of 'honourable love' seeks to be united spiritually as well as physically with their object of love which, naturally, is impossible, meaning that this type of love can never be satisfied, and is therefore limitless and infinite.[22] And as Elizabeth Pallitto has explained, 'Aragona's model pointedly rejects social class, gender, and even marriage as criteria for honourable love: noble lovers are determined by their integrity instead of by their bloodlines'.[23]

In a discussion with one of her interlocutors, Benedetto Varchi, a friend of Tullia's as well as a leading man of letters in Florence in the mid-1500s, Tullia wittily highlights what she sees as the hypocrisy of Renaissance Platonism. She remarks that 'Lucian wrote a dialogue in which he praised this vice, as did Plato'. Varchi, whose verses for beautiful male youths were well known, replies that Tullia is 'greatly mistaken' for 'equating Lucian with Plato'.[24] The dialogue continues:

> TULLIA: Pardon me. I had understood that Socrates and Plato not only loved young men publicly, but they gave them eternal glory through their dialogues, telling of love most lovingly, as one sees in the *Alcibiades* and the *Phaedrus* . . .

VARCHI: I do not say that Socrates and Plato did not love young men publicly and that they did not glorify them in their dialogues, telling of love most lovingly; but I do say that they didn't love them in that way that the common crowd thinks of it . . .

TULLIA: I will believe it is as you say. But tell me: were they lovers?

Varchi replies with an emphatic yes, and then goes on to explain that the souls of Socrates and Plato were pregnant with goodness and that they wished to generate something similar to themselves, at which point Varchi interrupts himself to say, 'but we are treading on very difficult ground and besides you know everything already'.[25] And it is the issue of Tullia's knowledge that is at stake here and throughout the dialogue. As a woman, Tullia presents herself as not trying to compete intellectually with Varchi the Florentine scholar. Rather she employs humour to undermine his point of view, by 'equating' the pseudo-Lucianic *Erotes*, in which one speaker defends pederasty, with Plato's dialogues. Tullia positions herself as the Lucianic, satirical foil to Varchi who speaks on behalf of Renaissance Platonism.[26] In response to Varchi's defence she replies, 'I believe you', which wittily implies that it is an opinion to be believed that Varchi has offered, rather than some absolute truth. But Tullia's belief in Varchi is immediately undercut, when she asks whether Socrates and Plato were lovers. Finally, after Varchi starts to provide his answer, he gives up, saying that Tullia knows everything already. And then the dialogue moves onto the issue of whether women can also be honest and honourable lovers. In this exchange, then, the difficulty for women to assume a position of intellectual authority over the classical texts in a male-dominated environment is emphasised as Tullia uses humour and satire to question Varchi's position. In the end, the reader does not receive a complete and satisfactory understanding of what it meant for Socrates and Plato to be lovers, as Varchi abandons his explanation, deferring to Tullia's knowledge, even though Tullia had been accused of equating Lucian with Plato. The exchange shows not only how difficult it was for a Renaissance woman to stake a claim of knowledge among humanist scholars, but the presence of a woman in the dialogue provocatively demonstrates how tricky it becomes to explain what Platonic love actually is, once those who are traditionally excluded from discussion of such matters – women – gain access to the male space of Italian Renaissance scholarship. Indeed, Tullia's argument that anyone could be a noble lover, and the fact that she wrote in Italian and not Latin, suggested that the interpretation of Platonic love might not solely be under the control of a small group of privileged men.[27]

It was precisely the trouble that women could cause that concerned many male scholars and intellectuals. The voices of women such as Tullia were countered by many others which anxiously expressed concern about the possibility of female rule over men. Numerous political tracts emphasised the importance of the masculinity of the sovereign, in a period when certain states – such as England – worryingly, had an unmarried queen. And while the rise of Protestantism underlined the need for harmony and mutual companionship in a Christian marriage, both Protestant and Catholic theologians re-accentuated the need for a husband's authority at the head of the family. The scientific debate about sexual reproduction clearly reflected the intense debates about the relative merits of being a man and being a woman. During the second half of the sixteenth century, female anatomy and physiology underwent more detailed medical inquiry. Inspired by ancient discussions, sixteenth-century Aristotelians mostly argued that women produce no semen or any comparable substance, and so contributed nothing meaningful to the foetus. Galenists, on the other hand, held that women did also produce semen and even needed to orgasm, in order to conceive. Nevertheless, the Aristotelians strove to argue that women's bodies were more prone to suffer desire as they were imperfect beings that strived after the perfection of male bodies. Although the Galenists saw men and women as equally perfect opposites in their sex, the idea that women had less control over their desires than men did not go away.

The anxiety over Tullia persisted into the seventeenth century, as reflected by the *Satyra Sotadica de Arcanis Amoris et Veneris* (*Sotadic*

Satires on the Secrets of Love and Sex). First appearing in print in the 1660s, this book seemingly offered a comprehensive account of sex, far outstripping Romano's mere 16 positions. The title page claimed it was a Latin translation by the Dutch classical scholar Jan van Meurs or Meursius (1579–1639) of a Spanish dialogue by Aloisia Sigea or Louise Sigée. A contemporary of Tullia, Sigée had been a linguist and poet, famous for her writings and her campaign for women's education, before she died in 1560. And van Meurs wrote treatises on ancient festivals, including phallic rituals, and penned erotic verse. Sigée had also produced such poetry as well as a dialogue in Latin between two women talking about court life. When the reader opened his copy of *Satyra Sotadica* in the 1660s, he would have found it furnished with a biography of the Spanish authoress and, if he then flicked through the text, he would also have noticed gaps, where the manuscript had lacunae. But all this was an elaborate front: there was no original Spanish work and the Latin text was in fact written by a Dauphinois attorney and historian by the name of Nicolas Chorier. The *Satyra Sotadica*, then, comprise a series of dialogues in which a woman called Tullia educates her younger cousin Octavia in the matters of sex on the eve of the Octavia's wedding and throughout her marriage. Whereas Tullia d'Aragona had represented herself as a satirist who questioned the truth of Renaissance Platonic philosophy, in Chorier's *Satyra Sotadica* the woman called Tullia is being satirised by the male author, who is mocking the idea of classically educated women. We saw that Ovid, as a male author, appropriates for himself a tradition of writing supposedly invented by a woman, Astyanassa, Helen's maid, and offers men advice in a battle of the sexes, in which men are adviced to be like Proteus, constantly changing and adapting to get what they want while, at the same time, undermining his position of authority as he emphasises how women can get the better of men. Chorier, on the other hand, presents two women who show how Protean a woman's sex life can be, by showing how Protean classical Latin can be, as they misquote and re-write Ovid's texts, as well as Virgil and Horace, in their quest for sexual pleasure. Chorier provides a satirical fantasy for his male readers to enjoy, a fantasy which also reflects contemporary male anxieties about educated, knowledgeable women.

Chorier's protean Latin

Before we turn to the *Satyra Sotadica* itself, then, we should take note of two significant contexts, out of which this work emerged in the seventeenth century. Firstly, it was by no means coincidental that it was a Frenchman who should have written this text: by the mid-seventeenth century, French monarchs and noblemen had been enviously eyeing Italian collections of classical art for over a century. François I and Louis XIII, as well as French ministers like Richelieu, had sought out ancient sculptures to decorate their houses. But the ambitions of Louis XIV, who had assumed power in 1661, were of a different order altogether: his decision to convert his father's hunting lodge at Versailles became the most spectacular and sensational attempt ever to procure the most famous ancient sculpture at Rome. As his finance minister Jean-Baptiste Colbert remarked, 'we need to ensure everything of beauty in Italy is in France'. By 1682 the *Mercure galant*, a French magazine, could indeed confirm that 'Italy is in France and Paris is the new Rome'.[28]

Chorier's work also emerged out of seventeenth-century debates between European intellectuals writing in Latin, interested in the body's passions and the relationship between desire and reason, debates which were in dialogue with Lucretius' *De Rerum Natura* and Virgil's *Georgics*. Lucretius' celebration in Book 1 of his poem, of 'sweet Venus' as a cosmic, social and artistic force that arouses the procreative will in all creatures and soothes Mars in the politically turbulent Rome of the late Republic, became particularly influential. Of course, Virgil in his *Georgics* had already demonstrated his interest in Lucretius when he wrote 'Venus herself gave the mind' ('mentem Venus ipsa dedit', 3.267) and all of nature is furnished with the procreative urge ('amor omnibus idem', 'love is the same for all', 3.244). Lucretius and Virgil were crucial in seventeenth-century articulations of materialism, which sought to understand the physical mechanics of our bodies. As Susan James explains, for many seventeenth-century philosophers, desire became 'the central appetitive force which enables us to stay alive and governs all our actions'.[29] Thinkers like Thomas Hobbes and Baruch Spinoza viewed the human subject as driven by an all-encompassing master-drive. As Hobbes put it in his *Humane Nature*, 'passion is one and the same indefinite desire of different Sex, as natural as Hunger' (the allusion to Virgil's 'amor omnibus idem' is clear).[30] Even René Descartes, the philosopher who argued that we exist because we can think ('cogito ergo sum'), was influenced by seventeenth-century materialism when he theorised that the body was 'driven by surges of hot fluid (the animal spirits) and was commanded by a tiny bud of flesh, the pineal gland', as James Turner has examined.[31] Seeing the world and our bodies as material, concrete objects was also important for contemporary educational theory, such as Jan Amos Comenius' *Didactica magna*, in which Comenius, one of the earliest champions of universal education, argued that children should negotiate their environment 'ad vivam autopsiam' – that is, understand it through feeling and experiencing the sensible world.[32] Chorier's *Satyrica Sotadica* applied the lessons of seventeenth-century Latin materialism to argue that knowledge is indeed gained through the sensations of the body – that is, through sex. Tullia teaches her protégée Octavia: 'as Lucretius says, all things are borne along by the force of steel [*impetu ferri*], which only the powers of Venus can soothe' (II, 38): 'the force of steel' also meaning 'the drive of the penis'.[33]

Latinity could facilitate innuendo and double entendre, and it also made generic ambiguity possible. Ovid's *Ars Amatoria* had, of course, artfully blurred the boundary between didactic advice and erotic stimulation. And so, just as a European community of male intellectuals was intent on using Latin to understand and organise the mechanics of the body, so Chorier's *Satyra Sotadica* brings two fictitious educated women to the debate. Chorier's book, then, questions what it might mean to know about desire in Latin: what would be the difference between the scientific attempts of seventeenth-century materialist philosophy and Tullia's and Octavia's Latinate knowledges? Indeed, as Ovid had already pondered, what would be the difference between men's and women's knowledge of desire? Tullia's and Octavia's dialogue reflects contemporary male scholars' concerns about women's access to education and intellectual debate more generally, as this fantasy of two women's intimate conversation questions what it meant to find reason and order in Latin. The very beginning of the dialogue shows what would supposedly happen if women started getting a classical education. Octavia praises her elder cousin Tullia:

> all your learning [*eruditio*] ought to have opened secrets up [*adyta . . . aperuisse*] for you. I have often heard you praised to the sky because you have been trained [*imbueris*] in Latin and Greek literature [*litteris Latinis Graecisque*], as well as almost all the liberal arts, so that it seems there is nothing left that you don't know (I, 24).

At the beginning of the *Satyrica Sotadica*, Octavia, knowing nothing about sex, needs her more educated cousin. And yet, the Latin that Octavia herself uses is filled with innuendo and double entendre: Tullia's 'eruditio' has opened up secret passages, just as later on, Tullia will peer into Octavia's vagina. And, just as Tullia has been literally 'moistened' ('imbueris') by Latin and Greek, so Tullia and Octavia will repeatedly describe sexual encounters in which they have been made wet by the 'rain' ('imber') of their partners. Just how knowing or how ignorant is Octavia to seem? She goes on to say that men worry about educated women and say that 'erudition is like a fountain of all things bad and disgraceful for us women' (I, 25). Octavia sounds chaste as well as experienced, making the Latin sound both respectable and pornographic. Tullia d'Aragona had positioned herself as the satirist in dialogue with Renaissance philosophy, which reflected the difficulty Renaissance women had in making claims to knowledge. In Chorier's text, Octavia's Latin makes her appear knowing and unknowing at the same time, so that she becomes a satirical image for Chorier's male reader, as he fantasises about a young woman on the eve of her wedding about to lose her virginity and innocence.

This fantasy was, however, an anxious one. Octavia describes to Tullia Caviceus' (her fiancé's) previous – unsuccessful – attempts to have sex with her. (It is later revealed that Octavia does not have penetrative sex with Caviceus until their wedding night.) Octavia says that Caviceus awakened a strange feeling, which she doesn't understand: 'Since that day, Caviceus is much more agreeable to me, and my mind is driven mad by some [*nescio qua*] violent desire. [. . .] I desire nothing, and yet I desire [*cupio nihil, et cupio tamen*]' (I, 28). Desire ('cupio') seems to be beyond understanding ('nescio qua'), just as the word 'desire' itself means more than one thing: 'cupio nihil, et cupio tamen'. And that was precisely the concern for male humanists and philosophers – that Latin might not make sense and might mean more than one thing. And the language of sex was the domain where language didn't always mean what it said: Ovid had taught his readers that the art of seduction lay in the ability to change the meanings of words, so that you say something but mean another. Now Tullia's tutorial for Octavia reinterprets the classical texts, undermining male humanistic attempts to understand their meaning. Indeed, Tullia's sexual curriculum runs riot with the classical canon – especially Ovid, Virgil and Horace.[34] In fourteenth-century France, a long poem called *Ovide moralisé* had been composed, in which the authors adapted Ovid's *Metamorphoses*, so that his stories made moral sense.[35] In the *Satyra Sotadica*, however, Tullia reads the *Metamorphoses* in a very different way. To explain Octavia's 'desire', the well-read Tullia quotes a long passage from Ovid's famous epic (9.456–7, 464–5, 468–75, 479–84): the story of Byblis' incestuous love for her brother Caunus, which drives her mad, causing her to dissolve into a fountain of her own tears. Tullia cites the first part of the tale, when a dreaming Byblis doesn't realise that her desires are transgressive:

> At first she did not understand these fires,
> And did not think there was anything wrong in planting kisses
>   on her brother
> (I, 28, and Ovid *Met.* 9.456–7)

Tullia's Byblis goes on:

> Provided that I do not try anything while awake,
> May sleep often return with a similar vision
> (I, 28 and Ovid *Met.* 9.479–80)

Tullia's language turns Octavia on, who then asks her elder cousin to teach her about her desires. What Tullia does *not* do is reveal whom Byblis loves and how she suffers. Ovid's story continued with Byblis' long love-letter, an epistle which did *not* follow Ovid's own instructions for letter-writing in his *Ars Amatoria*.[36] She foolishly reveals her name to Caunus, which causes her brother to reject her angrily (*Met.* 9.574), as Byblis laments:

> I should have tested out his feelings
> beforehand in ambiguous words [*ambiguis . . . dictis*] (*Met.* 9.588–9)

Byblis didn't understand that the art of seduction is conducted in 'ambiguous language', a lesson Tullia, however, has learnt, in quoting from Ovid's story so selectively. Whereas, in the *Metamorphoses*, Ovid presents the tale as 'a warning that girls should love what is permitted' (9.454), a moral eagerly taken up by medieval and Renaissance readers, Tullia rewrites Ovid's Latin in order to arouse Octavia's desires, so that the two cousins, family relations like Byblis and Caunus, can enjoy each other's bodies. Latin that had delineated 'what is permitted' becomes Latin to turn Chorier's reader on.

The contest between men's and women's knowledge of Latin and of sex becomes the focus of the brutal and painful defloration scenes described in the book. Of course, the metaphor of love as war was a central theme in Roman elegiac and erotic poetry. 'Every lover is a soldier', as Ovid wrote (*Amores*, 1.7.1, 19–20). Ovid's *Ars Amatoria* had viewed the art of seduction as a duel between a mutually suspicious man and woman trying to outwit one another. Chorier takes this theme and turns the wedding night into a bloody battle, in which the phallus conquers the woman. Tullia describes the loss of her virginity:

> He shot his tongue into my mouth and at the very same moment he drove his spear [*pilum*] into my fatal wound [*perniciem*]. I shriek and shout; rivers of tears flow from my eyes. 'Poor me!' I said, 'you're killing me. Stop for a little while from such a savage and wild attack [*ab hoc impetu tam saevo, tam fero*]' [. . .] At last with a final effort he succeeded in getting the whole of his enemy into my defences [*ut totus intra vallum meum subiret hostis*], but with such a force that I never sustained before' (IV, 65).

The violent Latin fetishises the loss of virginity with the bloody rupture of the hymen. The penis is a weapon: the vagina a wound.

Chorier's language resonates with Virgilian epic battle. Indeed Virgil's *Aeneid* is repeatedly invoked. The importance of this narrative of authority – a narrative of civic and political order – in a young man's Renaissance education was enormous. But where Aeneas battles for control against a series of chaotic female figures (Juno, Dido, Camilla . . .), in the *Satyra Sotadica* we read a very different sort of battle between the sexes: the deflowered vagina smells like the underworld in *Aeneid* 6 (III, 47). Sex with a woman is like 'itque reditque viam totiens' (IV, 75, citing *Aeneid* 6.122), going down the road to the underworld again and again. After hearing Tullia's account of her wedding night, Octavia is 'spemque metumque inter' (IV, 72): 'between hope and fear', like Aeneas' comrades, not knowing whether to hope or mourn for their friends after the cataclysmic storm (*Aeneid* 1.218).

Even Tullia's husband's orgasm sounds like Virgil:

> *intorquet summis innixus viribus hastam*, implet fecundo rore uterum.

> 'With all his strength he twisted in his spear and filled my uterus with fertile dew' (IV, 72; my italics).

Only, this time, the Latin comes from a poem called the *Cento Nuptialis*. Written by Ausonius, a fourth-century Latin poet from Bordeaux, the *Cento* is a wedding song in celebration of the marriage of Gratian, son of the emperor Valentinian, to Constantia. Ausonius' poem, consisting entirely of half-lines from Virgil's poetry, is a sexually explicit celebration of Gratian's wedding. So the scholarly Tullia cites a late-antique Latin author, who had rewritten Virgil's Latin in order to praise the erotics of marriage: Chorier's learned ladies demonstrate the erotic possibilities of protean Latinity for married life. In a defence of his poem, Ausonius had already rehearsed Catullus' argument about rude verse. He also argued that Virgil had planted obscene connotations in his Latin for those who were able to see it. Ausonius presented himself as a practitioner of *cacemphaton*, which Quintilian, in his *Institutio Oratoria*, had condemned as 'twisting language into obscenity' (8.3.44). Quintilian, a contemporary of Martial and worried about the state of the Latin language, had been concerned that certain devious readers of the classical canon had 'seized the opportunity for shamelessness from words that are furthest from obscenity' (8.3.47). When women become humanists and learn Latin, then, they too cannot help but see something else in the classical text: female sexuality questioned what Latin was supposed to have meant.[37] When read by women, the Latin language incites – creates – sexual desire. Just as Tullia was violently conquered, so Octavia feels like she is dying of an orgasm, just from listening: 'you're killing me with this discourse [*hoc sermone*], see, look, I'm dying in expectation of such pleasure!' (IV, 67). And as Octavia says to Tullia when it comes to describing her own wedding night: 'with an itch-inducing description [*pruriginosa descriptione*], I shall distil pleasures through your ears into your soul, pleasures which the god Hymen rained into my body (V, 82). Latin rains in the ear like semen in the vagina.

Indeed Octavia follows her mentor's lessons well when she herself rewrites a couple of lines from the *Aeneid*. Here is what Octavia says:

> Est hic, est animus pili contemptor, et illum
> qui cunno bene credit emi, quo tendit amorem

> True, our mind scorns the spear, and even believes
> that love it aims at can be bought by the cunt (IV, 68)

Women foolishly think, Octavia says, that 'amor' can be obtained by the 'cunnus' without the man's 'pilum'. But these two cousins know the phallic 'truth' only too well. Octavia's Latin makes a mockery of *Aeneid* 9.205–6:

> Est hic, est animus lucis contemptor et istum
> Qui vita bene credit emi, quo tendis, honorem
>
> True, I have here a heart that despises the light, that
> Would gladly spend life to buy the honour, to which you strive.

At this the point in Virgil's narrative, the Trojans are encamped and encircled by Turnus' forces, when the Trojan guardsmen Nisus and Euryalus plot a nocturnal attack. In the lines that Octavia parodies, Euryalus offers his service to his beloved companion Nisus. A bond between two heroic, comradely men is transformed ('immutasti', Chorier's Latin says) into a sexual bond between husband and wife. Euryalus offers to give up his life ('lucis contemptor'), whereas Octavia realises it is ridiculous to give up the penis ('pili contemptor'). Nisus and Euryalus strive for 'honor', whereas Octavia and Tullia want 'amor'.

As Tullia says, loving in Latin is an ingenious thing ('ingeniosa res est amor', IV, 85). Latinity allows something to look like one thing as well as the other: in Virgilian *honor* Octavia sees *amor*. Octavia's substitution makes heroic Latin look quite different. Ovid's *Ars Amatoria* had taught his male and female readers never to trust appearances and yet always to conceal one's true self. That seduction manual had depicted a battle for power between the sexes; in Chorier's portrayal of the wedding night, the confrontation between man and woman becomes a painful duel. But this is not the end of the fight, as Tullia goes on to explain the power-games of married life, where telling the difference between *honor* and *amor* becomes truly impossible. As she explains to Octavia, the phallus-wielding husband does not hold all the cards. She cites Horace's *Satires* (1.1.106):

> Recte dictum est,
> *esse modum in rebus, esse certos denique fines.*
> Non in rebus constitit laus et vituperium, sed in rerum usu.
>
> It's rightly said that 'things have a certain proportion, that is, there are defined limits'. Praise and blame do not consist in the things themselves, but in the use we make of them (V, 111: my italics).

Praise and blame, then, are nothing but words to be used, and don't reflect anything essential. Praise can be administered to anyone who looks praiseworthy. As Tullia says, 'Whatever you can conveniently do, without scandal to your husband or family, be convinced that everything is permitted to you [*tibi licere omne*]' (V, 111). She continues: 'the next lesson in wifely wisdom' is to 'cover one's life with a veil of sanctity. She who adorns [*honestat*] wicked deeds with the appearance of probity, is much more useful to civic life [*civili vitae*], than those who hide their good deeds under a shadow of disgrace' (V, 113). What looks like *honor*, Tullia teaches, can be extramarital *amor*, as the scholar of sex instructs her protégée how to be both a wife *and* a mistress. As we saw earlier in the chapter, Ficino had contrasted 'true love' that flies up 'to divine beauty' with 'adulterous love [*adulterinus*]' which was 'a falling down from sight to touch'.[38] Tullia, however, doesn't distinguish between marital and adulterous pleasure. Tullia d'Aragona had differentiated between 'disonesto' and 'onesto' love. Her namesake in Chorier, on the other hand, teaches her cousin to give wicked deeds the appearance that they are correct ('honestat'). Both the Renaissance philosopher and his female interlocutor, Tullia d'Aragona, are mocked in the *Satyra Sotadica*. And the quotation of Horace in this context is also significant. Horace's *Satires* had offered Renaissance poets such as Ludovico Ariosto a model for negotiating the tricky issues of patronage and friendship between men.[39] In Chorier's *Satyra Sotadica*, Horace's advice about knowing one's limits and finding a middle ground between different political factions, between different groups of men, becomes a lesson for women in how to position themselves between husband and lover. Horace – the author who had helped male humanists articulate their relationships among themselves – becomes, in the hands of learned women, a lesson in the exploration of feminine desire. Just as classical Latin could be both two things at once, so can Tullia and Octavia: 'you will be happy and blessed, when you mix one with the other' (V, 114) – that is, being wife and mistress.

Like all the other neo-Latin didactic texts of her day, Tullia's sexual curriculum worked from simple to advanced, from elementary to complex: beginning with Octavia's tale of Caviceus' hapless attempts at sex, to Tullia's initiation of Octavia into sexual pleasure, to Octavia's wedding night, then to Tullia's syllabus of extra-marital affairs, leading ultimately to her outline of possible group-sex positions. The *Satyrica Sotadica* was an erotic curriculum, in which the Latin language taught the early-modern male reader about sexual desire. Not surprisingly, it became very popular with French, Italian and English gentlemen who relished being taught the arts of love by this mistress of a text. Casanova claimed to have learnt from it and Diderot enjoyed it. Libertine writers John Wilmot, Earl of Rochester and John Oldham were profoundly influenced by it. Numerous editions were published on both sides of the English Channel, and the book remained in print until the end of the nineteenth century.[40] Copies found their way into princely libraries across Europe, and scholars on antiquity even began citing it. And yet, as Tullia says, invoking Ovid, near the very end of her tuition, 'Love as Proteus loves to change', 'mutari amat Proteus Amor' (VII, 278). Tullia's re-readings of classical Latin reflect the metamorphic nature of their desires, as these insatiable women keep on wanting something else. Despite Tullia's attempts to know everything about sex, the mind produces 'more things than can actually be done' – 'the body cannot easily do all that the mind persuades' (VI, 215).

In the hands of Tullia and Octavia, the classical Latin texts keep on changing, just like their desires. The stability of the canon is undermined as Chorier fantasises about a female Latinity which incites and stimulates sexual desire just as much as Latin might have instructed anyone. Ovid had professed his knowledge in the arts of love, only to confess he was no real expert in the matter, as he depicted a mistrusting world of men and women trying to outsmart each other in order to get what they want. Ovid, a male author in a bid for textual authority, appropriated the legendary genre of sex manuals that had supposedly been invented by women. In the *Satyra Sotadica*, on the other hand, the texts of Ovid himself, and his Roman colleagues Virgil and Horace, become the arsenal in the sexual battles between married men and women. Ovid is re-read by Tullia to turn Octavia on, so that the two cousins can have sex with one another before the latter is wed; Tullia uses Virgil to teach Octavia that she will have to submit to her husband's phallic weapons; and Horace is commandeered by Tullia to instruct Octavia in the art of outwitting her husband for the sake of Octavia's extra-marital sexual pleasures. Chorier presents for his male readers a fantasy which was indeed much enjoyed across Western Europe. And yet, this fantasy also bespeaks an anxiety about women's access to the classics and to an education. While Tullia and Octavia are shown to be capable of re-reading and re-writing Latin texts, this is ultimately for the sake of the male reader as the two cousins' abilities to engage with Latin never go beyond the sexual. Chorier's literary creations are a satire on women such as Tullia d'Aragona who *did* use classical texts to question male authority and structures of knowledge in a bid for some sort of female inclusion in the masculine world of Renaissance scholarship. In Chapter I, Beccadelli had provoked the question of who was vested to use Latin authoritatively when the language of sex is used. In this chapter, we have seen how it is through the language of sex that the issue of women's abilities and powers to learn and appropriate the classics is addressed and negotiated, at a time when the issue of Platonic love was of great interest to the humanist scholar. We can now turn to Chapter III, where we will see how the texts of Beccadelli and Chorier become co-opted into nineteenth-century sexological discourse, which sought to exercise its powers not only over women but all sorts of other subjects, by means of a catalogue of sexual identities.

CHAPTER III

SEXUAL ENLIGHTENMENT? FROM ARCHAEOLOGY TO SCIENCE

This chapter begins in the eighteenth century, when the newly rediscovered sites of ancient Herculaneum and Pompeii were yielding some spectacular artefacts. The number of phallic objects that emerged from the ground swiftly attracted interest around Europe, as intellectuals tried to understand the meaning of these articles. Very quickly a sophisticated market for collecting ancient erotica and curiosa developed out of the enthusiasm for Pompeii and Herculaneum, while many of these objects – whether they were authentically ancient or modern fakes – were either acquired by or donated to museums where they were then cordoned off into private cabinets, separated from the main collections. It was at this time, at the end of the eighteenth century, when anthologies of priapic and obscene poetry were published, and poems from Beccadelli's *Hermaphrodite* were included in one such publication. These material and printed collections came together at the same time as intense debates about the protocols of classical scholarship were being held in German universities, where the notion of classical studies (or *Altertumswissenschaft*) as a science which could provide truthful and objective knowledge about the ancient world was being formulated, institutionalised and professionalised. It was in this environment that one philologist, Friedrich Karl Forberg, apparently discovered a manuscript of Beccadelli's poetry in a library in Coburg, Bavaria. His edition of *The Hermaphrodite* was appended by a long essay which also made liberal use of the prose of the *Satyra Sotadica* to explain in an objective and scholarly manner the intricate vocabulary of sex in Latin.

With Forberg's publication, the study of ancient sex acts and behaviours had become a specific area of serious study within the broader project of classical studies in German culture. This chapter goes on to examine how the language of Latin epigram provided a lexicon of technical terms to map out ancient sexual activity for nineteenth-century medical research on venereal disease, which formed the basis for the 'termini technici' in Richard von Krafft-Ebing's *Psychopathia Sexualis*. Whereas Beccadelli's poetry and Chorier's prose had posed questions for their readers about how one could speak in Latin about sex with authority, with Forberg's essay the sexual vocabulary of Latin itself becomes an authoritative instrument for the nineteenth-century physician and sexologist. But could the Latin of Catullus' and Martial's epigrams really become a scientific language? This chapter explores this question.

The nature of the phallus

Tullia had taught her cousin Octavia that the word 'mentula' (dick) derives from 'mens' (mind), and 'cunnus' (cunt) comes from 'konnein' (Tullia's Greek for 'understand'): her bawdy lesson reflected seventeenth-century attempts to see reason behind the passions of the body. Tullia, however, eventually gave up trying to formulate a complete knowledge of sex: the mind could think up more things than the body could ever do. The materialist inquiries of the seventeenth century, however, paved the way towards eighteenth-century efforts to rationalise sexual desire. During the 1700s, many European rulers, statesmen and intellectuals became particularly concerned with the monitoring of their populations, the surveillance of the strength of their states and the control of public order. Although these issues had obviously been sources of anxiety to heads of state earlier in history, understanding the population's sexual habits became one of the principal ways in which to control and regulate a society's well-being by the end of the nineteenth century. Whereas earlier Christian writers had been concerned with the definition of sin, eighteenth-century thinkers became interested in how modern society might benefit from understanding the logic of nature – in particular, the sexual logic of the natural world. Building on early debates from the seventeenth century, sexual pleasure, many argued, was natural. But the philosophers of the Enlightenment oscillated between viewing nature as ordered, rational and harmonious, and as disruptive, chaotic and anarchic. And similarly, sexual activity was seen as the bedrock of society *and* as potentially wildly subversive. This ambivalence about sexuality meant that Enlightenment thinkers more often than not sought to understand how the power of sexuality might be harnessed for the good of society.[1]

Whereas Chorier's *Satyra Sotadica* showed its readers how classical Latinity could incite one to find something new in the text – to think up new forms of sexual desire – eighteenth-century thinkers, on the other hand, began to consider the rationality of sex. While Chorier's Latin had enflamed its readers to artificial inventiveness, so, in the eighteenth century, classical antiquity came to be viewed as a time when one was in tune with nature. While Chorier had depicted marriage as a battle between the sexes competing to outwit and win in the game of desire, eighteenth-century inquiries into married life examined how couples might complement and understand one another's desires in order to fulfil the logical workings of the natural world, to the wider benefit of modern society. The science of botany became an important discourse in the debates about the naturalness of sexual desire. This was evidenced in works such as Erasmus Darwin's *The Loves of the Plants* (1791), a promotion and illustration of Linnaeus' system, which described the sexual relations of plant life in epic verse; or, for instance, in *The Temple of Nature or, The Origin of Society* (1803), where Darwin depicted nature as made up of sexual drives that underpin our world.[2]

By the end of the seventeenth century, serious medical advice on happy married life had already become widely read. In 1690, an anonymously written work entitled *Aristotle's Masterpiece* appeared, offering young married couples detailed instructions on the correct age of marriage, tricks for successful conception, information on why children resemble their parents, advice on how to behave during pregnancy, guidelines on how to cope with the birth, and so on. The book heartily emphasised 'the plastic power of Nature' to 'go forth and multiply'. For the author of *Aristotle's Masterpiece*, as Roy Porter and Lesley Hall have summarised, marriage 'was companionable, sexually fulfilling, healthy for the couple concerned, and, along mercantilist lines, productive for the body politic'.[3] The book went through numerous editions and continued to be published into the twentieth century. Its mixture of medical expertise (anatomical 'knowledge' that drew haphazardly from both Aristotelians and Galenists) and homespun advice found a broad and diverse audience. A few years before, in 1686 in France, Nicolas Venette had published his *Tableau de l'amour conjugal*. Although it was aimed at a more educated high-brow market (Venette had studied medicine and was a respected medical author), the hodge-podge of medical theory and stories from classical and biblical texts ensured that it became a more popular read, although it was not taken altogether seriously by the medical establishment in France. Nevertheless, like *Aristotle's Masterpiece*, it too went through numerous editions not only in French, but also later in English. And, like *Aristotle's Masterpiece*, Venette too was interested in promoting a healthily sexual marriage. As Porter and Hall put it, for Venette, 'it [was] the translation of sexual desire into the public estate of matrimony that [would] transform the chaos of the passions into order'.[4]

The emphasis on the naturalness of heteroerotic sexual desire ensured that sex began to be seen as more of an object of scientific and legal inquiry. And it seemed that classical antiquity confirmed these modern ideas about the importance of knowing about fertility and conception for the welfare of society. Indeed, the discovery of numerous bizarrely shaped phallic objects in the 1750s and 1760s at Pompeii and Herculaneum was central to these debates. The phallic objects excavated were – and remain – strange to behold: for instance, a cock's head with a phallus for a nose; winged phalli with tails and bells hanging off; and phallic door-knockers. In his 1762 *Sendschreiben von den Herculanischen Entdeckungen* (*Letter on the Herculanean Discoveries*), the historian of ancient art Johann

Joachim Winckelmann had described such phallic 'amulets or pendants, which one wore against curses, against the evil eye, and against sorcery'.[5] These objects, unsurprisingly, were of great interest to antiquarians across Europe. One such figure was the grandly named art historian Baron d'Hancarville (a pseudonym for Pierre-François Hugues), who wrote a three-volume work called *Recherches sur l'origine, l'esprit et les progrès des arts de la Grèce* (published in 1785), in which he argued that ancient art was ultimately erotic in origin. Ancient representations of gods and goddesses in Greek, Roman and Indian art could be traced back to even earlier representations of a generative, creative force or deity. Ancient phallic artefacts and other ithyphallic objects and images were simply relics of mankind's original religion, the worship of the 'Être Générateur'. D'Hancarville's theory of art was in direct competition with Winckelmann's, which contended that the best art encouraged the viewer to look beyond the concrete, embodied sculpture, to contemplate abstract truths and beauties, as he imagined when looking at the Apollo Belvedere. D'Hancarville, conversely, was interested in how the abstract principle of generation became embodied and concretised in material and visual representations, such as phallic objects, and gems and cameos representing Bacchus. Whereas for Winckelmann ancient art moved the viewer from looking at the physical body to contemplating the abstract, for d'Hancarville the history of ancient material culture was essentially attempt after attempt to represent materially the generative, creative First Cause, to make concrete the abstract.[6]

Antiquarian publications about 'phallic worship' started appearing. One of the continent's greatest collectors of antiquities, Sir William Hamilton, British Ambassador to the court at Naples (the capital of the Kingdom of Two Sicilies), had a particular interest in these artefacts. He had already published his ancient Greek and Italian vase collection with a commentary written by d'Hancarville. The publication was one of the major antiquarian publications of the eighteenth century, lavishly reproducing in red and black Hamilton's sensational collection. But it was also the sexual frankness of some of the images that made the publication so interesting.

On Hamilton's vases were ithyphallic herms, groups of male lovers and prostitutes at symposia, and even, d'Hancarville argued, an all-male brothel.[7] In 1781, Hamilton sent a report to his friend Sir Joseph Banks, the well-known botanist and (like Hamilton) fellow of the Society of Dilettanti, about a strange case of phallic worship in a small, out-of-the-way town called Isernia, some way from Naples. Here, wives apparently offered waxen simulacra of phalli to the 'great toe' of St Cosmas and Damian. Hamilton continues: 'Those who have an infirmity in any of their members, present themselves at the great altar, and uncover the member affected (not even excepting that which is most frequently represented by the *ex-voti*)'.[8] Hamilton's letter then went on to say that the wives would spend the night in the church under the guardianship of the local priests, suggesting that it was the officers of the church who would be curing the wives' lack of fertility with their own penises. For the British ambassador Hamilton, the festival was simply evidence of 'Popish' backwardness and (sexual) corruption.

For another fellow of the Society of Dilettanti, Hamilton's discovery offered the opportunity to write a book-length study of phallic worship. Richard Payne Knight, a highly respected connoisseur and collector of antiquities, published his *Discourse on the Worship of Priapus and its Connexion with the Mystic Religion of the Ancients* in 1786, to be distributed among a select group of readers.[9] In this work, Payne Knight argued that society was originally founded upon and organised around a profoundly philosophical understanding of fertility and procreation. The world's oldest theologians established a system that worshipped the reproductive powers of Nature. Or, as Payne Knight put it, 'Because these symbols were intended to express abstract ideas by objects of sight, the contrivers of them naturally selected those objects whose characteristic properties seemed to have the greatest analogy with the divine attributes which they wished to represent'.[10] Payne Knight's enlightened ancients knew that they could not imagine the infinite reproductivity of the universe. Instead, they visualised through representations of the male and female 'Organs of Generation' Nature's logic of reproduction:

> The ancient Theologists knew that we could form no positive idea of infinity, whether of power, space or time; it being fleeting and fugitive, and eluding the understanding by a continued and boundless progression. The only notion we have of it is from the addition or division of finite things, which suggest the idea of infinite, only from a power we feel in ourselves of still multiplying and dividing without end'.[11]

With time, however,

> the grand and exalted system of a general First Cause, universally expanded, did not suit the gross conceptions of the multitude; who had no other way of conceiving the idea of an omnipotent God, but by forming an exaggerated image of their own Despot [the penis], and supposing his power to consist in an unlimited gratification of his passions and appetites'.[12]

So, the Roman god Priapus was simply a belated relic of an earlier, more philosophical, more rational system of thought. Payne Knight's most provocative statement was that Christianity had unwittingly taken on phallic worship, as he wrote of the Christian cross: 'the form of the letter T [. . .] served as the emblem of creation and generation, before the Church adopted it as the sign of salvation; a lucky coincidence of ideas, which, without doubt, facilitated the reception of it among the Faithful'.[13] The phallic worship that Hamilton had uncovered at Isernia, then, was nothing but a corrupted, hypocritical remnant. Payne Knight's anti-clericalism was a fulminating critique of Christianity's duplicitous stance against pagan sexuality.

The seemingly abundant supply of ancient phallic artefacts that emerged from the southern Italian soil saw to it that, by 1819, Naples had established a Secret Museum to house these objects that were to be considered erotic or obscene. Educated gentlemen, including eminent figures such as Goethe, began to build collections of *phallica*.[14] These erotic collections provided a market for d'Hancarville's *Monumens de la vie privée des XII*

Césars (first published in 1780) and *Monumens du culte secret des dames romaines* (1784). These volumes comprised images of fictional cameos – extremely collectable items in the eighteenth century – depicting the sexual activities of the Roman emperors and their lovers. While Romano's *Modi* had focused solely on male–female couplings, d'Hancarville's *Monumens* catalogued and illustrated a fully polysexual range of accomplishments that had been described in the classical texts. These tomes became popular, and numerous pirated editions had appeared by the start of the nineteenth century. Just like the *phallica* they illustrated, they themselves soon became collectors' items. Then, in 1791, the sculptor James Tassie produced a huge catalogue of ancient and modern gems, including priapic examples, which were supplied across Europe. By 1865, the British Museum had founded its own 'Secretum', when it acquired a collection of 'Symbols of the Early Worship of Mankind', owned by George Witt. By the end of the nineteenth century, a semi-clandestine publishing industry was booming with the publication of numerous titles on the subject of 'phallicism', or ancient phallic worship.[15] Indeed, the collections of various phallic objects and images depicting phalli demonstrated the different uses to which a penis could be put. Such collections visualised classical Latin's own rich sexual vocabulary which was structured around phallic penetration (an issue to which we shall return very shortly). Moreover, Payne Knight's attack on Christianity had been highly influential over French republican *idéologues,* who were keen on critiquing the hypocrisy of the Christianity of the *ancien régime*. One prominent example was *Origine de Tous les Cultes, ou Religion universelle* by Charles-François Dupuis, a huge publication, seven volumes in all. Dupuis was an important political figure and *savant* in France in the 1790s: he had been elected to the National Convention, where he sat on the Council of Five Hundred. His *Origine de Tous les Cultes* reflected contemporary anti-clerical suspicions targeted at the Roman Catholic Church.[16]

Just as European gentlemen enjoyed collecting *phallica*, and just as d'Hancarville banked on this market with the publication of fake erotic cameo collections, so scholars also became interested in collecting the language and literature of ancient sexual behaviours. The first attempt at a comprehensive lexicon of terms for sexual acts was a manuscript written in 1791, the *Carmina Ithyphallica: Dictionnaire érotique Latin–Francais*. In the same year, also influenced by the interest in collecting erotica, an anthology of erotic Renaissance Latin epigrams appeared, comprising Beccadelli's epigrams along with other Renaissance epigrammatists inspired and inflamed by his verses. This frank tome of free-speaking poetry, *Quinque illustrium poetarum*, must have been well received in revolutionary France, as the following year the editor, Barthélemy Mercier de Saint-Léger, was appointed to a commission on monuments which was charged with saving libraries for the public. Then, in 1798, a scholar called François Noël published *Erotopaegnion, sive Priapeia Veterum et Recentiorum, Veneris jocosae sacrum*, an even more comprehensive volume of ancient Roman, Renaissance and contemporary Latin priapic verse. This also included a lexicon of ancient sexual vocabulary larger than Barthélemy Mercier's work and paved the way for an illustrious career for Noël in producing dictionaries of French, Latin and fables. Noël was soon named a member of the Tribunat, and by 1802 he was inspector-general of public education.[17] Out of the anti-clerical fulminations of the *ideologues*, then, the study of ancient sexuality was slowly becoming a serious subject of scholarly analysis. Just as for Payne Knight the original worship of the 'Organ of Generation' was 'a very natural symbol of a very natural and philosophical system of religion', so for his readers the penis would become a self-evident representation of sexual desire.[18] The collecting of *phallica* and the anthologising of Latinate epigrammatic verse paved the way for the invention of a very specific area of knowledge in the nineteenth century: the phallic vocabulary of classical Latin was soon to offer the basis for the development of a fully institutionalised *Sexualwissenschaft*, the sciencific study of sex.

The priapic scholar

At this time, German scholars were also thinking very seriously about the relationship between the ancient and the modern worlds. German intellectuals were entangled in profound debate about what made historical investigation a scientific occupation: what methods made scholarly accounts about the past truthful and objective? Understanding the nature of the relationship between the past and the present became the object of scientific enquiry, which dealt with a series of complex questions: in particular, how is modern Europe different from, and similar to, classical antiquity? In what ways should the ancient past be seen as analogous to the present? What counts as anachronism? The dialectic of progress and decline became a key frame for the organisation of historical narrative, as scholars sought to make historical scholarship a *Wissenschaft* – a science – in its own right. The science of classical scholarship, *Altertumswissenschaft*, developed in institutional confidence at this time. By the end of the eighteenth century, classical philologists were busily positioning themselves as inhabitants of a specific intellectual discipline with its own rules, protocols and practices for historicising the past in an objective manner. This meant understanding the relationship between ancient and modern (how were they similar, how were they different?). In his lectures while a professor at the University of Göttingen, Christian Gottlob Heyne (often seen as one of the founding fathers of Classics as a discipline) examined the Social Wars of ancient Rome through a comparison with the American War of Independence; he assessed the similarities and differences between exile to an island in the ancient Roman empire and the British transportation of convicts to New South Wales, and when he lectured on Roman agrarian laws he also talked about the expropriations made in revolutionary France. By the 1810s, eminent German classical scholars such as Barthold Georg Niebuhr could say that 'everything ancient was alien to him'. As Anthony Grafton has put it, 'they insisted that the true scholar abandon the assumptions and mental categories of his own world and time'. The ambition of German historicism was such that Grafton has labelled it '*the will to replace the text* [. . .] [as] scholars tended to try to dissolve the texts before them in order to recreate something lost', the lost, othered world of antiquity, to inhabit it in all its difference.[19]

The Enlightenment critique of Christianity, the emergence of ancient phallic worship in English and French scholarship and the debates about historicism in German universities provided the opportunity for one German scholar to broach the issue of ancient sexual behaviour in real detail. Indeed this subject could be seen as a test case for the objectives – the objectivity – of historicist scholarship. Friedrich Karl Forberg (b. 1770), Conservator of the Aulic Library at Coburg, discovered a manuscript which included a part of Beccadelli's *The Hermaphrodite*. Seeing that Mercier's 1791 anthology also only contained some of Beccadelli's epigrams along with numerous errors, Forberg set to work on his own, complete edition which appeared in 1824. His preface sets out the scholarly nature of the work, as he explains how he has numbered each epigram; how he has carefully corrected the many mistakes found in Mercier's edition; how he has diligently compared the variant readings in the extant manuscripts and printed books containing Beccadelli's poems; how he has noted verbal similarities in ancient texts; and finally how he has put aside any shame about the subject matter in order to explain openly and clearly the more obscene sections which have been avoided in previous discussions of Beccadelli's work.[20]

Forberg also uses the preface to position himself within the world of professional German scholarship: he thanks the renowned Johann Gottfried Eichhorn (1753–1827) for allowing him to consult a Venetian edition of Beccadelli's works in the library at the University of Göttingen. Eichhorn is a very important figure in the history of biblical criticism, and his work exerted much influence on classicists working on Greek and Latin textual criticism. By 1824, he had been professor for many years at Göttingen, one of the first modern research universities in Europe, which was to have a significant influence on the history of university education in the West. Forberg also expresses his gratitude to Johann Gottfried Ludwig Kosegarten, a professor of Oriental languages at Jena, for copying out a few of Beccadelli's epigrams found in another manuscript. Forberg continues to say that he cannot name all those who have helped: in his studies he has been assisted by 'many other very learned men', to whom he is very happy to return any favours.[21] Forberg's name-dropping did not simply publicly proclaim his place within a network of institionalised and professional scholars. His description of a world of male professors granting access to and copying out texts, which in turn incur return favours, is reminiscent of the world of humanists inhabited by Beccadelli. Just as the texts of Catullus and Martial were difficult to obtain in the early 1400s, so Beccadelli's own text becomes tricky to get hold of in the nineteenth century. In Beccadelli's poetry, the elusiveness of Catullus and Martial works as a metaphor for the difficulty of reading these texts and using their Latin with authority. In Forberg's preface, however, the circulation of Beccadelli's epigrams becomes a sign of the authority of his edition of Beccadelli's poetry, as it advertises his command over Beccadelli's Latin through his placement in a world of modern scholarship.

Beccadelli had made fun of the 'rigid Catos', the censors, who professed their disgust at obscene poetry while being aroused by it. In the final poem in *The Hermaphrodite*, Beccadelli addresses his book, 'parve liber', saying 'you will fuck and will be fucked' (2.37.2, 32). He sends his book on its way in the knowledge that it will be welcomed and assaulted in equal measure. Forberg closes his preface in a similar way: 'Go, little book [*parve liber*], and undergo your fate. Do not be frightened of the censors and the Catos who have fallen from the heavens. Know that there will be those who will condemn you in public with their faces covered, but in secret will read you avidly having taken off their mask of pride'. While the author's farewell to his book was a common trope in Roman poetry, Forberg and Beccadelli look back to Martial when they dispatch their 'little book' to its public.[22]

But if Beccadelli sent his book out to the brothel, to be prostituted in the literary marketplace, and Martial's *libellus* had been sent out as a slave, Forberg's book, on the other hand, was addressed to the 'lectori ingenuo et simplici', the unnamed, anonymous, male 'well-born and honest reader', that is, the educated gentleman.[23] Whereas Forberg tries to construct a more confident relationship with his readers (in contrast to Martial's book, the slave, and Beccadelli's, the whore), he is more than aware of the possibility of a hostile reception. Indeed Forberg relies on the learnedness of his readers who could detect Forberg's own ironic self-awareness in his opening preface. For when he writes that he has put aside any shame about the subject matter ('pudore . . . posito'), he is alluding to Poem 29 in *Carmina Priapea* (a book of some 90 short poems in classical Latin pertaining to the phallic god Priapus):

> May I die of shame, Priapus, if I use obscene and shameless words,
> But since you're a deity, who has put aside his shame [*posito . . . pudore*],
> And show me your balls openly,
> Then I have to use the words 'mentula' and 'cunnus'.[24]

Here the poet is ashamed of using impure language but then goes on to use it. Forberg also finds himself in this situation, forced, as it were, to use obscene language to comment on Beccadelli's poetry. At the same time, Forberg is also impersonating Priapus – putting shame aside – to speak openly about sexual matters. By positioning himself as a careful scholar *and* Priapus, he knowingly comments on the possibility that his edition of Beccadelli might be seen as serious erudition as well as titillating reading.

Beccadelli's *Hermaphrodite* with Forberg's commentary only comprises the first half of the book. The second half is taken up by an essay by Forberg called 'Apophoreta: De Figuris Veneris', or 'Party Gifts: On the Shapes of Love'. The term 'Apophoreta' takes its name from a book of Martial's poems (book 14), consisting of epigrams describing gifts taken home after a party. The scene is the Roman festival of the Saturnalia, where social hierarchies organising relations between free and unfree were supposedly relaxed, and Martial the epigrammatist could mock and lampoon Roman characters without fear of punishment during the dangerous and uncertain times of Domitian's and Nerva's rule.[25] Forberg, on the other hand, imagines a community of readers 'well-born and honest' enough to enjoy and savour his essay of *apophoreta*, which was basically an anthology of obscene and erotic poems and passages culled mostly from Aristophanes, Catullus, Horace, Ovid, Juvenal, Martial, the *Carmina Priapea*, neo-Latin epigram, the *Satyra Sotadica* and d'Hancarville's *Monumens* publications. The collection of texts was bought together by Forberg to explain the 'active' and 'passive' pleasures of sex as he puts it, and he divides his essay into the following sections[26]:

De fututione
De paedicando
De irrumando
De masturbando
De cunnilingis
De tribadibus
De coitu cum brutis
De spintriis

Forberg's anthological essay, then, emerged out of the collecting culture that had been busy since the second half of the eighteenth century. And so, reflecting the interest in phallic collecting and priapic anthologising, Forberg organised his essay around whether one is penetrating with or being penetrated by the penis. In one footnote, Forberg suggests that the structure of the essay follows that set out in *Carmina Priapeia* 13:

Percidere puer moneo, futuere puella,
barbatum furem tertia poena manet.

I warn you boy, I'll bugger you; girl, I'll fuck you in the vagina,
A third punishment awaits the bearded thief.[27]

Forberg, the priapic scholar, begins with sex involving the insertion of a penis into a vagina ('De fututione'), moves onto the insertion of the penis into the arse ('De paedicando'), and then continues with sex involving the insertion of a penis into a mouth ('De irrumando'). The essay continues with a section on masturbation, followed by 'De cunnilingis' which concerns 'those who lick cunt', and the section after that focuses on 'tribads', or women who are equipped with enlarged clitorises, according to Forberg, to stimulate, fuck and bugger other women. The term 'tribas' in Latin derived from the Greek word for 'rub'. The essay closes with two much shorter sections, one on 'sex with animals' ('De coitu cum brutis') and finally 'group sex' ('De spintriis'). Penetration and being penetrated, whether by a penis, tongue or clitoris, become the defining axes of sexual experience, as excerpts from ancient and early-modern texts are collated under these headings.

Forberg opened each section with a definition of these Latin terms. The section on *fututio* begins with the following: 'Ac primum quidem videamus de opere, quod fit per mentulam cunno commissam. Id quidem proprie dicitur futuere'. In English, that is: 'Let's first consider that which is accomplished by the dick joined to the cunt. That is, properly speaking, fucking'.[28] *Fututio*, 'fucking' is, 'properly speaking', the use of the 'mentula' and 'cunnus'; these terms are used 'properly' as this 'fucking' is a term that is designed to shock. Forberg's priapic scholarship has to speak properly about the improper. 'De paedicando', 'On pedicating', opens with the following definition: 'quod quidem mentula perficit ope culi. Si quis opus peragit mentula culo, sive maris, sive feminae, immissa, paedicat'. This can be rendered as: 'that which is accomplished by the dick with the assistance of the ass. If he completes the work by inserting the penis in the ass of either a male or a female, he pedicates'.[29] And the third section, 'De irrumando,' 'On irrumating', starts off with this explanation: 'Penem in os arrigere dicitur irrumare, quod proprie est mammam praebere'. In English, this can be expressed as: '*irrumare* means to erect the penis into the mouth, which in its proper sense means to give the breast'.[30] 'De masturbando', 'On masturbating', begins with this definition: 'masturbare dicitur, qui manu perfricando mentulam semen elicit; or in English: 'the one who brings out semen by rubbing the dick with the hand is said to masturbate'.[31]

What we see from these definitions is that it is repeatedly the completion of the sex act that defines it. Pedicating is what the 'mentula perficit' and 'peragit', that is, what the cock executes to a conclusion, which means ejaculation.[32] Masturbation is the bringing out of semen by the rubbing of the penis by the hand. And the tribad 'does everything which the fucker and pedicator do, except for producing the flow of semen, although not even this form of sex is always completely dry, as women are accustomed to dissolve when their pleasure is dancing'.[33] In a footnote at this point, Forberg refers to a moment in the *Satyra Sotadica*, when Tullia tells Octavia that she often ejaculates on her husband's hand when he is tickling her clitoris.[34] We have already noted in the previous chapter how Octavia had praised Tullia for being 'trained', or literally 'moistened in Latin and Greek literature' ('litteris Latinis Graecisque . . . imbueris', I, 24). Almost every sex scene in the *Satyra Sotadica* ends in orgasm (either male or female, and sometimes both), and Forberg cites numerous such passages from Chorier's work when explaining *futuere* and *pedicare*.[35] And in his discussions of *irrumare* and cunnilingus, this theme is extended to swallowing semen and drinking menses.[36] In this way, then, Forberg organised the references to sex scattered across ancient and early-modern Greek and Latin literature into a tight structure of penetrator and penetrated who respectively produced and received bodily fluids.

Sexual medicine

Forberg's efforts to organise the sexual vocabulary into this structure clearly show that his book was a serious contribution to *Altertumswissenschaft*, to be consumed within a community of scholarly readers. Forberg turns the language of Latin epigram into something approaching a lexicon for classifying sexual practice. Latin had of course been used in the eighteenth century as a language of taxonomy, and Forberg could not have conceived of his project without figures like Carl Linnaeus, whose Latinate publications on botany had classified plant life. Late eighteenth-century freethinkers had argued that phallic worship reflected an enlightened, philosophical understanding of natural processes of creation. Forberg's organisation of ancient sexual behaviour also reflected an attempt to show that there was an underlying, logical structure to sexual experience. While Catullus' and Martial's obscene language had provoked fiery debate during the Renaissance about how such language might be used with authority, in Forberg's book, written after eighteenth-century enquiry into the naturalness of sexual desire, these terms of abuse and mockery are used to demonstrate how sexual practice can be shown to possess a timeless, ahistorical structure.

Sex is nevertheless seen as a relationship between active and passive phallic penetration, and so Forberg hardly avoided presenting sex as a relationship of authority and power. This should not be surprising, considering the epigrammatic poetry and prose by Chorier, which Forberg was using to write his essay. The Roman language of sex was used to mark out and distinguish relations of authority between the empowered and the powerless, as evidenced by Catullus' threat to butt- and face-fuck his readers, Beccadelli's mockery of women and pederasts, and the battle-scenes of marriage in the *Satyra Sotadica*.[37] But Catullus' poem also reflected his insecurity about his position, just as Martial would worry about his own relationship with his readers and just as Chorier's Latin reflected a masculine anxiety about the relations between men and women. Similarly, when Beccadelli sent his book off to the brothel, he knew that the book would 'fuck and be fucked' (2.37.32) by its readers, that is, its language would titillate some and appal others. His poetry displayed his command over Latin just as much as his jokes backfired, as they indeed did, failing to get his patronage from Cosimo de' Medici, the poetry book's principal reader. Just as these epigrammatists sought to control how their Latin obscenities were to be read, so they realised the impossibility of doing so. Forberg was also well aware that the language of Latin obscenity might not be a language of straightforward authority and that his own authority over the Latin language might be challenged, mocked or misunderstood.

In anticipation of such responses, he notes, as already mentioned, that the structure of the 'Apophoreta' essay mimics an epigram from the *Carmina Priapeia*, and he wittily characterises himself as Priapus 'putting aside his shame' in order to produce his edition of Beccadelli. Forberg was very conscious of the possibility that his book might fall into the hands of readers other than those men to whom it was addressed.[38] Right at the end of his essay, he himself plays the role of Latin epigrammatist, and concludes with an epigram of his own, which reflects this very issue:

> Haec prima est, lector cordate, et mensa secunda.
> Ut sileas, videor velle videre tuum.
> Cernere vis patrantes. *Εἰκοσιμήχανον* offert.
> Bibliopola dabit. Virgo pudica fuge.[39]

> That is the first and the second course, wise reader.
> Although you're silent, I seem to see what you want.
> You want to see them in action. The *Eikosimechanon* provides that.
> You can get it at the bookstore. Modest virgin, take flight.

Just before this closure, Forberg rounds off the 'Apophoreta' with a list of 90 sex positions, summarising the various possibilities of fucking, buggery, irrumation, masturbation, cunnilingus, tribad sex, sex with animals and group sex that are mentioned in the book. Forberg signs off, then, with an epigram advertising a booklet which contains 20 plates illustrating these positions.[40] The epigram is addressed to the male reader – indeed, the 'wise male reader' – who has enjoyed the Beccadelli and the 'Apophoreta', the first two courses. The second line is lifted from *The Hermaphrodite* (2.1.2), where Beccadelli had jokingly addressed Cosimo de' Medici, whose silence is interpreted by the Renaissance poet as meaning that Cosimo doesn't want to hear more obscenity but 'strenuous wars in mighty meter' (2.1.4). Beccadelli will, of course, not comply with this wish, but will continue with his lewd poetry in Book 2. Forberg, on the other hand, also knows what his wise reader wants, that is, actually to see the acts that have been described in the pages of his edition! But instead of being disseminated via manuscript as Beccadelli had been in the 1420s, Forberg's nineteenth-century reader, 400 years later in the 1820s, can visit the 'bookstore'. However, just as Forberg advertises this publication, we are also reminded of Martial's reader, Quintus (in Martial 4.72), who asks Martial to give him a free copy of his book because he, Quintus, has no desire to spend money on Martial's trivial poetry at the 'bookstore'. Forberg addresses himself to a wise and learned male readership, while at the same time, wittily alluding to Martial and Beccadelli, thereby suggesting that his book isn't worth the money either: it's just smut. The epigram closes with another lift from Beccadelli (1.4.2), where the Renaissance writer in an opening poem had advised 'chaste virgins' to stay away from reading his lines. Beccadelli's poem continues, however, by saying that sexually voracious women like Ursa (whom we met in Chapter I) are free to enjoy his writing. Similarly, Martial had warned women off from reading his obscene epigrams, and yet they continue to read:

> I already told and warned you before, chaste lady,
> Not to read the rude part of my book, but here you are reading it (3.86.1–2).

Martial then suggests the 'chaste lady' read on. Forberg also realises that women might be reading his book: he is literally addressing such a reader – a 'modest virgin' – at the end of his tome. So, we might very well ask then, who did read Forberg's edition? Who did get the opportunity to read his Latin?

As Forberg cleverly predicted, his Latin was disseminated way beyond the community of classicists it was initially aimed at. He might not, however, have anticipated quite how his work was about to be appropriated. We have concentrated so closely on his Latinate definitions of Roman sexual vocabulary because it was exactly these sentences that were to form the backbone of the technical terminology of sexology in the nineteenth century. What is more, Forberg's *Altertumswissenschaft* provided the basis for the burgeoning *Sexualwissenschaft* that was to concern doctors Europe-wide by the end of the nineteenth century. In 1839, 15 years after Forberg published his work, a medical historian in Halle, Julius Rosenbaum (1807–74) published the first part of a (never to be completed) trilogy: *Die Lustseuche im Alterthume* (*The Plague of Lust in Antiquity*) designed to prove that the origins of venereal disease could be found in the ancient world. Rosenbaum 'gladly acknowledg[ed] the no small assistance we have received' from the classical philologist Forberg.[41] While Forberg had tried to produce an objective work of scholarship for other educated men, for Rosenbaum, however, the ancient world had literally infected the modern. It was not simply the case that the classics might have a malign influence on nineteenth-century readers. Rather, Rosenbaum was concerned to prove that the ancient world had a very physical impact on the modern. The ancient misuse of the genitals had, he contended, created the environment for the development of venereal disease itself.[42]

Just as the naturalness of sexual desire was seen as crucial for the well-being of civic society, so it was that during the early decades of the nineteenth century prostitution, sex outside marriage and venereal disease became topics that received huge amounts of debate. The safeguarding of the pleasures of marriage became paramount during this period. Masturbation, anal sex and sex with prostitutes were heavily stigmatised as dangers to conjugal ties and to the burgeoning nuclear family. In the first half of the 1800s, there was a growing corpus of tracts and writings of a medical and pseudo-medical nature seeking to explain the specifically pathological aspects of sexuality.[43] Rosenbaum's work reflected these anxieties, which would reach high and emotive levels by the end of the century. In the middle of the century, much confusion still circulated around the causes of venereal disease. Still, in 1858, Sir Samuel Solly, President of the Royal Medical and Chirurgical Society in England could say, during a government inquiry into the problem, that syphilis was 'intended as a punishment for our sins and we should not interfere in the matter'.[44] (Worried about the sexual health of the armed forces, the British parliament would pass three Contagious Diseases Acts in the 1860s).[45] Rosenbaum's own history of venereal disease also did not offer any cures other than exhortations to moral probity and uprightness. Indeed, his *Lustseuche im Alterthume* aimed at frightening its readers from sexual contact, with its highly unpleasant descriptions of the death scenes venereal disease could cause. Classical antiquity was being used by Rosenbaum as a weapon of authority over the nineteenth-century reader.

Rosenbaum appropriated Forberg's sexual taxonomy wholeheartedly for the uses of medical science. Indeed, Rosenbaum's definitions of sexual practices were lifted straight from Forberg's Latin. *Irrumare* is described by both as 'penem in os arrigere' ('to erect the penis into the mouth') and the *cunnilingus* is someone who 'peragit opus linguam arrigendo in cunnum eumque lambit' ('completes the deed by introducing his tongue into the cunt and licks it'), which also appropriates Forberg's phraseology.[46] The authority of the obscene and abusive Latin epigrammatist is replaced by the authority of the medical doctor. In its new context, the Latin of Roman and Renaissance epigram, via Forberg, became part of the new medical vocabulary of sex in the middle of the nineteenth century. Indeed classical Latin itself becomes a diagnostic tool for the modern pathologist. Whereas Forberg's Latin had sought to clarify the sexual practices in Martial's texts for the classical scholar, now, with Rosenbaum, Martial's poetry was reframed to become medical-textbook Latin. For example, the ancient epigrammatist successfully diagnoses a case of paralysis of the tongue due to habitual cunnilungus:

> Excluding from consideration the pale complexion and evil smell from the mouth, which were equally consequences of the other forms of vice already mentioned, we have paralysis of the tongue mentioned at any rate in one passage:
>
> > Sidere percussa est subito tibi, Zoile, lingua,
> > dum lingis. Certe, Zoile, nunc futuis.
>
> > Your tongue, Zoilus, has been stricken with a sudden doom, while in the act of licking. Why! Surely, Zoilus, you copulate now.[47]

In Rosenbaum, the poems of Martial and other epigrammatists, 'to whom we are indebted for the proofs of our assertions', become part of a very different sort of anthology – the medical encyclopaedia – in order to warn the modern reader about the dangers of numerous sexual practices.[48] The fellator, for example, is prone to ulcers in the throat, which cause a 'deplorable death':

> The pain is a cutting and burning pain, as in anthrax [. . .] the breath foul-smelling, the patient exhaling an intensely offensive breath, and re-inhaling into the chest another no less so. Patients are so loathsome to themselves they cannot tolerate their own smell; the face is pale or livid, the temperature excessively high, the thirst as distressing as in fever. Yet they reject drink when offered from dread of the pain of swallowing; they undergo great agony both by the compression of the palate and by the return of the liquid through the nose.[49]

Catullus and Martial had used their epigrammatic voice as an authoritative gesture over their addressees, which, as we have seen, triggered off a debate about such language during the Renaissance and early-modern period. Martial's mockery of Zoilus, for instance, takes advantage of the supposed fact that Zoilus cannot speak back to Martial's abuse due to his paralysed tongue. And Martial's pose looks back to Catullus' threat to orally rape readers that defamed him. With Rosenbaum, however, Latin epigram becomes evidence for the authoritative diagnosis of the nineteenth-century doctor. Rosenbaum's fulminatory prose reflected many doctors' responses to venereal disease in the middle of the nineteenth century. His book was well received, with a second edition coming out in 1845. The problem of modern city-life was beginning to attract much attention. Before his death in 1836, the French doctor Alexandre Parent-Duchatelet had written *De la prostitution dans la ville de Paris*, which was posthumously published and very widely read. Through the 1850s and 1860s, Henry Mayhew documented the evidence for his *London Labour and the London Poor*. By the end of the 1860s, the British government had passed three acts designed to protect the armed forces, and therefore the nation, against the threat of venereal disease. The concern about the figure of the prostitute and the pernicious spread of sexually transmitted infection began to develop into a more complex set of anxieties about the significance of sexual practices more generally.

Through the second half of the nineteenth century, numerous doctors and criminologists began to categorise and pathologise sexual experience. By the 1880s there was a busy industry across Western Europe and North America. In 1876 Cesare Lombroso, the Italian criminologist, brought out *L'uomo delinquente*, which anatomised sexual criminality in horrifying detail and appeared in numerous editions and translations until the beginning of the new century. In 1880, the Frenchman Paul Moreau published *Des aberrations du sens génésique*, and in 1886 the work of Russian sexologist Benjamin Tarnowsky was translated into German, finding a broad and interested audience. At the same time, Forberg and Rosenbaum continued to be read and cited by these legal and medical authorities. A third edition of *Die Lustseuche im Alterthume* came out in 1882 and reached its seventh edition, including an English translation, by 1901. Forberg's book became a highly sought-after collector's item in its own right. The French publisher Isidore Liseux produced an underground French translation in 1882 and, somewhere between 1895 and 1900, Charles Carrington brought out a better English edition, furnished with further notes. Another more luxurious English edition, printed in Paris, appeared in 1907, reprinting with it the 20 obscene plates that could be bought with the original edition in 1824.

The German classical philologist Paul Brandt (who would later produce a very widely read three-volume social history of Greece, under the name Hans Licht) prepared the index for the German edition that came out in 1908. Along with his partner, Werner von Bleichroeder, Brandt possessed one of the largest collections of book and art erotica at the beginning the twentieth century, and they were affiliated to well-known anthropologist Magnus Hirschfeld's Institut für Sexualwissenschaft in Berlin. They also contributed to the four-volume pictorial encyclopaedia of eroticism published by the Institut für Sexualforschung in Vienna.[50] This publication was to have a lasting impact, not least on twentieth-century sex researchers such as Alfred Kinsey some 20 years later.[51] The re-publication of Beccadelli's epigrams, accompanied by Forberg's essay, which emerged out of the connoisseurs' collections of *phallica*, was, then, an important moment in the nineteenth-century development of the scientific study of sex. Indeed, Forberg's Latin, via Rosenbaum, formed an important intellectual platform for one of the most important texts about sex in the nineteenth century: Richard von Krafft-Ebing's *Psychopathia Sexualis.*

Sex, science and the classics

> Sexuality is the most powerful factor in individual and social existence; the strongest incentive to the exertion of strength and acquisition of property, to the foundation of a home, and to the awakening of altruistic feelings, first for a person of the opposite sex, then for the offspring, and, in a wider sense, for all humanity.[52]

This sentence, which appeared on the opening page of Krafft-Ebing's (1840–1902) famous book, reflected the beliefs of a larger cohort of thinkers at the end of the nineteenth century, for whom the truth of our existence – our achievements and our problems – could be explained with reference to a sexual identity. Indeed, if the organisation of society depended upon understanding the processes of sexual interaction, then the drives of sexual pleasure became the key to understanding the self. Krafft-Ebing himself was a highly respected Austro-German psychiatrist who became a favoured forensic witness and was invited to provide expertise on the sexual misdemeanours of defendants in court. Whereas medical men earlier in the century had thought that such deviants deserved punishment, Krafft-Ebing's experience in court and in his sanatorium led him to believe that such individuals should receive medical attention rather than legal penalties.[53] 'Modern social life', Krafft-Ebing argued, 'begets defective individuals, excites the sexual instinct, leads to sexual abuse, and, with continuance of lasciviousness associated with diminished sexual power, induces perverse sexual acts'.[54] The legal process offers a merely superficial solution in its incarceration of delinquents. Scientific investigation has shown, however, that 'a man mentally and sexually degenerate *ab origine*, and therefore irresponsible, must be removed from society for life, but not as a punishment'.[55] And so Krafft-Ebing collated the numerous case studies to be found in various articles and books, to produce his *Psychopathia Sexualis*. And it would be no exaggeration to say that Krafft-Ebing's anthology of sex, which first appeared in 1886, mapped out the landscape of sexual identities in which Western societies live today. He classified numerous sexual practices, standardising several terms such as *sadism*, *masochism*, *fetishism* and *homosexuality*. The book was very widely read, both inside and outside the medical establishment, reaching its twelfth edition by the time of the author's death, having been translated into several languages.

Krafft-Ebing grouped sexual deviances into two classes: perversions, which were symptoms of an innate morbidity; and perversities, which were immoral acts performed by corrupt, but reformable individuals.[56] Altogether more interested in the curability of those subjects sick with perversions, Krafft-Ebing's book comprised an anthology of case studies which were designed to show that such individuals had been sick from birth. The case study itself in *Psychopathia Sexualis* was an autobiographical report, in which the subject would give an account of their family background, followed by a candid and detailed description of their sexual proclivities. Never before had a single book collected together so many sexually detailed reports of peoples' lives to be read by a wider, educated public. Indeed, the anonymous autobiography was the key to Krafft-Ebing's success; not only did it seem to guarantee scientific accuracy, but it encouraged other members of the public to send in their own life stories, which Krafft-Ebing included in each new, ever expanding edition. Hundreds of readers wrote to the psychiatrist to tell him their own personal history.

The notion of the past was central to Krafft-Ebing's understanding of sexual perversion in that he heavily stressed the role of heredity in mental and sexual pathology. Krafft-Ebing claimed that he had studied the family trees of numerous patients to support his argument that sexual perversion was inborn and inherited.[57] Rosenbaum had himself contended that venereal disease in the present could be traced back to irregular and immoral sexual practices in the ancient world. Krafft-Ebing's book also understood modern sexuality in relation to antiquity, but in a somewhat different way. He was writing at the *fin de siècle*, at the end of the nineteenth century, a time marked in European culture and thinking by great optimism and pessimism. Many marvelled at the industrial and technological advances of the modern world and eagerly anticipated an even more glittering twentieth century. Others, however, were concerned that European civilisation could progress no further and was about to degenerate in a regressive direction into barbarism.[58] *Psychopathia Sexualis* reflects this *fin-de-siècle* ambivalence. 'Today', writes Krafft-Ebing on the one hand,

> we are far beyond the sexual conditions which, as shown in the sodomitic worship of the gods, in the life of the people, and in the laws and religious practices, existed among the ancient Greeks – to say nothing of the worship of the phallus and Priapus among the Athenians and Babylonians, of the bacchanals of ancient Rome, and the prominent place prostitutes took among these peoples.[59]

On the other hand, however, the development of civilisation through history brings with it a nervous tension leading to perverse sexual habits:

> Exaggerated tension of the nervous system stimulates sensuality, leads the individual as well as the masses to excess [. . .] Greece, the Roman Empire and France under Louis XIV and XV, are striking examples of this assertion. [. . .] Large cities are hotbeds in which neuroses and low morality are bred: see the history of Babylon, Nineveh and Rome and the mysteries of modern metropolitan life.[60]

However modern late nineteenth-century Europe might consider itself to be, it also risked sliding back in time:

> In spite of all the aids which religion, law, education and morality give civilised man in the bridling of his passions, he is always in

> danger of sinking from the clear height of pure, chaste love into the mire of common sensuality.[61]

If one were to take a look at the works consulted by Krafft-Ebing in writing *Psychopathia Sexualis*, one would see that, along with other contemporary sexological and criminological writings, Krafft-Ebing's bibliography only lists Rosenbaum's *Lustseuche im Alterthume* and two other nineteenth-century German works of classical scholarship on imperial Rome. This historical scholarship provided the vocabulary for Krafft-Ebing's history of civilisation, more broadly. These two other works on ancient Rome are Ludwig Friedländer's *Darstellungen aus Sittengeschichte Roms* (first published in 1862, and translated as *Roman Life and Manners under the Early Empire* by J. H. Freese and Leonard A. Magnus), and Friedrich Wiedemeister's *Der Cäsarenwahnsinn* (or *The Madness of the Caesars*, first published in 1875). Both works examined how the height of Roman luxury and decadence were also signs of the degeneration of Roman society, thereby providing Krafft-Ebing with a detailed historical image for his own *fin de siècle*. Wiedemeister's interest in the insanity of the Caesars supplied Krafft-Ebing with the possibility of linking Roman history with theories of heredity and degeneration, as Wiedemeister argued that the key to the madness of the Julio-Claudians lay in their family history. This infamous tale of 'Familiendegeneration', as Wiedemeister described it, offered a potent image for the family trees that Krafft-Ebing constructed of his patients.[62]

If, on the one side, the end of the nineteenth century seemed so modern, Krafft-Ebing's times also seemed very ancient. Indeed, Krafft-Ebing could not help but make comparisons between ancient Rome and modern sexual practices in the various case studies. So, in *Psychopathia Sexualis*, modern women, 'inflamed to lasciviousness', are like Roman wives who have themselves been whipped by priests as described by Juvenal (2.140–3).[63] One young man bereft of sexual desire wishes he could 'open his veins as Seneca did in the bath'.[64] Grandmothers horny for boys and women lusty for power are 'Messalinas'.[65] Sexual sadists who cut up and eat their victims claim to have learnt their trade from the tales in Suetonius' imperial biographies.[66]

One sadist who enjoys whipping the 'nates' – buttocks – of women, researched his interests by consulting the punishments meted out to Roman slaves.[67] A certain 'Count N.' enjoys 'osculum ad nates', kissing the buttocks of prostitutes, Krafft-Ebing punning 'os + culum', the mouth on the bum, as Catullus had once also punned (at Catullus 97.2).[68] Another young man, 'Mr Z', enjoys being flagellated 'ad podicem' – 'on the bum' – a word that appeared in literature such as Juvenal (2.12), when the satirist is making fun of strict censors who nevertheless like having a depilated anus. 'Mr Z' also pretends to be a page to a prostitute, dressed as lady of the manor, and gets off 'ope digitis' – with a little 'help from the fingers' up the anus.[69] Martial, on the other hand, had once joked to a girlfriend that 'there's no need for fingers' ('nil opus est digitis'), after she fails to erect his flaccid member (11.29). Another young man reaches orgasm from mouth-to-mouth kissing and ejaculates 'ante portam', that is, outside either the girl's vagina or anus. The word 'porta' had already been used in Catullus (15.18) and the *Carmina Priapea* (52.5) to mean 'anus', but was defined as 'vagina' by Tullia in the *Satyra Sotadica* as reported by Forberg.[70]

In the last couple of examples we see that the Latin language itself crept into Krafft-Ebing's text. Perhaps we should not be surprised to see subtle allusions to Latin epigram if we keep in mind Krafft-Ebing's reading of Rosenbaum's book. It should also be noted, though, that the autobiographies received by the psychiatrist were edited before publication in that Krafft-Ebing translated certain portions of them into Latin 'in order that unqualified persons should not become readers'. He 'saw himself compelled to choose a title understood only by the learned, and also, where possible, to express himself in *terminis technicis*'.[71] The scientificity of the autobiographies was to be vouchsafed by Krafft-Ebing's Latinity which, of course, came from a particular source – directly out of Julius Rosenbaum's borrowings of Friedrich Forberg's Latin. Whenever a subject came to describe their genitals, penetration or the transmission of bodily fluids, Krafft-Ebing switched into the Latin he had read in Rosenbaum. A few examples will suffice: 'membrum meum in os recepit', ('he receives my member in the mouth'); 'linguam meam in os eius immitto', ('I insert my tongue into his mouth'); 'magna mentula puellam futuat', ('he fucks the girl with his big cock'); 'penem aliorum puerorum in os arrigere' ('he erects his penis into the mouth of other boys'). And terms like 'cunnilingus', 'irrumare' and 'paedicatio' pepper Krafft-Ebing's text.[72]

While Beccadelli's Latin had provoked debate about the obscene language of classical Latin poetry and Chorier's *Satyra Sotadica* had suggested that all sorts of sexual innuendo could be found in canonical Latin texts – via Forberg's philology and Rosenbaum's medical history – such language could operate as a technical vocabulary in Krafft-Ebing's book, thereby bolstering the authority of the youthful intellectual discipline of sexology; the use of Latin reserved his book for a highly educated and professional audience. Krafft-Ebing's critique of the legal profession's treatment of sexual delinquents was part of larger strategy in the second half of the nineteenth century, when psychiatrists and psychologists were seeking professional respect and institutional stability. Across Europe, specialists were setting up private practices and sanatoria which catered for well-heeled clients, ensuring that psychiatry could break out of the confines of the asylum, so enhancing the social prestige of the discipline.[73] By writing in Latin, Krafft-Ebing was able to represent in precise terms the sexual activities of his correspondents. In this way, then, he was able to convey to his readers what homosexuals, fetishists, sadists and other 'perverts' actually did.

Forberg had organised his essay into a structure of active and passive sexual acts, which reflected the Roman conceptualisation of sex as a discourse of power and authority. Rosenbaum had utilised Forberg's vocabulary to map venereal disease. In Krafft-Ebing's text, however, Roman imperial texts were used to represent the debauchery of the *fin de siècle*, when relations of power and authority seemed to have gone wrong. The previous examples show women enjoying being whipped, grandmothers lusty for sex, sadists who enjoy cutting up their victims' bodies, and men who like being flagellated, licking prostitutes' buttocks and pretending to be pages to ladies of the manor. Those Roman texts which depicted the passivity of men and the active rapaciousness of women, as well as the sexual cruelty of the emperors and empresses, offered resonant images to Krafft-Ebing, whose case studies painted a modern world populated by sadists, masochists and sexual criminals. Krafft-Ebing used Latin to emphasise his medical authority over his patients and the *populus* at large, at a time when *fin-de-siècle* hierarchies of order and authority seemed to have gone awry. Just as the phallic vocabulary and depiction of sex in ancient Rome saw sexual relations in terms of active and passive, so Krafft-Ebing theorised that sadism and masochism were the most fundamental forms of psychosexual perversion and that other forms are mutations from these. He even coined the words 'sadism' and 'masochism' in 1890. Krafft-Ebing's Latin, then, sought to underline the doctor's authority and to position his work for a professional, scientific, educated readership at the same time as it pictured the unruly nature of modern society.[74]

Nevertheless, the tone of Krafft-Ebing's so-called technical Latin is itself quite difficult to read. Interestingly, Krafft-Ebing uses obscene words such as 'mentula' and 'futuat' interchangeably with neutral terms like 'penis' and 'membrum' and euphemisms such as 'immitto' ('I insert') and 'recepit' ('he receives). The vocabulary of Roman and Renaissance epigram and the definitions of Forberg and Rosenbaum become jumbled up, so that when we read Krafft-Ebing's Latin it becomes very difficult to judge its register. The following example comes from a case history of a man who is classified as an 'Urning' (a person with a woman's soul trapped inside a man's body – we will discuss this term more fully in the next chapter):

> At the same time, I have a very lively fancy, and spend most of my leisure hours thinking of handsome men with strong limbs; and I would be delighted to look on when a powerful fellow, using force, *magna mentula praeditus me praesente puellam futuat*; mihi persuasum est, fore ut hoc aspectu sensus mei vehementissima perturbatione afficiantur et dum futuit corpus adolescentis pulchri tangam et, si liceat, ascendam in eum dum cum puella concumbit atque idem cum eo faciam et *membrum meum in eius anum immittam* [*endowed with a large cock might fuck a girl in my presence*; I was convinced that with this sight my senses would be affected by the most violent passion

> and while he fucks, I will touch the body of the beautiful adolescent and, if allowed, I would mount him while he is lying with the girl and do the same to him and *insert my member into his anus*]'.[75]

The fantasy represented here is typical of what appears in *Psychopathia Sexualis* in that the one sexual partner is aroused at the possibility that another is being treated violently. Krafft-Ebing's case studies repeatedly present their sexual practitioners in terms of active or passive, reflecting his use of Latin terminology and his theories about sadistic and masochistic pleasures. Krafft-Ebing reverts into Latin when the subject starts using sexually explicit language ('large cock', 'fuck'), but then closes the section with 'insert my member into his anus'. The Latin segment contains what sounds like the subject's most sexually explicit confession (a fantasy of witnessing a rape), but then ends with a circumlocution which, as we now know, can be traced back to the medical and scholarly Latin of the middle of the nineteenth century. Forberg had used the verb 'immitto' to describe what the penis does in anal sex.[76] Did the original words of Krafft-Ebing's correspondent also shift in register? Is that what Krafft-Ebing meant to suggest? When he turns to Latin to represent the sexual practices and fantasies expressed by his correspondents, the language of the layperson and the language of the doctor become blurred, so that the reader of *Psychopathia Sexualis* is left to wonder how technical or how obscene Krafft-Ebing actually meant his Latin to seem.[77]

If Krafft-Ebing's Latin can look like both an obscene *and* a scientific language, then this reflected the fact that *Psychopathia Sexualis* became one of the most public statements of a discourse that blurred the boundaries between the healthy and the pathological: Krafft-Ebing's book was filled with numerous case studies of bourgeois individuals who, in appearance, were respectable members of their communities, but nevertheless enjoyed strange sexual activities and fantasised about weird sexual encounters and desires.[78] His *fin-de-siècle* book depicted a seemingly high-functioning modern world peopled by individuals of responsibility and of moral value who, at the same time, concealed uncivilised and regressive sexual identities within. The ambivalence of Krafft-Ebing's book was encapsulated in his Latin: it was the respectable language of scientific taxonomy and classification and a sign of education and civilisation, but was also an obscene language of debauchery and sexual perversion.

But if Krafft-Ebing began his project with the intention of proving how unwell the modern world was despite all appearances, he then began to doubt his own reasoning with each new edition published, and became more compassionate towards his correspondents. And so the line between healthy and pathological became even more difficult to draw. We can glimpse moments of Krafft-Ebing's uncertainty in various case studies. For instance, one from a later edition depicts a 'psychical hermaphrodite' (someone attracted to their own sex who also still possessed a weaker desire for the opposite sex), who reaches orgasm by kissing his partners on the mouth rather than having penetrative, genital sex.[79] The young man presents himself as highly cultured (he enjoys Chopin, Schumann, Schubert and Wagner), and hopes that the 'present prejudice' again men like him 'will disappear [. . .] One need but recall the Greeks and their friendships, which were nothing but sexual love [. . .] The Greeks are still regarded as an unattainable example, and held up for imitation'. This man's autobiography is a long, meandering tale: in one episode he describes his love for a soldier, whose long absences in a garrison in Hungary he is forced to endure. When they see each other – Krafft-Ebing translates into Latin – 'usus sexualis in osculis et amplexionibus solis constitit' – the young man finds sexual stimulation in kisses and embraces alone. Indeed, it seems that the psychiatrist was so taken with the narrative that his Latin, far from being scientific, nods to Dido kissing and holding onto Cupid in the *Aeneid* (1.687, 'amplexus atque oscula'): just as Aeneas will leave Carthage, so this young man is 'forced to be separated from him [his lover] for an indefinite period'. Certainly, at least, the 'psychical hermaphrodite' is reminiscent of the leitmotif of the ancient heroine (Ariadne, Penelope, Dido, etc.) waiting for her lover to return.

This individual embodies the *fin-de-siècle* moment when Krafft-Ebing was writing. He presents himself as a well-heeled member of the bourgeoisie (he is an official in a factory and he had attended a German Gymnasium; he mentions that his family has a cook and other servants; he is cultured in that he enjoys dancing lessons, fine art and music). And yet this status is a façade for a man who is constantly attracted to all that is 'ugly and dirty', that is, servant-girls, prostitutes in brothels and soldiers, even though 'intellectually and socially, everything common in speech and conduct is repugnant to me'. This 'psychical hermaphrodite' is a complex hybrid, with a 'masculine face' and 'girlish form'.[80] He is both cultured and debauched, socially respectable and sexually perverted, both eloquent and obscene – like Krafft-Ebing's Latin, which provides a literal account of the subject's enjoyment of kissing, thereby providing a scientific description of the subject's fetish – but at the same time has the power of reminding educated readers of classical heroines. The Latin purports to be a verbatim representation of the man's abnormal sexual desires, and yet also reflects the man's own more romantic view of his relationship with the soldier. Here Krafft-Ebing reports the technical truth of sexual deviancy while at the same time injecting pathos into the man's story. The Latin language signifies obscene behaviour as well as a moment comparable to a scene from Western civilisation's most admired poetry.[81] Just as the man looks outwardly respectable as well as sexually abnormal, both healthy and sick, so the Latin reflects such an ambivalence in Krafft-Ebing's own thinking, as he became more and more sympathetic to the so-called 'perverts' he tried to treat, to the extent that by the end of his life he supported the campaign in Germany for the decriminalisation of same-sex practices.[82] The end of the nineteenth century in Europe marked a time of great optimism and pessimism about the achievements and state of modernity. The lines between the civilised and the uncivilised, the normal and the abnormal, seemed especially hard to draw at the *fin de siècle*. Rather than an aura of scientific professionalism and authority, then, Krafft-Ebing's Latin comes to reflect such a sense of uncertainty.

Already in earlier articles, before Krafft-Ebing published his magnum opus, he had printed opinions of his correspondents that directly conflicted with his own theories of sexual perversion. For instance, in an article printed in 1882, Krafft-Ebing detailed case studies in which eloquent, educated and professional men compared their sexual desires for other men to Frederick the Great and Plato, unapologetically saying that they were 'certainly no filthy swine'.[83] After the original publication of *Psychopathia Sexualis*, while some of Krafft-Ebing's readers were convinced by his diagnoses and categorisations, other readers, however, began to question his sexual historiography by turning to other areas of classical literature and history to counter Krafft-Ebing's arguments about perversion. And so, as *Psychopathia Sexualis* grew with each edition as more of Krafft-Ebing's readers sent him their sexual histories, so did the dissenting voices.[84] The 'psychical hermaphrodite' just discussed voiced a hope that modern society might adopt the tolerance that the ancient Greek supposedly bore to same-sex practices, in complete contradiction to Krafft-Ebing's appropriations of ancient texts and ideas. So even if Krafft-Ebing had hoped that his Latin provided a scientific understanding of sex, some educated readers countered with their own understandings of classical antiquity. The authority of Krafft-Ebing's Latin vocabulary of sex did not remain uncontested. What it meant, to claim that classical scholarship could support so-called medical and scientific truths about sex, was opened to questioning.

Psychopathia Sexualis emerged from a history that has been traced out in this chapter. We analysed how late eighteenth-century freethinkers, fascinated by the discoveries of Pompeii and Herculaneum, argued that phallic worship originated out of a logical and philosophical understanding of natural processes of creation and propagation. Scientific interest in the naturalness of sexual desire impacted on historical research conducted at the beginning of the nineteenth century, as collectors around Europe started building collections of sexual artefacts. The eighteenth-century culture of Linnaean taxonomy created widespread interest in processes of scientific classification and categorisation. At a similar time, the calls for objective, unprejudiced historical scholarship provided the context for the possibility of classical philology on ancient sexual words and their meanings. Forberg sought to map out and depict sexual experience as a coherent structure of penetrator and penetrated in a list of 90 sex positions, by turning back to

Renaissance and classical Latin epigram. Forberg's work was quickly used for a very different sort of science in the mid-nineteenth century, as Rosenbaum's writing on the ancient origins of venereal disease reflected European concerns about the health of the modern city. In various sorts of ways, then, sex became an object of scientific study which was continually informed by understanding ancient sexual desires and pleasures, from the late eighteenth- and early nineteenth-century cultures of collecting to Krafft-Ebing's anthology of case studies.

This chapter does not, however, uncover how the obscenities anthologised in collections of priapic epigram and neo-Latin writing simply became an accepted scientific terminology by the end of the nineteenth century. The Renaissance and early-modern debates about how erotic Latinity was to be used authoritatively were not finally put to rest with Krafft-Ebing's 'termini technici'. Rather, we have begun to see that, in contrast to Krafft-Ebing's use of Latin, one 'psychical hermaphrodite' turned to the ancient Greeks in order to defend his sexuality. The relationship between the ancient past and the modern present was a highly contested issue at the *fin de siècle*. While Krafft-Ebing relied on historicist scholarship developed earlier in the nineteenth century, what ancient history might be able to teach modernity about sex was not going to be a story for just the scientific establishment to tell. The next chapter looks more closely at one of Krafft-Ebing's most careful contemporary late nineteenth-century readers, who turned away from the psychiatrist's Latin to ancient Greek and questioned the idea that objective historical scholarship could authoritatively educate the modern age about sexual pleasure.

CHAPTER IV

SEXOLOGY, HISTORICISM AND ANCIENT GREECE

Psychopathia Sexualis became a very complicated document in which different voices competed for the reader's attention. The words of the doctor and the pervert confronted one another on the page, ensuring that many were to criticise Krafft-Ebing for disseminating 'homosexual propaganda' while others lambasted his work as pornography.[1] Many case studies were, in fact, long, even expansive narratives, in which the subject was given space by Krafft-Ebing to provide a detailed account of their (sexual) lives. These accounts reflected the huge impact of the *Bildungsroman* on the bourgeois, educated readers of the *Psychopathia Sexualis*. This German term, which literally means 'novel of formation', describes a genre of fictional writing, in which the journey of the protagonist's life from infancy into intellectual and spiritual maturity is laid out. The art of autobiography in the nineteenth century had become an important strategy for understanding the self. Towards the end of the eighteenth century, Jean-Jacques Rousseau's *Confessions* had provided European readers with a detailed examination of a subject in all its difference and uniqueness. The narrative that revealed the idiosyncratic self became a hugely popular mode of writing, as bourgeois subjects analysed themselves in their diaries, published their memoirs and letters and retold stories of peoples' lives in novels. Krafft-Ebing's correspondents would have been well-read in such narratives of individualisation, which depicted the subject's progress against the complexities of the industrialised and urbanised environment of the modern world, an issue which of course elicits the question of the authenticity of the narratives submitted for inclusion in *Psychopathia Sexualis*.[2]

It is impossible to prove the veracity of all the accounts given about the sex lives in Krafft-Ebing's book, and we saw in Chapter III how the Latin in the case study of the 'psychical hermaphrodite' reflected this tension, being both a technical and a literary language.[3] More significantly for the context of this chapter, this man, clearly dissatisfied with the sexological perspective on his perversion, turned to the Greeks in the hope that in them he might find an alternative language for his desires. In Chapter II, we saw how Ficino was very keen to turn back to Plato's texts in the original Greek in order to clear up any misunderstandings other humanists had expressed in Latin about sex and love. While the historical scholarship of the early nineteenth century had provided Krafft-Ebing's sexology with a technical vocabulary which supposedly represented the truth about sex, the 'psychical hermaphrodite' was making use of another strain of nineteenth-century German historical scholarship which focused on ancient Greece. Interestingly, this German engagement with the Greeks arose out of debates about the nature of historicism, as German intellectuals sought to understand the applicability of ancient Greece to the problems, dilemmas and events of the modern world. Back in 1755, the budding historian of ancient art, Johann Joachim Winckelmann, encouraged his German contemporaries to embrace Greek forms in order to produce real art. Or, as he put it, 'the only way for us to become great, or if this be possible, inimitable, is to imitate the ancients'.[4] Paradoxically, then, if moderns imitated the Greeks, who seemed inimitable, then the moderns will become so, too. Winckelmann's statement encapsulated what would develop into German philhellenism over the following 200 years, whereby ancient Greek culture was venerated as a timeless exemplar and yet, because of the prodigious German scholarship produced during this time, highlighted the historical specificities of the ancient Greek world.[5] Krafft-Ebing's 'psychical hermaphrodite' reflected this two-sided perspective: for him the Greeks were to be 'held up for imitation' *and* nevertheless 'an unattainable example'.

On the one hand, German historical scholarship uncovered cultures of same-sex love in ancient Greece which allured and excited nineteenth-century men who were sexually attracted to other males. On the other, however, such scholarship often engendered the belief that ancient Greek culture was a product of particular circumstances, and therefore unrepeatable. This chapter focuses on those nineteenth-century men who were interested in revivifying Greek love in the face of the condemnatory discourses of psychology and criminology. The protagonist of the chapter will be John Addington Symonds, a highly eminent late-Victorian intellectual, who struggled in private with his desires for men and boys. We will see how Symonds constructed an epistemology of his sexual passions by turning to ancient Greece in an effort to integrate his knowledge into the context of sexology and psychology. Krafft-Ebing had attempted to make use of classical Latin as a technical terminology and yet could not help make altogether more literary comparisons between ancient Rome and the *fin de siècle*. While his 'psychical hermaphrodite' yearned for ancient Greece, Symonds, on the other hand, was to make a concerted effort to think about what ancient Greek literature might contribute to modern sexology. But the historicism of *Altertumswissenschaft*, which made the Greeks both exemplary and inimitable, would make this adoption of Greek very tricky indeed. With the Greeks hovering between real historical people and ideal, timeless – even fantastical – models, the issue of how real or how metaphorical the nineteenth century's relationship to the ancient past was to be was of profound interest and concern to Symonds, in his need to provide a more tolerant sexology.

It's all Greek to me . . .

From the love of Greek art to the truths spoken in Greek tragedy and philosophy, and to the fascination with Athenian democracy, European culture from the 1760s and into the nineteenth century became obsessed with the impossible example of Greece. The labours of German scholars are expansively reflected in the massive *Allgemeine Encyclopädie der Wissenschaften und Künste* (*General Encyclopaedia in the Sciences and*

Arts), a reference work that had been begun in 1813 and remained unfinished in 1889, by which time it had reached a gargantuan 167 volumes. At the time it was viewed as the epitome of German scholarly industriousness and endeavour, and more recently Robert Collison has called it 'the greatest Western encyclopaedia ever attempted'.[6] The entry on 'Griechenland' was the longest in the entire work, spanning eight volumes (80–7) and covering 3,668 pages. In 1837, Moritz Hermann Eduard Meier, one of the editors on the encyclopaedia, provided a highly comprehensive article on pederasty and its practice all over the ancient Greek world. Meier, a legal scholar, emphasised that we 'want the truth and nothing but the truth', as he argued that 'noble pederasty was for the Greeks not something purely spiritual/intellectual [*nicht etwas rein Geistiges*]' but 'something material/sensual [*etwas Sinnliches*] was mixed in'. The noble form of pederasty took 'pleasure/satisfaction [*Wohlgefallen*] in physical beauty [*körperlichen Schönheit*]'. Although Meier was keen to contend that 'noble pederasty' was not sodomitical, he did allow that ancient Greek men could appreciate male bodily beauty, however 'disgusting' ('widerlich') that might seem to his nineteenth-century readers.[7]

Such German scholarship provided educated nineteenth-century men with data on ancient sexual practices and behaviours between males. But, even if for Krafft-Ebing's 'psychical hermaphrodite' ancient Greece offered a fantastical place to fulfil his desires, Greek was to be no straightforward 'code' for the expression of passion between males in the nineteenth century.[8] What such desire even meant was far from clear. For Krafft-Ebing the world was not simply divided into heterosexual and homosexual people. Men attracted to women and women attracted to men enjoyed all sorts of sexual liaisons (sadistic, masochistic, fetishistic and so on). People attracted to their own sex also comprised various different types. In *Psychopathia Sexualis*, Krafft-Ebing classified such subjects into two principal groups (those who acquired their habits and those who were born with their desires), however, within both groups there were several gradations:

> Thus, in the milder cases, there is simple hermaphroditism; in more pronounced cases, only homosexual feeling and instinct, but limited to the *vita sexualis*; in still more complete cases, the whole psychical personality, and even the bodily sensations, are transformed to correspond with the sexual perversion; and in complete cases, the physical form is correspondingly altered.[9]

To begin with, then, there are individuals who are mainly attracted to the other sex but also possess desire at varying levels for their own ('hermaphroditism'). Then there are people who seem heterosexual, but in their sex lives behave homosexually. Then there are others whose whole personality seems homosexual, which leads Krafft-Ebing to posit others again for whom the sexual perversion of homosexuality corresponds with a physiological alteration of gender. Krafft-Ebing's complicated typology reflected the prevalence of several competing conceptualisations of same-sex desire that were circulating at the end of the nineteenth and into the twentieth century.

In particular, he was influenced by the writings of Karl Heinrich Ulrichs, a civil servant who lived in Hanover. During the 1860s, under the pseudonym Numa Numantius (after Numa the legendary Roman king and lawmaker), Ulrichs produced several pamphlets arguing that anti-sodomy laws in the German states should be repealed. When Germany was unified in 1871, the new country's legislation generalised the Prussian legislation that criminalised sexual activity between men, leading Ulrichs to redouble his efforts. Indeed, Ulrichs is often described as the 'first gay man' to come out: in 1868 he dropped his *nom de plume*.[10]

His theory of 'same-sex' sexuality can be summed up in his formula *anima muliebris in corpore virili inclusa*, 'a woman's soul contained in a man's body'. He argued that two hermaphroditic seeds existed in the embryo: one controlled the biological sexual organs and the other regulated the psychological sexual drives. Both seeds should develop in the same direction, but it was possible, Ulrichs postulated, that the two seeds could be misaligned, resulting in a person who would be neither completely man nor completely woman, but a member of a third sex. Ulrichs explicitly referred to Aristophanes' speech in Plato's *Symposium* (189c–193e), which had posited aboriginal beings made up of two halves, our sexual desires reflecting our urge to return to that blissful state. As Ulrichs put it in one of his pamphlets (helpfully translated by Sebastian Matzner):

> It is a matter of fact that among mankind there are individuals whose bodies have a male physique but who nevertheless feel sexual attraction towards men, sexual horror for women, i.e. a horror of sexual contact with women. These individuals I shall call in what follows 'Uranians' [*Urninge*] whilst I shall call those individuals, who are commonly simply called 'men', 'Dionians' [*Dioninge*], i.e. those whose bodies have a male physique and who feel sexual attraction towards women, sexual horror for men. The love of the Uranians I shall call 'uranian' or man-manly love, the love of the Dionians 'dionian'. [. . .] My terms are based on the names of the gods Uranus and Dione; for a poetic fiction of Plato relates the origin of man-manly love to the god Uranus, and that of love towards women to Dione (see Plato's *Symposium*).[11]

But Ulrichs' theory was not a replication of Aristophanes' myth. He assumed that sexual attraction could only take place between male and female, and so the Urning (a woman's soul in a man's body) could only be attracted to a Dioning. Quickly realising that this logic meant that the Urning would never be lucky in love, Ulrichs went on to develop his thesis, positing two classes of Urning, the 'Weiblinge' or 'muliebriores' (the womanly, passive and feminine) and the 'Mannlinge' or 'viriliores', (the manly, virile and masculine), who could be attracted to one another. While Ulrichs, who himself identified as an Urning, did, then, elaborate a theory for relationships between Urnings, such sexual encounters followed the line that a masculine individual could only desire a feminine individual and vice versa.[12]

Such individuals became known in sexological texts as 'inverts'. In 1868, however, an Austrian-born Hungarian journalist, also sympathetic to the legal rights of those who seemed attracted to 'their own' sex, postulated quite a different position by inventing the word 'homosexuality'. The term, it seems, first appeared in a letter by Karl-Maria Kertbeny to Ulrichs, dated 6 May. Kertbeny claimed to have become interested in sexual rights after experiencing the death of a close friend, a 'homosexual' who had killed himself after being blackmailed. Having served in the army, Kertbeny supported himself as a journalist and travel writer, while at the same time writing extensively on sexual matters. In his letter to Ulrichs he divided people into four categories: 'monosexual' (masturbators), 'homosexual', 'heterosexual' and 'heterogenit' (bestialists). The terms 'homosexual' and 'heterosexual' reflected Kertbeny's belief in the existence of *two* sexes as opposed to Ulrichs' *three*. For Ulrichs this was unacceptable: he could not agree to Kertbeny's neologisms, which suggested that homosexuals were individuals who were attracted to individuals *like themselves*.[13]

Early readers did not always distinguish between the terms invented by Ulrichs and Kertbeny: Krafft-Ebing used both 'homosexual' and 'Urning' when he described sexual practices between men. One German campaigner for sexual rights, Benedict Friedländer, however, certainly did recognise the difference. He was greatly troubled by Ulrichs' association of same-sex desires with any kind of femininity. In 1903, this well-to-do gentleman founded with Adolf Brandt Die Gemeinschaft der Eigenen ('Community of the Special'), which became Germany's second largest organisation for men attracted to men, established in response to Magnus Hirschfeld's Wissenschaftlich–humanitäres Kommittee ('Scientific–Humanitarian Committee), an association set up to campaign for the rights of Urnings. In his writings, Friedländer found fault with the Aristophanic theory as expounded by Ulrichs. He contended that love between men was precisely that – between men who were like one another – as opposed to Ulrichs' differentiated Urnings. For Friedländer, the ideal state of society was a patriarchy in which men married women to reproduce but were also free to have intense, although chaste, relations with other men. Whereas Ulrichs saw the Urning as possessing a woman's soul, Friedländer saw men and women as opposing forces in society, and men were the superior species. Friedländer also turned back to antiquity for a model of the society he envisioned: 'Already the ancients knew this, by the way, for example, when Aristotle calls the acceptance of homoerotic love a remedy against gynaecocracy'.[14] Whereas, for Ulrichs, Urnings represented a third sex, a position in between man and woman, for Friedländer, Uranian lovers embodied the most manly and virile of men, naturally interested in all the affairs of their fellow males. As such, then, Friedländer fervently argued for the *differences* between the sexes, going as far as blaming women's increasing socio-economic status in modern times for the demise of the homoerotic patriarchy of ancient societies.

So, different theories of 'same-sex' desire utilised different ancient models for different agendas. For Ulrichs, the Aristophanic myth provided a biography for the inverted Urning, a thesis which informed the philosophy at the heart of the German sexologist Magnus Hirschfeld's Scientific–Humanitarian Committee, dedicated as it was to the rights of those not of the male gender – that is, Urnings and women. For Friedländer, on the other hand, the modern world could only look back in wonder at a lost ancient patriarchy. And these were not the only conceptualisations of same-sex desire circulating at the end of the nineteenth and into the beginning of the twentieth century. The older legislative discourse on sodomy still prevailed. Although Krafft-Ebing's medical *Psychopathia Sexualis* argued that a medical understanding of sexuality was preferable to the legal treatment of sexual criminals, he provided a detailed picture of what he called 'cultivated pederasty'. Relying on the criminological texts with which he finds fault, Krafft-Ebing describes an underground scene in Paris:

> old roués [rakes or libertines] that have supersatiated in normal sexual indulgence, and who find in pederasty a means of exciting sensual pleasure, the act being a new method of stimulation [. . .] This kind of pederast is the most dangerous, since they deal mostly with boys, and ruin them in body and soul.

Such old 'aunts' cultivate 'petits jesus' or 'lost, depraved children' and pimp them out. 'Cultivated pederasty' was also supposedly taken up by those whom certain environments might cause them to act in such a way, on 'long voyages', 'in prison, in watering places, etc'. The origins of this form of sexuality were also traced back to ancient times, as Krafft-Ebing puts it:

> this vice seems to have come through Crete from Asia to Greece, and, in the times of classic Hellas, to have been widespread. Thence it spread to Rome, where it flourished luxuriantly. In Persia and China (where it is actually tolerated) it is widespread, as it also is in Europe.[15]

At the same time in England, Greek pederasty, or love between an older man and boy, provided several men with a justification for writing poetry about and addressed to male youths. William Johnson, a Classics master at Eton, privately published a slim volume of poetry called *Ionica*, which became a source of inspiration for later 'Uranians', as they came to call themselves. Johnson, a popular and brilliant tutor, was nevertheless asked to leave Eton in 1872 under mysterious circumstances. Some have read between the lines suggesting that this was due to improper relationships with his pupils, whereas others have argued an incriminating letter to a boy was intercepted by the child's parents. Whatever the truth, Johnson took on the name Cory (after his paternal grandmother) and later moved to Madeira where he married and had a son. And, despite any misdemeanours, Johnson was fondly remembered: at Eton he had taught and befriended many boys who would go on to become important statesmen, including three prime ministers (Rosebery, Balfour and Asquith) 'who at Eton learnt the elements of high politics' from their favourite classics master, as Reginald Baliol Brett, 2nd Viscount Esher, one of the most powerful men of his time, put it in his 1924 memoir of Johnson's life.[16]

Ancient Greek did not so much supply a code but *codes* – a plurality of competing models – for the theorisation of same-sex sexuality at the end of the nineteenth century. It was at this time that a well-known, widely read writer penned his own memoirs in which he explored his sexual desires for boys and men. John Addington Symonds (1840–93), named after his father (an eminent physician and himself a writer on criminal responsibility, dreams, sleep and beauty), had been educated at Harrow School and went on to Balliol College, Oxford, to read Classics. After graduating, Symonds obtained a fellowship at Magdalen College, only to be forced to resign from his position due to poor health brought on by an accusation that he had had an affair with a young college chorister. Wealthy enough to live off a private income, he became a highly successful public intellectual, producing biographies of English poets and a seven-volume history of the Italian Renaissance as well as two widely read books on ancient Greek poetry. Only a few of his closest friends knew that Symonds, outwardly a successful and happily married man and father, was far from contented.

In 1873, his attraction to a 19-year-old male youth inspired him to investigate the relationship between ancient Greek pederasty and modern sexual relations between men. His research eventually saw the light of day in 1883, but only just: Symonds anonymously published *A Problem in Greek Ethics* in a tiny edition of ten copies. In 1889 he decided to write his autobiography, a highly candid account of his sex life, which, of course, was never published in his lifetime. This was followed by *A Problem in Modern Ethics* in 1891, also published anonymously in a small edition, in which Symonds discussed the plethora of nineteenth-century theories about sexual practices between men. Perhaps more than any other writer discussed so far in this chapter, Symonds made a point of really thinking about how a *historical* understanding of ancient Greece might help him understand – even facilitate – his desires for other men, and how his classical studies helped or hindered the possibility of a kinder, more accepting science of sex.[17]

Knowing about ancient Greece

Symonds' reception of ancient Greece was profoundly informed by his tutor Benjamin Jowett, Regius Professor of Greek at Oxford. It was under the influence of this don that the undergraduate Symonds read the dialogues of Plato. Jowett's teaching at Oxford paved the way for his translations of all of Plato's dialogues, which appeared in three editions during his lifetime. And Jowett did not avoid discussing the issue of Greek pederasty. In his introduction to the *Symposium*, he refers his reader to 'the admirable and exhaustive article of Meier'.[18] Jowett was indeed a close and careful reader of German scholarship and philosophy, which emphasised a historicist approach to the ancient world, whereby an objective and ethically detached stance was deemed necessary for the production of truthful research. In such a vein, then, Jowett registered 'the great gulf' of difference between ancient and modern morality on the subject of pederasty. He also conceded that 'it is impossible to deny that some of the best and greatest of the Greeks indulged in attachments, which Plato in the *Laws*, no less than the universal opinion of Christendom, had stigmatised as unnatural'. And yet, he also claimed that pederasty in the dialogues of Plato was 'mainly a figure of speech' and that the physical aspects in Pausanias' speech in the *Symposium* were 'more words than matter'. Jowett's objective stance vis-à-vis the Greeks could only go so far, then.[19]

Even if Symonds was not able to remain at Oxford as a don for the rest of his life, the education he received there provided him with the theoretical framework to write a historically informed study of Greek pederasty. And so, in 1873, Symonds embarked on *A Problem in Greek Ethics*, saying:

> [T]he fact remains that the literature of the Greeks, upon which the best part of humanistic education rests, abounds in references to the paiderastic [*sic*] passion. The anomaly involved in these facts demands dispassionate interpretation. I do not, therefore, see why the inquiry should not be attempted.[20]

Symonds' essay represented the first attempt to produce, in the English language, a historically accurate and objective account of pederasty. Although Symonds claimed not to have read Meier until much later, Symonds' historicist depiction of Greek pederasty was remarkably similar. We should not be too surprised, however, since they were both working from a common source: Pausanias' speech in Plato's *Symposium*, which distinguished between common and heavenly Aphrodites. For Symonds, like Meier before him, these two forms of sexual desire were actually blended. And so the 'mixed pederasty' of classical Athens, as Symonds called 'Greek love', 'was a passionate and enthusiastic attachment subsisting between man and youth, recognised by society and protected by opinion, which, though it was not free from sensuality, did not degenerate into mere licentiousness'.[21] But Symonds' Greeks of the classical period looked back to an earlier age, exemplified by Homer's Achilles and Patroclus, when ideal and manly relationships between men blossomed. Relying on nineteenth-century German scholarship that posited an invasion of 'Dorian' invaders from the north into the Aegean south in pre-Archaic times, Symonds wrote:

> Instead of a πόλις [city-state], with its manifold complexities of social life, they [the Dorians] were reduced to the narrow limits and social conditions of a roving horde. Without sufficiency of women, without the sanctities of established domestic life, inspired by the memory of Achilles, and venerating their ancestor Herakles, the Dorian warriors had special opportunity for elevating comradeship to the rank of an enthusiasm.[22]

The historical relationship between Homer and his later, classical Greek readers was, then, a complex one:

> Homer stood in a double relation to the historical Greeks. On the one hand, he determined their development by the influence of his ideal characters. On the other, he underwent from them interpretations which varied with the spirit of each successive century. He created a national temperament, but received in turn the influx of new thoughts and emotions occurring in the course of its expansion.[23]

While Symonds' historical method led him to argue that ancient Athenians participated in pederastic relationships, this was itself a custom that looked back to an even further removed period in time, which had been captured in the poetry of Homer and lived out by the Dorian warriors before that again. *A Problem in Greek Ethics* portrayed Dorian comradeship as exerting an informative influence on 'historical Greeks', while at the same time remaining an irrecoverable feature of the past. Symonds' research contradicted Jowett's argument that ancient Greek relations between men and youths were merely 'figures of speech', and yet it reflected Jowett's emphasis on historicism, and consigned the best form of Greek love to a very ancient past.

This essay just saw the light of day about ten years later in 1883 with an edition of ten copies. It seems that Jowett had been entertaining but then gave up on the idea of writing an essay on Greek love.[24] In 1889, Symonds wrote a letter to his old tutor, Jowett, with whom he had maintained a friendship, saying that he was pleased that Jowett was no longer writing his essay:

> I am glad to hear from the last letter you wrote me that you have abandoned the idea of an essay on Greek love. Little good could come of such a treatise in your book. It surprises me to find you, with your knowledge of Greek history speaking of this in Plato as 'mainly a figure of speech'. – It surprises me as much as I seem to surprise you when I repeat that the study of Plato is injurious to a certain number of predisposed young men. Many forms of passion between males are matters of fact in English schools, colleges, cities, rural districts. Such passion is innate in some persons no less than the ordinary sexual appetite is innate in the majority. With the nobler of such predetermined temperaments the passion seeks a spiritual or ideal transformation. [. . .] For such students of Plato there is no question of 'figures of speech', but of concrete facts, facts in the social experience of Athens. [. . .] Greek history confirms, by a multitude of legends and of actual episodes, what Plato puts forth as a splendid vision. [. . .] It is futile by any evasion of the central difficulty, by any dexterity in the use of words, to escape from the stubborn fact that

> natures so exceptionally predisposed find in Plato the encouragement of their furtively cherished dreams. [. . .] Greek love was for Plato no 'figure of speech', but a present poignant reality. Greek love is for modern students of Plato no 'figure of speech' and no anachronism, but a present poignant reality. The facts of Greek history and the facts of contemporary life demonstrate these propositions only too conclusively.[25]

Symonds took issue with Jowett's historical method ('with your knowledge of Greek history') to suggest that Plato was using a 'figure of speech'. Symonds' historicism, on the other hand, relied on the 'concrete facts', the 'stubborn fact' of Greek pederasty – 'the facts of Greek history'. Whereas Jowett had registered the 'great gulf' between ancient and modern, for Symonds there was 'no anachronism' in comparing Plato's 'present poignant reality' with the 'present poignant reality' of the nineteenth century. If, back in 1873, Dorian culture seemed like an irretrievable aspect of the distant past then, by the late 1880s, Symonds' historicism had led him in the opposite direction to Jowett's historical inquiry, so that Symonds would emphasise the influence ancient Greek texts had on the minds of those 'predisposed young men' reading them. Whereas in 1873 Symonds had underlined the need for a 'dispassionate interpretation' of 'paiderastic passion', this possibility seemed less distinct in 1889. Symonds' quandary was that Greek love was both impossible to imitate *and* it encouraged and shaped the minds of certain modern men.

This letter was written at a time when legal circumstances and changing reading habits impacted profoundly on Symonds thoughts about the subject. In 1885, the Labouchère Amendment (Section 11 of the Criminal Law Amendment Act, 1885) made 'gross indecency' a crime in the United Kingdom. This replaced older legislation against sodomy, so that where sodomy could not be proved, relations of an intimate nature between males more generally became prosecutable.[26] Symonds was well aware and critical of the change in law and began to read criminology and sexology in earnest.[27] The autobiographical narratives found in Krafft-Ebing informed

Symonds' desire to write his own story. And so, in 1889, he began to write his memoirs, or his 'vita sexualis', as he calls it, a phrase he borrows from Krafft-Ebing.[28] And yet, 'it does not appear to me', writes Symonds that 'the school of neuropathical physicians have solved the problem offered by individuals of my type'.[29] Krafft-Ebing's theory of heredity just did not add up: 'The "neuropathic grandmother" is too common an occurrence in modern families to account for what is after all a somewhat rare aberration of sexual proclivities'.[30] Symonds' mocking use of the term 'neuropathic', which refers to the pathology of the nervous system, reflects Symonds' critical attitude towards Krafft-Ebing's diagnosis of the nervousness of modern society:

> It is notorious that in literature I have done a very large amount of work, not only brilliant, but solid and laborious, which has placed me in the front rank of English authors. My literary achievement is no doubt due in part at least to a high degree of nervous sensibility; and compared with the average of men, I may be pronounced to have exhibited an abnormal strain of nervous energy. This nervousness has been a condition of my performance. But is it logical or prudent to diagnose so marked a specimen of the artistic temperament as morbid?[31]

Symonds concedes that his 'brilliant' literary achievements which have positioned him 'in the front rank of English authors' might be down to an excess of nervous energy resulting from his struggles with his sexuality. Nevertheless, he questions the wisdom and logic that brilliant literary writing is a product of morbidity. Symonds used his memoirs to show himself that the ancient Greeks produced literature that reflected a healthy and beautiful love of the male body. In this way, then, his memoirs became his first attempt to correct the diagnoses of sexology by turning to Greek literature.

As befits an autobiography, Symonds begins with his childhood. An early chapter describes his time as a pupil at Harrow School, when he first discovered how Greek literature could offer him an alternative, more positive view of his sexuality. This discovery occurred, he says, during a time when he was forced to endure a brutal and violent regime at Harrow, where

> every boy of good looks had a female name, and was recognised as a public prostitute or as some bigger fellow's bitch. Bitch was the word in common usage to indicate a boy who yielded his person to his lover.

Symonds expresses his disgust at the 'priapic' behaviour in the boys' dormitories, describing one boy as 'the notissima fossa', 'or the most notorious ditch', quoting Juvenal (2.10), for the boy's capacity to receive a large penis in his mouth and anus. Harrow reminded Symonds of the scenes he had read in Latin priapic and satiric poetry.[32] The reference to Juvenal summed up Symonds' attitude to life at Harrow: in this poem, the Roman satirist had criticised those hypocrites who say one thing but do another: 'every street is full of stern-faced perverts. How can you castigate shameless acts, when you yourself are the most notorious ditch amongst the Socratic faggots?' (2.8–10). Harrow, we are to infer, is full of teachers who are in charge of youths but who also enjoy buggery.

This would appear to be just the case, as Symonds then goes on to relate how, in his last year at Harrow,

> in the month of January 1858 Alfred Pretor [a friend of Symonds'] wrote me a note in which he informed me that Vaughan had begun a love affair with him. I soon found that the boy was not lying, because he showed me a series of passionate letters written to him by our headmaster.[33]

Symonds did not tell anyone about the pederastic headmaster, Charles Vaughan, until an Oxford undergraduate on a reading trip to the Lake District with his Latin tutor John Conington who himself 'sympathized with romantic attachments for boys'.[34] Conington, supposedly a practitioner of chaste relationships with younger men, decided to inform Symonds' father who, in turn, wrote to Vaughan who, fearing scandal, was eventually persuaded to retire.[35] If Symonds' use of Latin to describe the debauched dormitories at Harrow might remind us of Krafft-Ebing's Latin to describe the decadent *fin de siècle*, then this was certainly not meant to reflect Symonds' own sexuality. Rather, Symonds contrasts his discovery of Plato in the sixth form with Vaughan's pederastic regime of Juvenalian 'Socratic faggots':

> We were reading Plato's *Apology* in the sixth form. I bought Cary's crib and took it with me to London on an *exeat* in March. My hostess, a Mrs Bain, who lived in Regent's Park, treated me to a comedy one evening at the Haymarket. [. . .] When we returned from the play, I went to bed and began to read my Cary's Plato. It so happened that I stumbled on the *Phaedrus*. I read on and on, till I reached the end. Then I began the *Symposium*; and the sun was shining on the shrubs outside the ground-floor in which I slept, before I shut the book up.[36]

Symonds draws a sharp distinction between what he read in Plato and his experiences at Harrow:

> The study of Plato proved decisive for my future. Coming at the moment when it did, it delivered me to a large extent from the torpid cynicism caused by the Vaughan episode. At the same time it confirmed my congenital inclination toward persons of the male sex, and filled my head with an impossible dream, which controlled my thoughts for many years.[37]

Just as Socrates went on into the following morning discussing the relationship between tragedy and comedy, so Symonds read these dialogues until 'the sun was shining on the shrubs'. Just as the *Symposium* ends with the amusing entrance of Alcibiades, with his comical portrait of Socrates, and with Socrates' own discussion of theatre, so Symonds' reading of that dialogue is prefaced by a comedy at the Haymarket. Symonds pictures himself as moving away from the *Apology*, the text in which Socrates answers his accusers' charges of introducing new gods and, more significantly, corrupting Athenian youths, towards the Platonic texts of beauty and pleasure, the *Phaedrus* and the *Symposium*. The sun 'shining on the shrubs' has us imagine a newly enlightened Symonds as being reborn in this bright new morning. At the same time, however, despite the power of the Platonic text to confirm Symonds' 'congenital inclination', it was nothing but 'an impossible dream'. He might have felt 'as though in some antenatal experience I had lived the life of [a] philosophical Greek lover', but the reality of his life proved that he could not really time-travel.[38] Harrow was nothing like a Platonic Academy or even a visit with Socrates to the palaestra but, rather, full of Socratic hypocrites such as those in Juvenal's satire.

Even if Symonds was critical of his old headmaster, he also 'felt a deeply rooted sympathy with Vaughan. If he had sinned, it had been by yielding to passions which already mastered me'.[39] Later on in the memoir, Symonds describes being blackmailed by a younger man at Oxford, who had managed to copy out extracts of Symonds' letters and poems. These were then sent to six dons at Magdalen College (where Symonds had become a fellow) in order to suggest that Symonds harboured desires for a College choirboy. Symonds found himself in a similar situation as Vaughan, although Symonds was exonerated of the false charges put to him.[40] A few years later, in 1868, by this point in time married, Symonds was given the opportunity of lecturing on Greek poetry at Clifton College in Bristol, which was where he got to know one of the pupils, Edward Norman Moor. Beguiled by his beauty, it was soon after this that Symonds started to write *A Problem in Greek Ethics*.

In the memoirs, he describes the physical relationship that developed with Moor in terms that makes it look like a Platonic lesson. Symonds appears to be keen to contrast his own pederastic relationship with Vaughan's, even if he admitted to feeling 'sympathy' with the Harrow headteacher. And yet, just as Platonism was 'an impossible dream' at Harrow, so Symonds presents himself as caught between Platonic philosophy and Athenian tragedy, between enlightenment and suffering. Ancient Greek literature offered him a language for the expression of his desires *and* an archive of myths about the impossibility of fulfilling his passions. At one point he compares his fate to that 'of Ajax or of Phaedra', either insane or illicitly desirous of a chaste, beautiful ephebe.[41] But, if he compares himself to Phaedra, at another point Symonds also feels like Hippolytus, whose 'tongue swore but [whose] heart remains unpledged', as Symonds quotes line 612 from Euripides' *Hippolytus*.[42] The metaphor of the desirable Greek ephebe, who dies before his time, reappears in one of the most sexually explicit episodes of the memoirs, the sex scene between Symonds and one of his pupils. It is here where we see the tension between Platonic enlightenment and Euripidean suffering emerging most clearly. When Symonds has sex with Norman, he has sex in Platonic *and* Euripidean Greek. The memoirs contain an extract from his diary dated 28 January 1870, not long before Norman was to begin at Oxford, when Symonds describes having sex with his younger lover:

> Oh, the strain of those delicate slight limbs and finely moulded breasts – the melting of that stately throat into the exquisite slim shoulders – as of the Genius of the Vatican – the στέρνα θ' ὡς ἀγάλματος κάλλιστα [and his most lovely breast, like that of a statue]. I find it hard to write of these things; yet I wish to dwell on them and to recall them, pen in hand: – the head that crowned all, pillowed with closely cut thick flocks of hair and features as of some bronze statue, sharp and clear – the chiselling mouth [. . .] His hips are narrow, hardened where the muscles brace the bone, but soft as down and sleek as satin in the hollows of the groin. Shy and modest, tender in the beauty-bloom of ladhood, is his part of sex κύπριν ποθοῦσαν ἤδη [now longing for passion] – fragrant to the searching touch, yet shrinking: for when the wandering hand rests there, the lad turns pleadingly into my arms as though he sought to be relieved of some delicious pang [. . .] Norman is all in all and wholly μελίχλωρος [honey-pale].[43]

'Pen[is?] in hand', quoting a line from one of his own poems, Symonds compares Norman to Cupid, 'the Genius of the Vatican'. The pederastic scene sounds emphatically like the writings of the English Uranian poets, such as William Johnson, focused as it is on Norman's tender youth ('delicate slight limbs', 'exquisite slim shoulders', his 'ladhood', 'the lad'). Symonds explicitly aestheticises the erotic experience with the boy, who is like 'some bronze statue'. The 'shy and modest' Norman, his erect penis 'shrinking', is reminiscent of ancient Greek discourse on the innocence of the *erōmenos* being chased by the *erastēs*.[44] From teacher and pupil to lovers, Symonds' relationship with Norman crosses the line between pedagogy and pederasty: it is Symonds' 'intention to educate Norman and to stimulate his intellect'.[45] The knowing Greek quotations from Plato and Euripides colour the scene. Norman is μελίχλωρος, 'honey-pale', a word used by Socrates in Plato's *Republic*, when describing men's love for the imperfections of their boyish lovers: a true lover 'feels affection' for his beloved 'as a whole', just as 'a philosopher's passions are for wisdom of every kind' (474d–475b). Symonds' map of the whole of Norman's body ('all in all and wholly') is an erotic application of Socrates' philosophy: Symonds' desire begets knowledge of Norman's physique, just as Symonds' knowledge of Greek shapes his desires for Norman. But Symonds' comparison of Norman to a Greek statue is not so straightforward. The quote comes from Euripides' *Hecuba* (560–1), when Talthybius the Greek messenger describes to Hecuba her daughter Polyxena's beautiful statuesque breast just before her death at the hands of the Greeks, as a sacrifice to the dead Achilles. Symonds' sex in Greek couches itself in ancient philosophical discourse, and yet his sexual conquest of Norman recalls Polyxena on the verge of stabbing herself to death. The moment of pleasure for Symonds results from his reading of Platonic philosophy *and* it violently marks the loss of Norman's virginity. The eroticised Socratic tutorial is also a moment of saying goodbye to Norman's body now that it has matured into adulthood.

The sex scene recalls the sense of loss that coloured so much English Uranian poetry about boys.[46] Several poems in William Johnson's *Ionica*, a book of pederastic poems he had privately and anonymously published while a master at Eton in 1858, had already mourned the maturation of a youth or the imminence of his adulthood.[47] One poem, 'ΑΛΙΟΣ ΑΜΜΙ ΔΕΔΥΚΕ' ('The Sun Has Sunk for Me'), laments the separation of Johnson from his young lover, although he is consoled by the fact that 'I play with those that still are here' under his pedagogic care.[48] The title is a reworking of a line in Theocritus *Idyll* 1.102, in a song where the shepherd Daphnis pines and dies for a lost love. The final poem in the book, 'An Apology', sums up Johnson's tome of erotic loss. This poem, which, despite the title, offers no Socratic defence, describes his desires as 'the temple of my love'. But by the end Johnson writes:

> The trophied arms and treasured gold
> Have passed beneath the spoiler's hand;
> The shrine is bare, the altar cold,
> But let the outer fabric stand.[49]

The relationships themselves have passed, but their shells, Johnson's poetry itself, like the ruins of a temple, still stand. An empty ruin, empty words . . . Johnson's *Ionica*, then, meditates upon the untimeliness of pederastic desires in the nineteenth century. Not only do his poems hope that 'two minds shall flow together, the English and the Greek', suggesting that modern England might never be (like) ancient Greece, but Johnson's poetry also observes that the pederast will always feel at a loss: either his beloved is too young to reciprocate his desires or the beloved is too old, grown up, departed from Eton.[50] Greek love is always already in the past – a looking forward to what one once had in the past.

It is not surprising that Johnson should have been engaging with the poetry of the Hellenistic writer Theocritus, whose idylls explored the sense of loss involved in pederastic passion. While Symonds was on Easter holidays from Harrow in the year he first read Plato's *Symposium*, he befriended a chorister, Willie Dyer. Symonds recounts his noble love, in contrast to Vaughan's Harrow: 'Twice only in my life did I kiss him on the lips'. In fact, it was the first time Symonds had kissed a boy. Looking back to this moment he writes:

> I still possess a white anemone gathered on the spot of that first kiss. It marks the place in my Theocritus, where this phrase occurs: 'there were men back then of the Golden Age, when he who was loved [that is, the beloved boy] returned one's love' (12.15–16).[51]

Theocritus' poem is about a man fast growing old who deludes himself that his love of a beautiful youth will one day be seen as a golden age of pederastic love by those in the future looking back into the distant past.[52] If Symonds, then, looked back to the ageing lover in Theocritus' poem, who anticipated a future reader looking back at him, he was all too aware of the irony, as he pictured his own boyhood as an irrecoverable past and he himself as that ageing lover. Nothing but an anemone connects him back to that place. Symonds' subtle sense of the historical, then, deeply informed his sexuality. Even if being a lover of boys seemed to help Symonds understand Greek all the better, his desires also reminded him of the impossibility of knowing ancient Greece all the more sorely. Despite his attempts to locate an epistemology of his passions in the discourse of Platonic philosophy, which might correct the diagnoses of contemporary sexology, ancient Greece continued to offer a tricky example.

If Symonds presents himself as a pederast (that is, a lover of youths and boys) at some points in his memoir, at later sections he starts to describe his love of adult men. In one sex scene, 'with a brawny young soldier', he revels in sex which is 'comradely and natural [. . .] I thoroughly enjoyed the close vicinity of that splendid naked piece of manhood'.[53] Symonds also records a trip made to Venice in 1881, when he fell for a 'manly' gondolier in Venice, Angelo Fusato, whose 'Mercurial poise upon the ankle' and 'wild glance of a Triton' made 'a simile of a sea-god' the best way of looking at him. The friendship, in Symonds' eyes at least, was a relationship 'between two men', 'comradeship' and 'masculine love'.[54] We have already seen that Greek literature and history offered different sorts of examples to nineteenth-century men attracted to the male form. Symonds' own sexuality, as he presents it in his memoirs, shifts between a pederasty, founded on an age-discrepant asymmetry, and a homosexuality, that is, a desire between two virile men who are alike. Even if, in 1883, he was publishing an essay that committed Doric love to the very ancient past, he was also imagining its possibility in the present. And, in the second half of the 1880s, the Dorians continued to occupy Symonds' thoughts. By the end of the decade, he was weighing up the chances that Doric Greek love might be revivified by modern homosexual men. In 1889, the year Symonds wrote his memoir, he sent a letter to Krafft-Ebing in which he critiqued Krafft-Ebing's theories of heredity and degeneracy and argued that any nervousness, weakness or mental incapacity that might be felt is brought on by the disadvantageous position the affected man holds in modern society. Far from pathological, then, the struggle undergone by men sexually attracted to other males is characterised by Symonds as 'the Iliad of their sufferings and constant nervous excitations'.[55] Symonds' reference to Homer was not merely rhetorical.

The legal position for homosexuals after the Labouchère Amendment, along with the growing body of medical work which pathologised same-sex desire, compelled Symonds to engage his classical knowledge in a more directly political context. In *Greek Ethics*, in 1883, Homer's heroes and the Dorians were described as an influence on, but also an irrecoverable ideal for, the ancient Athenians. In 1891, he anonymously published 50 copies of *A Problem in Modern Ethics*, in which he included the letter to Krafft-Ebing as part of a longer argument that Doric love offered the best example for modern homosexuals to follow, in the face of the theories of criminal sodomy, inversion and Krafft-Ebing's depiction of degenerate modern society. Indeed, Symonds sought to distinguish his depiction of Doric love from the Latin tradition of writing, out of which Krafft-Ebing's Latinity had emerged: 'those who can bring themselves to enquire into such matters' can read 'Forberg's annotations to "Hermaphroditus" [and] Rosenbaum's "Lustseuche"' which report on 'the wildest freaks and aberrations'.[56] In *Modern Ethics*, on the other hand, Symonds politicised his stance towards contemporary scientific writing on sex to argue that Doric Greek friendship and love was not a pathological aberration, but rather a uniquely egalitarian and manly pursuit, democratic in nature and worthy of emulation for Western democrats at a time when British law imperilled homosexual freedoms and rights.[57]

Modern Ethics concludes with a discussion of the American Walt Whitman's 'Calamus' poems from his collection *Leaves of Grass*. Whitman (1819–92) had been a successful journalist in Manhattan but retired from the hustle and bustle of the city to work with his father as a carpenter. It was at this time that he wrote and published the first edition of *Leaves* (in 1855), a suite of poems in celebration of democracy as embodied in the erotic beauty of the human form. In 1860, in the third edition, Whitman included the 'Calamus' poems, which looked back to antiquity just as much as they celebrated the possibilities of love and comradeship between men. By the 1870s, Whitman was being closely read by Englishmen such as the socialist activist and homosexual Edward Carpenter, who was very interested in disseminating Whitman's electrifying poetry to the English working class through his own book-long poem *Towards Democracy*, first published in 1883, the same year as *A Problem in Greek Ethics*.[58] The Symonds of *Modern Ethics* was well aware of this reception of Whitman, whose poetry, he argued, 'recalls to our mind the early Greek enthusiasm – that fellowship in arms which flourished among Dorian tribes'.[59] Whitman 'expects Democracy, the new social and political medium, the new religious ideal of mankind, to develop and extend "that fervid comradeship", and by its means to counterbalance and to spiritualise what is vulgar and materialistic in the modern world'.[60] Symonds, ever the eager letter-writer, also corresponded with Whitman, hoping that the poet would confirm his interpretation. However, as Symonds records in *Modern Ethics*, he received a reply from Camden, New Jersey, in which Whitman condemned Symonds' 'morbid inferences' as 'damnable'. Although Symonds tries to read Whitman's poetry contrary to Whitman's stated intention, he closes *Modern Ethics* despondently: 'The world cannot be invited to entertain' Doric Greek love.[61]

Despite this setback, the possibility that Greek literature could make a contribution to late nineteenth-century medical expertise and authority on the subject of male sexuality still interested Symonds. In 1890, he had begun to correspond with Henry Havelock Ellis, the author of *The New*

Spirit, which was published that year. This was a radical political tract that charted the emergence of a new world of science and social and cultural progress at the *fin de siècle*: 'anthropology, sociology and political science; the increasing importance of women; the disappearance of war; the substitution of art for religion', as Ellis ambitiously put it.[62] And the provocative author also shared Symonds' admiration for Whitman and democratic politics as well as Symonds' interest in contemporary sexology. But Ellis was no specialist in the field: his only medical qualification was a licence to practise from the Society of Apothecaries, and, as Phyllis Grosskurth has outlined in her biography, Ellis' 'medical' practice only ever stretched to a three-month post as superintendent of a hydropathic establishment in Harrogate, Yorkshire, where he advised 'the patients on the waters and [presided] at table'.[63] But, as Sean Brady has explained, it was the leftist politics of Symonds and his contemporaries, such as the playwright George Bernard Shaw, that led Ellis to conceive of his book *Sexual Inversion*, which would argue that sexual attraction between males and between females was congenital and should therefore not be punishable by the law.[64]

By 1892, Ellis and Symonds agreed that they would collaborate on the publication. Ellis dealt with the medical and psychological sections of the book, while Symonds provided the sections on literary and historical material. The collaboration made Ellis very uncomfortable: the sexologist and the classicist proffered very different sorts of defences for the legitimation of same-sex desire. Ellis argued that inversion was congenital, whereas the inclusion of *A Problem in Greek Ethics* in Ellis' and Symonds' *Sexual Inversion*, suggested that the existence of a Doric Greek love, although fine and noble, seemed, already to the ancient Athenians, 'almost too high above the realities of common life for imitation, yet stimulative of enthusiasm and exciting to the fancy'.[65] Ellis' attempts at a scientific approach clashed with Symonds' Hellenism, which looked back to the Dorians for a too-idealistic model of endless self-fashioning. For Ellis, sexuality was innate. However much purchase this idea also had on Symonds, the classicist could not stop believing that it was reading classical literature that shaped one's individual character, for better or for worse. Symonds died in

1893 with the issue of what ancient Greek literature might contribute to sexology open to debate. Their book appeared in German in 1896 and in English in 1897, leaving their readers to continue the discussion.[66]

Just as Renaissance humanists had rejected Latin epigrammatic poetry in favour of Plato's Greek in order to understand human desire, so nineteenth-century philhellenists in their own different ways turned away from Krafft-Ebing's depiction of modern decadence in ancient Roman terms. While Krafft-Ebing's reliance on classical historiography supposedly validated his Latinate vocabulary of sexuality, some of his readers questioned his historicist credentials. In this chapter, we have focused on how it was Symonds in particular who thought very carefully about what ancient history – specifically, ancient *Greek* history – might have to say about modern male sexuality. Platonic philosophy lent Symonds a language in which to express himself, and yet he was also turned on by the sense that Greek culture was perhaps utterly irrecoverable: when he desired the ephebic body, it was the imminent loss of that body – its innocence crushed, its virginity taken, with adulthood looming – that Symonds found so pleasurable. It was 'l'amour de l'impossible', as he called it.[67] Symonds' sexuality emerged in a context when different versions of same-sex desire were circulating: criminologists who adjudicated on sodomy; theorists of inversion who posited a third sex; older pederasts who adored and groomed younger boys; and homosexuals who professed to love the same sex. Indeed, 'same-sex' is a far from helpful adjective, as inverts, sodomites under the surveillance of criminologists and pederasts all viewed their sexual relations as predicated on specific asymmetries, hierarchies or differences between partners, whereas identified and self-identified homosexuals were seen and saw themselves as practising a relationship between two equal selves. Ancient Greek, then, didn't straightforwardly speak the truth of nineteenth-century men's desires. In Symonds alone, the language offered numerous different opportunities – various competing ways to describe, represent and understand his sexual desires. But if this chapter has focused so closely on male sexual pleasure, then what did ancient Greek texts teach nineteenth-century sexology and its readers about female same-sex sexuality? It is to this very issue that the next chapter turns.

CHAPTER V

FROM THE TRIBAD TO SAPPHO

Women's access to, and mastery of, Greek and Latin was a source of both humour and anxiety for Renaissance and early-modern male scholars and readers. Beccadelli's girlfriend, who had read Catullus, is called a 'domina', a 'mistress', in his poem (2.23.2). While the term was commonly used in Roman love elegy, in Beccadelli her authoritative nature is emphasised as she 'drives Beccadelli on with dire threats' (2.23.10), in case he doesn't deliver up a copy of Catullus for her. Tullia d'Aragona's satire on Renaissance philosophers of love also engendered anxiety and mockery in the form of Nicolas Chorier's fantastical cousins Tullia and Octavia, whose creative (mis)interpretations of Latin literature uncovered alternative reasons for reading the classics. The concern about women's knowledge of the classics was reflected in Beccadelli's and Chorier's presentations of women who appropriated and misused Greek and Latin for their own erotic ends. In an early part of *Satyra Sotadica*, this takes on a particular perspective when Tullia is teaching Octavia the art of the orgasm and she stimulates her younger cousin's imagination with her own version of Ovid's story about Iphis' passion for Ianthe, that is, one girl's love for another. Whereas, in the *Metamorphoses*, Isis transforms Iphis into a boy so that 'he' can marry and consummate 'his' desires with Ianthe, Tullia presents Iphis as endlessly burning for the girl (II, 36–7) in order to seduce her younger cousin to have sex with her. It seems that Tullia has appropriated Ovid's Latin so that she and Octavia, two women, can enjoy each other. But as in Ovid, so in Chorier, desire between women is a rehearsal for marriage between man and woman: Tullia's and Octavia's love-making is training for the bride-to-be's wedding night. Chorier writes female sexual pleasure in Latin for the enjoyment of men.

Beccadelli and Chorier were expressing their anxieties about who knows more about sex – men or women – a concern that emerged from Ovid's depictions of the battles of the sexes and ancient reports of women-authored sex manuals. But the issue of same-sex sexuality put into sharp focus the question of the relationship (the similarities and differences) between male and female pleasure. Sex between women in the classical tradition was repeatedly presented as a rehearsal for, or a pale imitation of, male–female sexual relations, whereby the tribad mimicked the man's phallic role. The issues of women's knowledge and female same-sex sexuality became intricately entangled in the second half of the nineteenth and into the early twentieth century, when the question of women's use and abuse of the classical languages took on specific coordinates as women, as well as certain men, campaigned for the admittance of women to higher education in various European countries. The growing possibilities for women studying Classics at English universities in the nineteenth century have been well researched in particular detail, where, in Oxford and Cambridge, colleges for women were founded in the 1870s onwards. The entrance of women was often unwelcome to other male undergraduates, especially since the learning of Greek– even more so than that of Latin – seemed an expressely masculine pursuit. Isobel Hurst records, for instance, the hostility of male undergraduates who were concerned over women reading works such as '*Oedipus Rex*, which is distinctly spicy in parts'. The 1888 Oxford undergraduate journal from which Hurst quotes goes on to discuss the comical embarrassment facing male tutors explaining to female students the 'chaste complications' of Sophocles' play.[1] Greek was seen to 'unsex' women, as they endeavoured to mimic men at university study.[2]

The issue of women in higher education was just one aspect of broader, controversial debates in Britain about relations between the sexes, as some women (and some men) began to question Victorian gender roles: how like or unlike were women and men, asked numerous voices at the *fin de siècle*. In North America and Europe, fierce debates waged about women's social and political status. The so-called 'New Woman' appeared in numerous guises in the last two decades of the nineteenth century: some championed free love; other women activists re-examined the role of motherhood; suffragettes contested constitutional politics; some joined socialist causes; others explored the place of women in literature and the arts; and some celebrated and demonised their supposed mannishness. Classical antiquity repeatedly supplied risqué images for the imagination of the *fin de siècle*. Oscar Wilde's play on the subject, *Salomé*, was initially not permitted a performance in London, and polarised audiences in Paris. Aubrey Beardsley's notorious, illustrated edition of the play appeared in 1894. And Beardsley scandalously explored women's political power in his obscenely illustrated edition of Aristophanes' *Lysistrata*. Then, in 1896, Leonard Smithers, the London publisher of erotica, exotica and anthropology, released an edition of Juvenal's *Sixth Satire*, accompanied by Beardsley's sadomasochistic illustrations – women impaled on columns being scourged by the satirist; and the actor Bathyllus displaying his anus to the viewer to be penetrated.[3]

This late nineteenth-century concern about the relationship between women and men as gender boundaries seemed to be eroding directed descriptions of sex between women. It was within this context that ancient descriptions of tribads, who possessed enlarged clitorises for penetrating other women, offered the principal image of female same-sex sexuality in medical science at the end of the nineteenth century. This chapter begins by providing the ancient background on tribads and then traces out the reception of these ancient depictions at the end of the 1800s, as the issues of women in higher education, women's access to Greek, and female same-sex sexuality became intertwined. The concern about women who imitated men as they sought access to Greek and Latin at university level shaped Symonds' understanding of sex between women, as he wrote up a new section on the subject in his *A Problem in Modern Ethics*, which became part of Havelock Ellis' *Sexual Inversion*. While Symonds had emphasised the links between male pederasty and pedagogy, he denied there was such a relationship for ancient Greek women. Sexology, informed by the image of the ancient tribad, deemed the woman who had sex with another woman to be nothing but a poor imitation of a real man. The chapter then turns to a remarkable discovery made in 1890, when a papyrus in British-occupied Egypt brought a new ancient poet to the world. Although the name 'Herodas' was already known to classical scholars, none of his poems actually were. An ambitious Cambridge classicist got the chance to produce a full commentary of his poetry that had been unearthed. The sixth poem was a dialogue between two women, engaging in lusty conversation with one another, in search of a dildo. Walter Headlam, the Cambridge man, could not help but see tribads in the poem. We examine, then, how the ancient Greek language was used by a male scholar to confirm the modern stereotype that sex between women was a mere mimicry of 'real' phallic sexuality.

It was against this anxiety about the tribad that the Victorian image of Sappho was constructed. But, as this chapter shows in its concluding section, the image of Sappho as a pure and chaste Victorian schoolmistress was difficult to control, as male writers could not help but appropriate Sappho's voice to express their own desires. Sappho's identification with a man in her poetic outpouring to a woman in Fragment 31 had already inspired men to identify with her in ancient Rome, when Catullus (in Poem 51) depicted his own desires for a woman in imitation of Sappho's poem. In the 1880s, we will see that another man – John Addington Symonds – also wrote his own English version of the fragment. Symonds was, of course, an extremely well-known Victorian intellectual who outwardly lived a conventional family life. So, despite the concern that women might be becoming too like men, the verses of the female poet's feelings for other women permitted a widely read and admired male Victorian writer, Symonds, to identify with a woman. And what is more, with closer reading Symonds' version comes to look very homoerotic in meaning. Symonds' use of Sappho's verses, then, for his own homoerotic ends flies in the face of what he had written in his private publication about the tribadic sexuality of ancient Greek women, which was a poor imitation of male pederasty.

It was not accidental that Sappho the schoolmistress and Sappho the voice of a homosexual Victorian man could have co-existed in the 1880s.

In the second half of the nineteenth century, the fragments of her poems were published for the first time since antiquity in Greek and in English with the correct pronouns, thereby showing the objects of affection in her verses to have been both women and men. There was clearly a range of different Sappho's on offer for the modern writer to identify with and imitate. The chapter ends with a reading of two female lovers' re-writing of Sappho in the 1880s, which showed great awareness of the contested reception of Sappho's fragments, and celebrated this diversity of modern Sapphic invention. Aunt and niece, and lovers, Katherine Bradley and Edith Cooper, wrote a book of Sappho-inspired poems under the pseudonym 'Michael Field', in which they turned away from male-authored scientific accounts to offer a different knowledge of women's experiences of sex and desire.

Female traditions and Greek pederasty for women?

A long history of medical texts stretching back to the ancient world related female same-sex sexuality to the phallic clitoris. Ancient medicine was well aware of clitoral stimulation: the pseudo-Aristotelian Book 10 of *Generation of Animals* (637a23–8) offers a rather clumsy description. In *On the Usefulness of the Parts of the Body*, Galen writes about a part which offers 'no small usefulness in inciting the female to the sexual act and in opening wide the neck of the womb [the vagina] during coitus'.[4] But, because ancient anatomy viewed the woman's sexual organs as homologous to a man's (albeit less perfect), the clitoris became the female equivalent for the penis.[5] This association emerged especially in texts written under imperial Rome, when the word 'tribas' ('tribad') started to appear in Latin in the second century CE.[6] The most well-known instances appear in Martial. In one epigram, 'the tribad Philaenis buggers boys and more savagely than a husband's lust penetrates eleven girls in one day' (7.67.1–3), and she returns a few poems later, called 'tribad of the tribads' (7.70.1).

The fifth dialogue in Lucian's *Dialogues of Hetairai*, satirical sketches written for an educated Roman audience, laddishly wondered how like a man women are who have sex with one another. Clonarium questions her friend Leaena about her friendship with the 'rich Lesbian' Megilla. Clonarium notices that Leaena is 'blushing' and Leaena is 'ashamed' to talk about it. Clonarium is puzzled: 'what do you do when you are together?' Leaena reveals that Megilla is 'terribly manly', to which Clonarium responds with a question: is she a *hetairistria*? Leaena divulges how they had sex 'like men'. Clonarium, laughing, asks whether Megilla, who asks to be called Megillus, has 'that manly thing' (*to andreion ekeino*). Leaena said she wondered if Megillus was a hermaphrodite, but 'she' says 'she' isn't – rather 'she' is 'all man' (*to pan anēr eimi*), continuing: 'I was born a woman like all you others, but I have the mind and desires and all other things of a man . . . I have something in place of the manly thing [*anti tou andreiou*] . . . you'll see'. So what is this 'something *anti tou andreiou*'? Is it a dildo? A clitoris? Lucian leaves the answer to his reader's imagination, as he asks them to question whether there is anything specific to female (homo)erotics: is there a specifically female pleasure? What did female desire feel like? The differences between sex with a boy and sex with a woman were also the subject of debate in imperial Roman texts fascinated by Plato's *Symposium*. Plutarch's dialogue *Erōtikos* examined the applicability of Platonic *erōs* to married life between men and women, whereas the Lucianic text *Erōtes* wittily debated the merits of sex with boys and sex with women. How like a boy is a woman was a source of philosophical contention among intellectuals in imperial Rome.[7]

Between its description in Soranus' *Gynaecology* of the second century CE and the early-modern period, there is very little discussion of the clitoris in Western medicine. With the development of modern anatomy during the Italian Renaissance, however, the clitoris became a focus of attention when it seems to have been identified again in medical writings. Charles Estienne published *La dissection des parties du corps humain* first in Latin and then in French translation in 1546, in which he linked the function of the clitoris to urination. Gabriele Falloppio also described the clitoris in his 1561 work *Observationes anatomicae*. But it was Realdo Colombo at Padua University, in his *De re anatomica* in 1559, who first emphasised its role in female sexual pleasure. This was part of a more general theoretical moment in anatomy, when male and female bodies came to be seen as opposites and as profoundly different (as opposed to ancient times, when women's bodies were often seen, in medical texts, as imperfect, inverted versions of male ones). And yet, the story is not so straightforward. Although the clitoris was for some anatomists a signifier of female sexuality, for others, such as Andrea Vesalius, an extremely eminent and influential anatomist, it was nothing but an aberration, not a sign of femininity but of the fact that such 'women' were 'hermaphrodites'. Just as the idea that women's bodies were fundamentally unlike men's developed, so ancient notions about the analogousness of men's and women's bodies persisted.[8] And the renewed interest in medical discourse in the clitoris saw to it that texts such as Lucian's became widely quoted as proof that a woman might be able to penetrate and provide phallic pleasure to another woman. In the early nineteenth century, then, Forberg could open his chapter on 'tribads' by citing Lucian, in order to justify his definition that women whose clitoris 'reaches such proportions [. . .] can use it as a cock, either for fucking the vagina or fucking the ass'.[9]

When Forberg was researching his book, an Englishwoman was also doing her own research on the figure of the tribad. Anne Lister (1791–1840) was a wealthy Yorkshire landowner and traveller whose diaries record in remarkable detail her sexual and romantic affairs with other women.[10] Her economic status permitted her not to have to marry, and she was therefore able to pursue her sexual desires for other women. Lister learnt to read Greek and Latin and her diaries reveal her attempts to find an identity by turning to ancient texts. Sappho's poems were generally bowdlerised in the early nineteenth century when Lister came to read them. Only in 1820, in Pierre Bayle's entry on Sappho in his *Historical and Critical Dictionary*, did Lister seem to find anything to do with the Greek poet's desires for other women. And yet, Bayle says nothing explicit, and merely explains Horace's description of 'masculine Sappho' as denoting that she was a 'tribad, and that it denotes the inclination she had for the sciences, instead of handling the spindle and the distaff'. Bayle's account lists contending interpretations for nearly every aspect of her life, so that all Lister could note in her diary about Bayle's 'Sappho' was the single word 'interesting'.[11] Finding a heritage was not going to be straightforward.

Entries in her diary later on in the same year record her explorations of Roman references to tribads and female same-sex sexuality in Horace, Juvenal and Martial. While many editions of the classics expurgated any sexual matter that seemed unsuitable for modern readers, Lister's eagerness to uncover sexuality between women brought her to an early seventeenth-century commentary on Juvenal by Eilert Lübben, which did explain the actions of Tullia and Maura in Juvenal's sixth satire. But, of course, these Roman writers often represented such desires obliquely and pejoratively. When reading Martial's abusive epigram aimed at a woman called Bassa, who seems chaste but actually 'fucks' women (1.90), Lister wonders whether Bassa used a dildo or not.[12] While Lister's diary claims to have found Juvenal's poem sexually stimulating, these texts did not become a source of inspiration in the way that the Greeks would do for Symonds' generation. Although Lister looked back to antiquity for a sense of heritage, she never developed these pieces of knowledge into a full-blown historical account.[13]

The tribad became a key image in later nineteenth-century medical discussions of female same-sex sexuality. While the topic was not discussed in as much detail by Krafft-Ebing and British researchers, mannish women, large clitorises and tribadism among prostitutes were subjects that interested French and Italian specialists in sexual deviancy and perversion.[14] And the pedagogic dialogue between an older and a younger woman continued to be popular topos into the nineteenth century, as Victorian pornography took pleasure in, and medical writers showed concern over, the sexual aspects of school friendships between girls.[15] Symonds also knew the French and Italian material well and, while Victorian pornography about girls being flagellated at school would not have been his chosen reading material, Symonds' own participation in the semi-clandestine world of late-Victorian sexological publishing would have made him very aware of all sorts of erotic writing.[16] When he came to revise *A Problem in Greek Ethics* for his collaboration on *Sexual Inversion* with Havelock Ellis, he included a discussion of sex between women which reflects his classical knowledge and reading of contemporary science. It should be no surprise, then, that knowing about female same-sex sexuality intersected with the theme of women's access to knowledge. At the time when Symonds was writing, there was much public debate in England, as well as across Western Europe, about women in university education.[17] Benjamin Jowett had encouraged his students to read Plato and came to be seen as a modern Socrates, as his pupils practised 'Jowett-worship'.[18] The homosocial settings of Plato's dialogues were viewed as a model of pedagogy for male teachers and their students at Oxford and Cambridge. The idea that knowledge was transmitted from an older man to his youthful counterpart sancitified this male-only environment. We have already seen Symonds' admiration of the Dorians in *A Problem in Greek Ethics*; relying on earlier German scholarship, as ever, he pictured the Dorian relationship as a pedagogical one, where the elder was called the 'inspirer' and the youth the 'hearer'.[19] The Spartan youth's hearing and heeding of his older lover's lessons was viewed by Symonds as an ideal model of pedagogy.

While it was deemed permissible to allow young ladies to learn Latin, letting them into the male world of Hellenic studies seemed simply beyond the pale. The founding of the women's colleges at Oxford and Cambridge elicited much concern from male dons and students while, at the same time, female intellectuals strove to learn and teach Greek in the turbulent 1890s, marked by so much political unrest and contestation. This anxiety is very visible in the new version of *A Problem in Greek Ethics* for *Sexual Inversion*, which included a new section about sex between women and was very condemnatory about the very possibility of ancient Greek female pederasty. In contrast to male *paiderastia*, 'feminine homosexual passions were never worked into the social system, never became educational and military agents'. Although 'Greek logic', as exemplified by Aristophanes' myth of the *Symposium*, 'admitted the homosexual female to equal rights with the homosexual male', Symonds can find 'no recorded example [. . .] of noble friendship between women'. 'Even Aeolian women', such as Sappho, 'did not found a glorious tradition corresponding to that of the Dorian men. If homosexual love between females assumed the form of an institution at one moment in Aeolia, this failed to strike roots deep into the subsoil of the nation'. Even if ancient Greek literature might have hinted at the possibility of 'equal rights' for the 'homosexual female', Symonds was not interested in the rights of such women in the nineteenth century: in terms of British law, they were invisible, there being no mention of gross indecency between women. Symonds' disapproval of lesbianism could not be clearer when he writes: 'while the Greeks utilised and ennobled boy-love, they left Lesbian love to follow the same course of degeneracy as it pursues in modern times'. The only explicit discussion of phallic sexuality in *A Problem in Greek Ethics* comes in this section, when he alludes to the strap-on dildos in Pseudo-Lucian's *Erotes* and Herodas' sixth mimiamb, in which two women search for a dildo. Ancient and modern female homosexuals are presented as a sterile, degenerate lot, incapable of reproducing themselves in a 'glorious tradition', as Dorian men had done – indeed they merely mimic the fecundity of the phallus with their 'monstrous instruments of lust'.[20]

It was not by accident that Symonds should have alluded to the *Mimiambs* of Herodas, a poet writing in Alexandria during the third century BCE. They had only very recently been discovered in Egypt, and their emergence produced a small stir in the British press.[21] It happened at a time when several interesting Greek texts, such as the Aristotelian *Constitution of Athens* and poetry by Bacchylides, emerged in dubious circumstances out of the British occupation of Egypt (the British had had an extensive military presence in the country since 1882).[22] When some in England were beginning to call for the abolition of compulsory Greek at Oxford and Cambridge, the arrival of the new papyri signalled a breath of fresh air in classical studies. Herodas was, however, not as warmly received as those other texts. In the *editio princeps*, Frederic Kenyon hoped that Herodas might portend the discovery of more poems by Sappho.[23] That something seemingly rather unusual might be readable about *women* in Herodas was also hinted at in a report of Herodas' discovery in *The Times* in 1891:

> In the sixth [poem], two ladies discuss a subject dear to the female heart in every age, that of dress (with an excursus on the iniquities of servants), and go into raptures over some mysterious article of attire unknown to the lexicons, conjectures as to the nature of which had better be referred to Girton or Lady Margaret's, rather, than to Balliol or Trinity'.[24]

Was the journalist knowingly making a satirical link between the new women's colleges and female same-sex sexuality? The emergence of a poem starring *Metro* (like the word *matēr*, 'mother') and *Koritto* (like the word *korē*, 'daughter') was bound to be food for thought. *Mimiamb 6*, a ribald fantasy about female eroticism, is a dialogue between Koritto and Metro, in search of a dildo. We have already seen how Tullia and Octavia in Chorier's *Satyra Sotadica* discussed what it meant for a woman to know the classics. Along with Forberg's commentary and Rosenbaum's work, the *Satyra Sotadica* was also republished in the original Latin, along with French and English translations in the 1880s. With women's access to ancient Greek being such a hot topic, the discovery of Herodas could not help but contribute to the discussion.

Philologists in France, Germany and England swiftly set to work on producing a definitive edition of Herodas out of the tattered papyrus. In England, it was arranged for a highly ambitious young classicist of King's College, Cambridge, to have a go. Walter Headlam (1866–1908) was directly descended, on his mother's side, from the great classical scholar Richard Bentley. He had gained a first class in the classical tripos in 1887, along with a clutch of university prizes. In 1890, he was appointed to a fellowship and soon after assumed his teaching duties. He was an eccentric character, but formidably erudite. He read and wrote ancient Greek with great fluency. He devoted much of his energy to the textual criticism of Aeschylus. Indeed, such was his drive for scholarly recognition that, in 1891, he acerbically attacked the recently published Aeschylus commentaries of his Trinity colleague, A. W. Verrall, a respected and senior classicist. The 162-page review by Headlam was vitriolic and extreme. Headlam was determined to get to the top (indeed later in his career, he was considered for the Regius Professorship of Greek, though did not get it). In such an intellectual environment, then, it was only natural that Headlam would set to work on writing a commentary on Herodas, a brand new ancient author, whose manuscript lay in enticing ruins. It was a task that would occupy much of his time until his death in 1908.[25]

Mimiamb 6 presents us with Koritto offering Metro a seat in her home, whereupon the latter delicately asks the former from where she had purchased that 'red baubōn', Herodas' word for dildo (more commonly *olisbos* in Greek, 6.18–19). Rather than answer her question, Koritto asks Metro where she saw her dildo. Metro replies that Nossis, Erinna's daughter had it. Koritto had, it appears, lent out her sexual aid, and now it seems lost. But Metro's interest does not abate: who made it, she asks. The answer is Kerdon but, tantalisingly, the search is not over yet: Metro knows two Kerdons – which one is it? Koritto replies, neither, but a third, a short bald-headed man. However, the quest is still not complete, as Koritto reports that her Kerdon was making two dildos when she saw him, and that the one she really wanted he was selling to someone else, whose name he wouldn't reveal. Now at the end of the poem, Metro asks for directions, which Koritto promptly gives, closing off with an order to her slave to check on the hens: she doesn't want one to fly out of her lap, presumably like her dildo did.

Despite the explicit-sounding subject of the poem, Herodas' language is subtle, suggestive and far from crudely obvious. He writes in double entendres: just as Metro looks for a dildo that recedes ever further out of her grasp, so the reader is encouraged to uncover the jokes hidden in the poem. But just as the dildo evades Metro's search, so Herodas presents female same-sex sexuality as endlessly tantalising and wanting in satisfaction. This is reflected in the repeated gag on rubbing in the poem, which exhibits the women's annoyance at their counterparts who keep on passing round this dildo without returning it to its owner. As early as line 12, before we know the reason for Metro's visit, we see Koritto barking at her slave. Metro replies: 'dear Koritto, you are rubbing the same yoke as I'. Within a few lines it becomes clear that Koritto's fidgetiness comes from the loss of her *baubōn*. The 'yoke' and the verb for 'rubbing' evoke a witty, but insistent phallic symbolism. Later, at line 27, when Koritto hears that her dildo is being passed round various women, she exclaims, 'women, this woman will be the end of me'. The verb used here, *ektribō*, shows just how badly Koritto is being rubbed up the wrong way.[26] Close readers of the poem will also see that Kerdon himself looks suspicious: he is described as bald-headed' and 'small', in Greek *phalakros* and *mikkos* (6.59). The *phal-* in *phalakros* reminds the reader of the word 'phallos' and the jocular emphasis on his size suggest the manufacturer himself resembles a dildo. Indeed the comparison of the man to a fig gently underlines the joke (6.60–1).[27] This poem, then, is a scene of sexual desire under erasure, in denial, composed of mutters, moans and frustration. Koritto says to her friend that her 'eyes bulged out' (*exekumēna*, 6.68) when she saw Kerdon's dildos. Although this dramatic dialogue entices the reader/viewer with the possibility that female bodily desire can be seen and visualised in the shape of a dildo, the moment when Koritto sees the signifier of her sexual desire, it is her eyes that swell. The only parts of this woman's body that bulges with pleasure are her eyes. The naked desire that the reader/viewer sees in this poem is precisely the seeing of desire.

Indeed, the whole point of a double entendre is that it playfully asks the reader whether the language in question has one single meaning or a dirty additional second. And the relationship between the one and the two is a leitmotif in Herodas' poem. We will remember that there were two dildos that Koritto saw, but she could only get her hands on one. The second was ultimately out of her grasp. Metro also knows two Kerdons and wants to know which *one* the dildo-maker was. The very title of the poem plays with this leitmotif: *Philiazousai e idiazousai*, literally 'Women who love or women who are alone'. Is this poem about two women who like to be together or a single woman who enjoys solitary self-pleasure? What is actually happening in this poem? Just as Lucian was to tantalise his reader a few centuries later, so the unsuccessful hunt for a dildo, veiled in double entendre, was also designed to tease and frustrate Herodas' reader, as female same-sex sexuality is presented as a continuous deferral of satisfaction.

Headlam's commentary on the word βαυβών ('baubon'), the word used by Herodas for 'dildo', positions Metro and Koritto within contemporary debates about women's study of the classics and female tribadism.[28] He opens by observing, 'Weil and Dr Jackson have discerned what needed only to be pointed out that βαυβών = ὄλισβος' ('olisbos' is the more common word for dildo in Greek and appears, for example, in Aristophanes' *Lysistrata* (109)). While the = suggests that nothing could be clearer – a straightforward synonym – Headlam's notes nevertheless go on to characterise Metro and Koritto in more detail. Headlam continues by citing, but not translating, from the *Suda* (the tenth-century Byzantine encyclopaedia) explaining what the *baubōn* actually was:

> leather genitals, the tip made of red hide, having the shape of male genitalia. Bacchants attach them to themselves strapping them round the neck and between the thighs, as they dance in honour of Dionysus.

Even though there is no mention of Dionysus in the poem itself, Headlam subtly alludes to contemporary turn-of-the-century debates about women inside and beyond classical scholarship. The lack of any translation of the quote from the *Suda* ensured that Headlam's text would be available only to educated readers. And it would have been Headlam's *female* colleagues who would have been very interested in what he had to say. Indeed, late-Victorian and Edwardian classical scholarship experienced a profound interest in the apparently violent, sexual rites of Dionysus. Headlam's colleague at Newnham, the eminent classicist Jane Harrison, was very interested in the figure of the maenad, a female follower of Dionysus. From 1894 into the early years of the 1900s she published on the topic, and in her teaching at Newnham she seemed, Yopie Prins has suggested, to

> self-consciously play the role of the inspired maenad. [. . .] In her teaching as in her scholarship, Harrison replayed the rituals of Dionysiac worship in order to initiate others into the expression of a highly aestheticized and eroticized enthusiasm.[29]

If Headlam had already openly lambasted Verrall, a senior colleague at Trinity, his commentary on Herodas also reveals his irreverent attitude to the classicists teaching and studying at the women's college not far from King's.

After listing several instances where dildos appear in Greek and Latin literature, Headlam's interest in the significance of ancient Greece for modern sexual politics reappears a few lines down, when he refers his reader to Richard Burton's infamous 1885 'Terminal Essay'. This 14,000-word essay appeared in Volume 10 of his translation of *The Book of a Thousand Nights and a Night* (more commonly known as the *Arabian Nights*), in which Burton argued that 'Sotadic Love', named after the pederastic Hellenistic poet Sotades, was prevalent in much of the Mediterranean, Asia, Africa and the native populations of North America.[30] Headlam directs his reader to 'see further [. . .] Burton *1001 Nights* and the *Terminal Essay* x (ed. Macm.), pp.208, 9', thereby pointing us to a particularly explicit moment in Burton's work where Burton had written:

> within the Sotadic zone there is a blending of the masculine and feminine temperaments, a crasis which elsewhere occurs only sporadically. Hence the male *féminisme* whereby the man becomes patiens as well as agens, and the woman a tribade, a votary of mascula Sappho, Queen of Frictrices or Rubbers.

In a footnote, Burton then refers to the verb *tribesthai*, defining it as 'the friction of the labia and insertion of the clitoris when unusually developed; or artificial by means of the fascinum, the artificial penis'.[31] Even though the word 'tribas' did not appear until the second century CE, way after Herodas was writing in the third century BCE, Headlam reads the tribad into the Greek text. Headlam does not say it, but it seems that he was connecting the innuendo in the verb 'tribo' with the tribad. Burton's understanding of sex in terms of active or passive, 'agens' and 'patiens', as he puts it, clearly emerges from the Roman conceptualisation of sexual experience. And so Martial's Latin, which had provided nineteenth-century doctors a term for a woman who has sex with another woman, also provided Headlam with a frame of reference.

That Headlam is thinking of the tribad emerges further on in his note on 'baubōn', when he comments that the word's 'accent is difficult'. Behind this seemingly dry and learned observation lies another of Headlam's own witticisms at the expense of the tribad. He continues: 'Leutz gives τρίβων. etc. For dissyllabic nouns ending in –βων except parts of the body such as βουβών'. Although it denotes 'rag', the word τρίβων roguishly refers back to Burton's text as well as the puns on the verb *tribo* in Herodas' own poem. Indeed, the word also means a 'rogue', a word with which we might characterise Headlam himself here, as he notes that the accent on *baubōn* is like those used for words describing parts of the body such as βουβών, meaning 'groin'. Headlam, the caustic classicist, seems to be enjoying himself in the manner of a Latin epigrammatist like Martial, as he suggests that *baubōn* be also considered as a part of the body. Just as texts produced under imperial Rome had conditioned a long history of male-authored observations on sex between women that stretched into the late nineteenth century, so this reception history in turn conditioned how a classical commentator around the year 1900 viewed female same-sex sexuality in ancient Greek culture.

So many Sapphos

Even if Herodas was an ancient Greek poet, he was also seen as a writer who spoke very candidly about the sexual politics of the 1890s for highly educated readers capable of enjoying his Greek. At a time when women who read Greek at university seemed to be a symptom of a wider problem with women attempting to usurp traditional masculine spaces and roles, Herodas' Greek offered male readers like Symonds and Headlam an opportunity to look down on educated women in a long tradition that goes back to Chorier and Beccadelli. It was against the image of the tribad that a chaste and unsexual Sappho was constructed in the nineteenth century. As Burton himself noted in his note on the tribad, a number of classicists 'have made Sappho a model of purity'.[32] Burton was referring to the German scholars, Karl Otfried Müller (1797–1840) and Friedrich Gottlieb Welcker (1784–1868), who cast Sappho 'as a friendly spinster teacher at a boarding school' which reflected 'an attempt to justify the role of and allay anxieties about the current regime of single-sex schools'.[33]

The wholesome image of Sappho was most widely propagated in late-Victorian British culture by, of all people, John Addington Symonds who, in private, was scathing about sex between women. In 1873, Symonds published *Studies of the Greek Poets*, which emerged from the lectures he had given at Clifton College, where he had met his young lover Norman Moor. In his book, which reached a broad readership beyond scholarly circles, he depicted Sappho as a member of an 'aesthetic club' comprised of ladies who 'were highly educated, and accustomed to express their sentiments to an extent unknown elsewhere in history – until, indeed, the present time'. Whereas Symonds some 20 years later would deny female pederasty an educational ethos, the Symonds of 1873 pictured 'the Lesbian ladies', that is the ladies who lived, like Sappho, on the island of Lesbos, as 'appl[ying] themselves successfully to literature', as 'they formed clubs for the cultivation of poetry and music' and 'they studied the art of beauty'.[34]

Symonds' depiction was used by the medical doctor and amateur classicist Dr Henry Wharton who, in 1885, published *Sappho: Memoir, Text, Selected Renderings, and a Literal Translation*. Wharton's book proved to be very popular, and was in its fifth edition by 1907, and so Symonds' image found a large audience. Utilising the latest German scholarship, Wharton sought to publish all the extant fragments along with a selection of poetic versions as well as a literal translation, as his title suggests. But, even if his book opened with a 'memoir' of Sappho's life, the fragmentary nature of her poetry saw to it that knowing who Sappho actually had been was no straightforward matter. Wharton poured cold water on the ancient reports that Sappho, propelled by maddening desire for a beautiful young man called Phaon, had thrown herself off the Leucadian cliff to plunge to her death. The story, Wharton argued, does 'not seem to rest on any firm historical basis', which gave him the opportunity to advocate for a chaste Sappho who enjoyed 'the purity of her love for her girl-friends'.[35] Wharton cites Strabo the ancient geographer's description of Sappho as 'a wonderful thing' which, as Prins puts it, made Sappho 'less a female person than an idealized feminine persona'.[36] Wharton's 'memoir' of Sappho, which introduces his edition, admitted to the lack of real and knowable facts that could be attached to Sappho's biography, and so turned her into an exemplary, disembodied poetic voice of lyrical passion.[37] It was in this way, then, that Sappho proved to be the inspiration for numerous imitators and adaptors since antiquity, which Wharton's edition sought to show, in that it was an anthology of various modern versions of Sappho's poems. Interestingly, Wharton's edition provided several male writers with the opportunity to express their own passions and desires.

'The purity of her love for her girl-friends' was reflected, according to Wharton, in Fragment 31, one of Sappho's best known poems. Among the versions he included in his edition, Wharton published one by Symonds, who had provided a number of renderings for the edition and 'much valuable criticism' as Wharton was careful to acknowledge in his preface.[38] It seems that it was the purity of Sappho's intentions that permitted many modern male imitators to appropriate her voice, in order to express their passions for a beloved woman. Here is Symonds' translation of Fragment 31:

> Peer of gods he seemeth to me, he blissful
> Man who sits and gazes at thee before him
> Close beside thee sits, and in silence hears thee
>   Silverly speaking
>
> Laughing Love's low laughter. Oh this, this only
> Stirs the troubled heart in my breast to tremble.
> For should I but see thee a little moment,
> Straight is my voice hushed;
>
> Yea, my tongue is broken, and through and through me
> 'Neath the flesh, impalpable fire runs tingling;

Nothing see mine eyes, a noise of roaring
Waves in my ear sounds;

Sweat runs down in rivers, a tremor seizes
All my limbs and paler than grass in autumn
Caught by pains of menacing death I falter
Lost in the love trance.

This poem had been a source of inspiration for male poets since classical antiquity. Catullus had provided his own Latin version:

Ille mi par esse deo videtur
ille, si fas est, superare divos . . .

That man seems to me to be equal to a god,
that man, if it is right, to outstrip the gods . . .
(51.1–2)

While Symonds was to denigrate the idea that love between women could live up to the ideals of Greek pederasty between an older man and a male youth, in public he was able to publish poetry to be widely read by a Victorian audience, in which he imitated a female poet and re-directed her expression of desire for a woman into a heteroerotic passion of a man for a woman. Sappho, it seemed, provided a very useful voice for men to verbalise their own desires for women in late-Victorian Britain.

Symonds wrote his Sapphic poem in 1883. In 1889, however, he wrote out the first two lines and a word of this poem in Greek in his memoirs, to record how he felt for the Venetian gondolier, Angelo Fusato:

φαίνεταί μοι κῆνος ἴσος θέοισιν
ἔμμεν' ὤνηρ ὄττις ἐνάντιός τοι
ἰσδάνει

He seems to me equal to gods that man
whoever he is who opposite you
sits . . .[39]

Wharton had attempted to put Sappho's fragments together in order to write her memoir. In Symonds' memoir, however, he re-fragments her poetry to turn it into a male homoerotic fragment, in which Symonds identifies with the woman and desires the man, in contrast to his public performance in Wharton's edition in which he identifies with a man in desire for a woman. Symonds admits just before this point in his memoirs that much of his publicly published poetry was actually written with Angelo Fusato in mind, whom he had first met in 1881, and this writing 'will be understood by anyone who reads the sonnets written about him in my published volumes'.[40] In 1889, Symonds could cite from Sappho Fragment 31 to express his jealousy for a woman sitting next to Angelo Fusato, not long before he will deny any significance to female sexual expression in *A Problem in Modern Ethics* in 1891. Did Symonds have Angelo in his thoughts when he translated Fragment 31 for Henry Wharton? While the opening word of his poem – 'peer' – suggests that Symonds is identifying with the man in his enjoyment of another woman, the word 'peer' also encourages us to take a closer look at Symonds' language. Indeed, the notion of sight persists through every verse of Symonds' poem ('gazes', 'see', 'Nothing see mine eyes', 'Lost in the love trance'). At whom is Symonds actually staring in this poem? The 'thee' in line 7 could refer to the woman who is the 'thee' in the first stanza, but could it also equally refer to the man?

The fragmentary nature of Sappho's poetic corpus meant that modern authors were free to develop and enlarge upon the tattered remains in whichever direction they wished.[41] Symonds' re-fragmentation is simply an inversion of this modern, inventive response to Sappho's words. Wharton's edition relied upon the authority of the text of Sappho, originally published in 1843 by the German classicist Theodor Bergk, which retained the female pronouns in Sappho's Greek, thereby showing Sappho as addressing herself to women as well as men in her poems.[42] Sappho presented her own passions as numerous and differing. The multiple Sapphos that emerge from the fragments, as well as her plentiful imitators collated in Wharton's book, encouraged two women to write a book of poetry that reflected on the contested and crowded reception of the ancient Greek poetess. It is with a female-authored Sappho, written in response to the male Sapphos of the nineteenth century, with which this chapter concludes.

Katherine Bradley (1846–1914) and Edith Cooper (1862–1913), aunt and niece, who lived as a couple, published, under the pseudonym 'Michael Field', a volume of Sapphic lyrics in 1889 entitled *Long Ago*. Bradley was born into a comfortable middle-class mercantile family in Birmingham. She had one sister, Emma, 11 years her elder, who married and went to live with her husband in Kenilworth, Warwickshire. Katherine joined her sister and brother-in-law around the time of Edith's birth, their first daughter, in 1862. Katherine was to play an important role in family life: after the birth of her second daughter, Emma became permanently invalided and Katherine, at 18, became the guardian of her niece Edith. They were to become more than aunt and niece: sisters, friends and, eventually, lovers. They were wealthy enough not to work (nor to seek husbands) and they were well educated: Bradley attended a summer course at Newnham College, Cambridge, and attended lectures at the Collège de France in 1868. In 1878, both women studied classics and philosophy at University College in Bristol. In 1875, Bradley had already published her first book of poetry and, in 1884, the pair published the verse-drama *Callirrhoë* under the pseudonym 'Michael Field', for the first time.

The identity of the new, exciting writer, discussed in literary circles, did not remain a secret for long. Nevertheless, Bradley and Cooper continued to publish as 'Michael Field', their first book of poetry under this name being the 1889 volume *Long Ago*. While there is continued discussion about the actual significance of this name, it seems that Bradley and Cooper did not adopt it because they identified as manly.[43] 'Nothing ever reported of Bradley and Cooper suggests this type' of the mannish female invert, as Marion Thain notes.[44] In their diaries, for example, they were repelled by the writer Vernon Lee's masculinity, and Bradley seems to have been attracted to the androgynous boyishness of Cooper rather than any pronounced virile masculinity. Furthermore, both women were also clearly enticed by and enjoyed flirting with men.[45] Marion Thain suggests that 'Bradley and Cooper created a deliberately amorphous sexual identity which avoided commitment to any one position'. As 'Michael Field' they attempted to 'inhabit an area between categories', 'outside of the realm of sexological categories'.[46]

The title of their poetry book, *Long Ago*, signals their sense of the past as a time before sexological categorisation, in contrast to Symonds who had turned back to the ancient Greeks in order to make a positive contribution to nineteenth-century sexual medicine. So, while *Long Ago* is structured around Sappho's painful and unrequited love for Phaon, it also includes poetry of passion for numerous other figures: Erinna, Aphrodite, the Graces, Adonis, Mnasidica, Alcaeus, Gorgo, Anactoria, Leto and Niobe, Selene, Anacreon. As Thain puts it, 'Sappho represented a sexual ambivalence: still the lover of Phaon, but now also clearly linked with a female homoerotic community'.[47] Bradley and Cooper's point of departure was Wharton's edition, which showcased a range of different Sapphos from a number of authors, so that *Long Ago* projected the reception history of Sappho back onto Sappho herself, as she is depicted as a woman of multifarious passions and diverse affective attachments. And, in contrast to the discourses of sexual medicine and classical scholarship, which saw the tribad as an imitation of real male phallic sexuality, for 'Michael Field', Sappho offered a more nuanced opportunity to think about the relationship between heterosexual love and female same-sex sexuality. In Poem XXXIII in *Long Ago*, the Sapphic authorial voice compares the love of men with the love of women:

ταὶς κάλαισ' ὔμμιν [τὸ] νόημμα τῶμον
οὐ διάμειπτον

Maids, not to you my mind doth change;
Men I defy, allure, estrange,
Prostrate, make bond or free:

Soft as the stream beneath the plane
To you I sing my love's refrain;
Between us is no thought of pain,
    Peril, satiety.

Soon doth a lover's patience tire,
But ye to manifold desire
Can yield response, ye know.
When for long, museful days I pine,
The presage at my heart divine;
To you I never breathe a sign
Of inward want or woe.

When injuries my spirit bruise,
Allaying virtue ye infuse
With unobstrusive skill:
And if care frets ye come to me
As fresh as nymph from stream or tree,
And with your soft vitality
    My weary bosom fill.

Each poem in the book opens with a fragment of Sappho taken from the Wharton edition, as does this one (here fragment 41). In the first line, 'Michael Field' begins with their rendering of Sappho's Greek, in which she addresses other 'maids' (literally, 'beautiful women', κάλαισ'). Michael Field's use of the fragment was highly self-conscious: Sappho says her mind does not change in a poem which has translated her Greek into English, changing its intent and meaning. Indeed the theme of change continues through the poem, as Sappho contrasts her love of men which is constantly altering, with the love she gives to women which is constant and never 'breathe[s] a sign / of inward want or woe'. With men, on the other hand, Sappho 'def[ies], allure[s], estrange[s], / Prostrate[s], make[s] bond or free'. But which is the preferable, Sappho never says: does Sappho like the pain and peril of men? This is a poem about 'manifold desire': a textual Sappho – whose love for 'maids' does not change, its constancy survives in Greek – and a bodily Sappho of changing passions, who 'pine[s]' and 'bruise[s]'. 'Michael Field', writing after Wharton's collation of Sappho's fragments and imitators, depicts a Sappho who remains the same *and* changes over time.

The figure of the tribad was used by male doctors and classicists in order to understand the relationship between male sexuality and female same-sex sexuality. Sappho's impassioned poetry addressed to women, on the other hand, offered male poets from Catullus onwards a vocabulary for their own desires. Bradley and Cooper, who were two woman writing as a man imitating the female poet, were clearly interested in the relationship between men's and women's experiences of desire and sex. This is reflected in Poem LII, where 'Michael Field' describes the story of Tiresias, who changed into a woman after having seen and struck with his staff two snakes having sex, while on a walk in the woods. Seven years later, when she sees the snakes again, she strikes them once more, and turns back into a man. Zeus and Hera are having an argument at this time about who felt more pleasure in sex: according to Zeus, women obtained nine of the ten parts of pleasure from sex, whereas Hera thought that men got most of the pleasure. And so the goddess asks Tiresias, 'In marriage who hath more delight' (52.33)? Tiresias sides with Zeus and says it is women, thereby incurring the wrath of Hera who then blinds Tiresias. In the traditional story, Zeus compensates Tiresias with the power of prophecy. In the poem by 'Michael Field', however, Tiresias received his powers of insight from his life as a woman: 'Thou hast been woman, and can'st see / therefore into futurity' (52.73–4).

The alteration to the story is significant. As a woman, Tiresias felt a 'finer sense for bliss and dole', a 'receptivity of soul' (52.15–16). As a woman, Tiresias can feel more and has more knowledge. Whereas 'man's strong nature' seems in control of the order of things, women's knowledge is of a different kind: 'Medea's penetrative charm', the ability of 'blossoming Daphne' to attract Apollo, and the 'child / Gathering a bunch of tulips wild / To feel the flowery hill-side rent / Convulsive for thy ravishment' (52.41, 53, 58–62). 'Michael Field' describes the disturbing and threatening power of Medea, Daphne's abilities to attract a god, and an innocent child's experience of rape. 'Michael Field' suggests that women's experience of 'bliss and dole', that is their joy and their fate, is beyond men's reductive comprehension, as it involves Medea's and Daphne's powers to charm heroes and gods as well as a girl's painful experience of sexual assault, an episode central to many classical myths. The voice of 'Michael Field' presented itself in stark contrast to contemporary sexual medicine and classical scholarship, which had professed to know about female same-sex sexuality by describing it as a poor imitation of male phallic pleasure, and in contrast to male authors who had appropriated Sappho's same-sex passions to verbalise their own hetero- and homoerotic desires, precisely at a time when many were concerned about and interested in women usurping the privileges and positions of the male gender. Tiresias made a fitting image for Bradley and Cooper, writing as a man 'Michael Field', who was imitating Sappho. As Tiresias, thinking as both a man and a woman, they suggested how different men's and women's experiences of sex were at the end of the nineteenth century; how little men understood women despite the claims of medical doctors and classical scholars; and how knowledge of female sexuality might be better understood by those inhabiting female bodies.[48]

The poetry of 'Michael Field' is an appropriate place to close this chapter. Bradley and Cooper proffered an alternative epistemology to the medical discourses which sought to define and categorise female same-sex sexuality at the end of the nineteenth century. Krafft-Ebing's *Psychopathia Sexualis* was inciting much contemporary debate about sexual relations between members of the same sex. Indeed, the subtitle of the 1892 American-English translation was *With Especial Reference to Contrary Sexual Instinct: A Medico-legal Study*, in reference to the centrality of the subject in the book. In Chapter IV, John Addington Symonds emerged as one of Krafft-Ebing's most careful readers and respondents, as he attempted to accommodate ancient Greek love to modern sex research. The ancient figure of the tribad, on the other hand, shaped medical descriptions of sex between women: Symonds denied the possibility of a female pederastic relationship which could match the ennobling and educational ethos of the love of an older man for a boy, while the discovery of Herodas provided further confirmation of the lusty and debauched nature of the tribad. In contrast to this image of the phallic woman, Symonds was at the same time influential among English readers in containing and neutralising Sappho's same-sex desires. Despite the late-Victorian concerns about women becoming like men, male authors enjoyed the privilege of using Sappho's voice to express in print their own desires for the female sex. Bradley and Cooper, as 'Michael Field', questioned this male appropriation of the female voice as they suggested that women's experiences of sex were much more varied – both more pleasurable and more painful – than men could appreciate. Even if some were concerned or excited about the prospect of the blurring of the differences between the sexes at the *fin de siècle*, the figure of Tiresias in the poem of 'Michael Field' underlined the dissimilarites between men and women. It was by living as a woman that Tiresias could comprehend the pleasure as well as the violence experienced by women. Women possessed a 'receptivity of soul' that was not recorded in the pages of medical classifications of sexuality authored by male doctors. Instead of trying to contribute to the male-dominated world of sexual pathology and classical scholarship at the end of the nineteenth century, Bradley and Cooper offered a poetic mode of knowing.[49]

To be highlighted, then, is the continual tension between scientific and literary discourses in the history of the development of sexual pathology and the responses which it provoked. The voice of 'Michael Field', inspired by Sappho, turned to lyric poetry which, as Thain puts it, 'is *not* intrinsically historical'.[50] In their turn away from a discourse steeped in historical facts and figures, Bradley and Cooper very consciously invented an alternative ancient past out of Sappho's fragments. Their poetry evidences the importance of the space of fantasy for sexual desire just as Symonds also imaginatively used Greek literature to describe his sex scene with Norman. The notion of fantasy leads to the next and final chapter, that is, to Sigmund Freud, for whom ancient Greece was less a historical place than a mythical fantasyland in the psyche.

CHAPTER VI

FREUD'S CLASSICAL MYTHOLOGY

This final chapter draws together three central themes that have informed this book. Firstly, this chapter examines how Freud's psychoanalysis questioned what sort of discourse should structure an authoritative understanding of sexuality. Whereas Krafft-Ebing and his readers were interested in how the history of the ancient world might inform modern sexual practices and behaviours, Sigmund Freud (1856–1939), on the other hand, was concerned to understand how ancient myth, especially that about the characters Oedipus and Narcissus, provided the key to sexual desire. With his fascination with classical mythology, Freud was unsure whether historical discourse offered the best way for comprehending sexuality. While Krafft-Ebing's *Psychopathia Sexualis* had encouraged readers to write down their autobiographies, Freud cared more about what we did *not* know about our pasts – that is, what we repressed. In particular, it was the repressed desire for the phallic mother that was to figure repeatedly in Freud's writing, which brings us to our second theme: the collecting and anthologising of sexual pleasures.

The Freudian phallic mother was a figure who satisfied all the desires of the child: the mother's breast fulfilled the child's wants at a time when the child had no inkling about sexual difference. Freud theorised that the infant imagined a figure which lacked nothing: the mother with a penis was the young boy's sole object of desire before he discovered that some beings have no penis. This discovery triggers in the boy's mind a fear that he might also lose his penis as he hypothesises the reason why some people – girls and women like his own mother – have no penis. The boy imagines that castration might come from the hands of his father, jealous of the boy's relationship with the mother. Freud's fearful young boy, then, has to turn away from and repress his desires for his mother and look for another woman. All the adult man ever desires when he desires a woman, or indeed another man, Freud was to argue, is ultimately the satisfaction he imagined he once had with his phallic maternal parent. When a little girl makes the discovery of sexual difference, she, however, is thrust into the path of penis envy, which is only satisfied when she gives birth to a child, a symbol of the penis she never bore.

This chapter traces out how the eighteenth-century interest in phallic worship provided some of the key contours for Freud's bizarre, remarkable and yet highly influential theorisation of the phallic mother. Chapter III examined the culture of collecting phallic artefacts, which was accompanied by the anthologising of ancient and modern Latin priapic poetry. This provided a context for Forberg's edition, which itself collated Beccadelli's poems and excerpts from Chorier, thereby providing an important resource for the medical taxonomies of Rosenbaum and Krafft-Ebing. In this chapter, however, we see Freud's own rather different reception of Richard Payne Knight's *Discourse on Priapus*. Payne Knight had argued that the ancients originally worshipped a deity of active and passive, and of male and female attributes. The phallic artefacts from classical antiquity were, according to Payne Knight, later corruptions of this original worship of a deity which embodied Nature's powers of generativity and reproduction. Just as ancient civilisations worshipped a deity of indeterminate sex, so Freud contended that the young child fantasises about a figure which lacked for nothing and could satisfy all his wants and desires. We have read about the history of collecting together sex positions, from ancient sex manuals to Beccadelli's *Hermaphrodite* – which was designed as a book for all tastes, for 'cock and cunt' – and Chorier's *Satyra Sotadica*, which brought together all possible sexual pleasures into one book, and on to the eighteenth-century collections of phallic objects and priapic epigrams, and nineteenth-century anthologies of sexual identities. Freud's phallic mother, emerging from this long history, was the figure who was supposed to be capable of gratifying all the desires of the child.

Even if Freud might have been pleased with uncovering the desires of the unconscious, he was also troubled by the phallic mother – a consternation which brings us to our third theme, that of the contest between male and female authority over sex and desire. From ancient stories about female-authored sex manuals to Beccadelli's Catullus-reading 'domina' to Chorier's satire on Tullia d'Aragona to the nineteenth-century reception of the tribad and Sappho, the issue of women's knowledge about sexual pleasure had repeatedly troubled male writers and scientists. Freud, too, continued to be concerned about the persistence of the phallic mother in our adult psyches. Near the end of his career, he wondered whether there was anything more to us than the fear of castration or penis envy. Whereas the Freud of the beginning of the twentieth century utilised classical mythology for the services of modern science, the Freud of the 1930s wondered whether there was any escaping the authority and influence of those ancient myths despite the efforts of the science of psychoanalysis. So how did the figure of the ancient phallic mother become so deeply buried in the Freudian psyche that 'she' was to underpin our identities into our adult lives? In order to answer this question, it is necessary to turn back to the beginning of Freud's career in psychoanalysis.

History and myth

The autobiographical plot was crucial for Krafft-Ebing's study in sexual pathology. His work was to influence a generation of sex research including Havelock Ellis. Looking back into the past became the principal way in which one could understand one's sexuality, the truth of one's self. Sex became understood within a firmly historical framework. When Sigmund Freud began analysing his patients for hysteria, he too became interested in his patients' pasts. But the idea that an autobiographical narrative could provide the explanation for his patients' symptoms seemed unhelpful to

Freud. In a footnote in his *Three Essays on Sexuality* (which was first published in 1905), he wrote:

> Havelock Ellis has published a number of autobiographical narratives. [. . .] These reports naturally suffer from the fact that they omit the prehistoric period of the writers' sexual lives, which is veiled by infantile amnesia and which can only be filled in by psychoanalysis in the case of an individual who has developed a neurosis.[1]

Chapter IV examined how understanding male sexuality became caught up in questions about the nature of history. Symonds' understanding of his sexuality emerged out of a historical investigation of ancient Greece – out of the belief that such an investigation could explain his sexuality to him. While Ellis was less keen to rely on the ancient Greeks in order to theorise sexual inversion, he too was invested in the autobiographical narrative: one's historical past provided the key to one's sexuality. Sex research applied the history of civilisation to the sexual history of the individual, just as that individualised sexual history then offered a model for thinking about the history of the West. Freud, on the other hand, was interested in the 'prehistoric period' which had been 'veiled by infantile amnesia'. Freud was thus responding to nineteenth-century debates about historicism in order to argue for the limits of the use of history for understanding one's sexual desires. Whereas Symonds had relied on respectable German historical scholarship, Freud turned from the world of Greek history to the stories of Greek myth.[2]

Barthold Georg Niebuhr, the authoritative ancient historian and author of *Römische Geschichte* (published 1811–32), had already argued that historical narratives of early Rome by Roman writers served psychological needs of the present rather than attempting to provide an accurate description of the past. This theory interested Freud, concerned as he was in how we wrote (about) our pasts, especially those very early ones.[3] And developing Niebuhr's argument, when people look back to those very early times, they generally told lies to understand their present. Our earliest memories were nothing but stories we have made up. When Freud's patients lay on his couch and he asked them to tell him about themselves, about their pasts, so that he could understand the cause of their psychological problems, he did not think their stories were entirely true. In fact, these stories covered up, re-ordered and re-arranged the actual, historical truth, in order to make sense to the patient in the present. Freud applied nineteenth-century historicist distrust to the autobiographical narratives of his patients. Just as ancient historiography seemed full of untruths (in contrast to the scientific historicism of the nineteenth century), so the early lives of Freud's patients were really nothing but myths (in contrast to the historically truthful account that the psychoanalyst was to reconstruct for the patient).

Freud was writing at a time when classical archaeology was becoming institutionalised as a university discipline. Since the rediscoveries of Pompeii and Herculaneum, the scientific status of archaeology had been bolstered through the nineteenth century as methods in excavation, recording, and cataloguing improved. Heinrich Schliemann's sensational 'discoveries' at Troy and Mycenae captivated the imaginations of the general public as well as specialised archaeologists.[4] Freud himself viewed his old friend Emmanuel Löwy, by the late 1890s an eminent professor of archaeology in Rome, 'as an *alternative ego*, a kind of fantasy-figure for an alternative life Freud could vicariously experience', as Richard Armstrong discusses.[5] By the end of the nineteenth century, one of the ways, if not the way, to imagine and conceptualise any sort of relationship between the ancient and the modern was through obviously archaeological metaphors of 'excavation', 'disinterment', and 'unearthing'. So much of archaeology was involved with the uncovering of burial sites that it seemed that the past could in some way be resurrected and brought back to life. Therefore, it is hardly surprising that Freud the psychoanalyst should have depicted himself as an archaeologist. The first time Freud described himself in these terms was when he was writing about hysteria in 1896:

> Imagine that an explorer arrives in a little-known region where his interest is aroused by an expanse of ruins, with remains of walls,

> fragments of columns, and tablets with half-effaced and unreadable inscriptions. He may content himself with inspecting what lies exposed to view, with questioning the inhabitants – perhaps semi-barbaric people – who live in the vicinity, about what tradition tells them of the history and meaning of these archaeological remains, and noting down what they tell him – and he may then proceed on his journey. But he may act differently. He may have brought picks, shovels and spades with him, and he may set the inhabitants to work with these implements. Together with them he may start upon the ruins, clear away the rubbish, and, beginning from the visible remains, uncover what is buried. If his work is crowned with success, the discoveries are self-explanatory: the ruined walls are part of the ramparts of a palace or a treasure-house; the fragments of columns can be filled out into a temple; the numerous inscriptions, which, by good luck, may be bilingual, reveal an alphabet and a language, and, when they have been deciphered and translated, yield undreamed-of information about the events of the remote past, to commemorate which the monuments were built. *Saxa loquuntur!* (*SE* 3:192)

For Freud, this depiction was no empty metaphor. The portrait of the psychoanalyst as explorer appeared in an article called 'The Aetiology of Hysteria', in which Freud criticised current methodologies for finding the causes of women's hysterical symptoms. This short but significant article saw Freud depart from the emphasis on patients' autobiographies and theories of heredity – significant aspects of medical discourse in the nineteenth century. Instead of listening to patients as they searched back into their family history, Freud felt it to be more scientific to possess a method 'in which we should feel less dependent on the assertions of the patients themselves' (*SE* 3:191). The aim of the essay, then, was to show that there are *two* aetiologies to hysteria: one that the patient herself gives (a story about a shocking or horrible experience that brings on the symptoms); and then a chronologically earlier one that the psychoanalyst disinters after questioning the patient about her childhood past. The hysterical symptoms are brought on because the later experience that the patient knows about somehow unconsciously reminds her of the repressed first experience. Freud posited that 'whatever case and whatever symptom we take as our point of departure, *in the end we have come to the field of sexual experience*' (Freud's emphasis, *SE* 3:199). Perhaps, argues Freud, the patient witnessed his parents *in coitu*, or he was sexually abused by a parent or another adult, or he had sexual intercourse with an older sibling. The trauma of this earlier experience was driven into the unconscious and only resurfaced as a symptom as a result of a second, lesser trauma which somehow became psychically associated with the first. And so, the full significance of Freud's archaeological metaphor emerges: he imagines something – a multilingual object or document – that can be used to decipher a hitherto unknown script. The two layers of antiquity are like the double aetiology of female hysteria. We can also see what Freud means about the 'prehistoric period' of the patient's story about herself, a period which exists before the beginning of her own historical narrative of who she was.

Freud's positing of a sexual aetiology at the heart of hysteria shocked the medical community. However, the idea that young children had been originally traumatised through a sexual experience – what became known as the 'seduction theory' – didn't fully satisfy Freud for another reason. His hysteric female patients would complain (once the psychoanalyst had explained the 'truth' behind their [hi]stories), 'But I can't *remember* having thought it . . .' which led Freud to wonder: '[Are] we to suppose that we are really dealing with thoughts which never came about, which merely had a *possibility* of existing, so that the treatment would lie in the accomplishment of a psychical act which did not take place at the time?' (*SE* 2:300). In 1897 (a year after his hysteria paper), he came up with a very radical answer to this question: in a letter to his friend Wilhelm Fliess, an otolaryngologist in Berlin, Freud mentioned in writing, for the first time, his theory about Oedipus: 'I have found, in my own case too, [the phenomenon of] being in love with my mother and jealous of my father, and I now consider it a universal event in childhood'.[6] In *The Interpretation of Dreams* (first published just over two years later), Freud turned his personal discovery into a universal fate:

> The discovery is confirmed by a legend that has come down to us from classical antiquity: a legend whose profound and universal power to move can only be understood if the hypothesis I have put forward in regard to the psychology of children has an equally universal validity. What I have in mind is the legend of King Oedipus and Sophocles' drama which bears his name (*SE* 4:261).

Rather than finding a straightforwardly historical event at the origins of his patients' condition, Freud came to see that everyone 'relived' the myth of Oedipus. The recording of our earliest experiences were not simply fabrications (in order to make sense of our present), but these experiences were in an important sense themselves mythical – in that they were fantasies played out in our minds, but which would have huge consequences for the rest of our lives. Freud was indeed very interested in the 'prehistorical'.

Freud's analysis of hysteria saw the male psychoanalyst confront the female hysteric, the scientific male interpreting the female patients' stories of their pasts, of hysteric patients stuck in their pasts. Freud's turn to Oedipus, however, was to profoundly change the import of his work: from analyst to self-analyst, from a negotiation between male scientist and female storyteller to everyone, *men as well as women, both analyst and patient*, replaying the destiny of the mythical king Oedipus. To proclaim that 'we were all Oedipus' sounded idiosyncratic to many of Freud's readers, and yet the universalisation of the myth had already had a long history in German thought. Friedrich Schelling had seen Oedipus' fate as an investigation of the forces of freedom and necessity, and Georg Hegel viewed Oedipus' solution to the riddle of the Sphinx as a myth through which 'humanity in general is summoned to self-knowledge'. Oedipus had become a symbol of the philosopher.[7]

In 1808, Jean-August-Dominique Ingres exhibited his *Oedipus and the Sphinx*, in which Oedipus is depicted as an enlightened challenger of the monster. In 1864, Gustav Moreau painted his own version of *Oedipus and the Sphinx*, only this time the monster has leapt defiantly onto the chest of Oedipus, who seems to resist. Whereas the Sphinx's head looks frighteningly inhuman in Ingres, Moreau's Sphinx possesses a beautiful woman's head. Contemporary responses to this painting interpreted her as an image of 'modern female beauty', an alluring face hiding a 'bestial humanity', as Simon Goldhill has discussed.[8] By 1890, Franz von Stuck's *The Kiss of the Sphinx* presents the artist's self-portrait pinned down, kissing an irresistible monster. With Freud, however, the battle between male subject and female monstrosity becomes slightly skewed, in that we are *all* Oedipus, *women and men*. Or, to put this more accurately, everyone, for Freud, is destined for a drama whose dramatis personae are human subjects not defined by sexual difference but living in a world of castrated and non-castrated beings, an issue which requires further explanation.

Freud's fascination with Oedipus developed over the course of his career. After *The Interpretation of Dreams*, Freud's first most detailed theorisation came in 1905 in *Three Essays on Sexuality*, in which Freud suggested that the real riddle of the Sphinx for mankind – the most profound question a child can ask of itself – is 'where [do] babies comes from?' (*SE* 7:195). Just as for Hegel, solving the puzzle represented man's greater understanding of himself, for Freud, man's most important question about himself is his origins. But the solution to this riddle does not bring the Freudian subject to an elevated position of knowledge. Indeed, the drive for knowledge first occurs 'at about the same time as the sexual life of children reaches its first peak' (*SE* 7:194). That's to say, the pleasure derived from sucking at the breast, from defecating and then from infantile masturbation converge, so that by the time they are three to four years old, 'the instinct for knowledge in children is attracted unexpectedly early and intensively to sexual problems and is in fact possibly first aroused by them' (*SE* 7:194). The drive to knowledge, then, emerges from the child's interest in sexuality. But the child's question, 'where do children come from?', occasioned, according to Freud, as a result of 'the arrival of a new baby', for instance a sibling, does *not* bring the child to any enlightened state (*SE* 7:195). The child ponders the question deeply, and many come up with the answer that 'people get babies by eating some particular thing (as they do in fairy tales) and babies are born through the bowel like a discharge of faeces' (*SE* 7:196). At the same time, however, from the riddle of the Sphinx the Freudian child formulates a certain theory of sexual difference, which will have long-lasting consequences:

> it is self-evident to a male child that a genital like his own is to be attributed to everyone he knows, and he cannot make its absence tally with his picture of these other people. This conviction is energetically maintained by boys, is obstinately defended against the contradictions which soon result from observation, and is only abandoned after severe internal struggles (the castration complex). [. . .] The assumption that all human beings have the same (male) form of genital is the first of the many remarkable and momentous sexual theories of children. [. . .] Little girls do not resort to denial of this kind when they see that boys' genitals are formed differently from their own. They are ready to recognise them immediately and are overcome by envy for the penis – an envy culminating in the wish, which is so important in its consequences, to be boys themselves (*SE* 7:195).

While the myth of Oedipus does not figure centrally in *Three Essays on Sexuality*, Freud nevertheless characterises the child as an Oedipus trying to solve the mystery of his existence. Rather than as a figure of enlightenment, though, Freud's Oedipus is typified by his ignorance: his answer to the riddle is wrong. And as Lisa Appignanesi and John Forrester have put it, 'In an important sense, in the unconscious, no one ever solves the mystery of the origin of babies – it remains the riddle of the Sphinx'.[9] The little boy never really gives up his fear of castration, just as the girl never really stops envying the penis. It is these feelings that lie at the heart of human sexuality for Freud.

As Freud goes on to explain in *Three Essays*, our desires reflect our longing to return to a time before we feared or mourned the loss of a penis – the time when we were at our mother's breast. When Freud wrote that 'the finding of an object [of desire] is in fact a refinding of it' (*SE* 7:222), he meant that every erotic choice we make is designed to resuscitate the feelings of pleasure we enjoyed as a baby in our mother's arms. At the beginning of *Three Essays*, Freud had already characterised infantile sexuality as 'polysexual' in nature: the mouth, the anus, and then the genitals are all in turn explored in different phases because of their excitability. 'A child's intercourse with anyone responsible for his care', as Freud puts it, 'affords him an unending source of sexual excitation and satisfaction from his erotogenic [or erogenous] zones' (*SE* 7:223). The child, in blissful ignorance of its 'true' sex, not needing to distinguish itself as masculine or feminine, enjoys a totalising source of pleasure from its carer, who again need not be defined according to anatomical sex. Whereas Krafft-Ebing's correspondents wrote in great detail about the origins of their particular sexual predilection, Freud's child experiences a plurisexual stimulation and satisfaction of erogenous zones, and is therefore unclassifiable as homo-, hetero- or even bisexual, nor as an invert, nor a fetishist, and so on. It is not until puberty, so the third of the *Three Essays* contended, 'that the sharp distinction is established between masculine and feminine characters' (*SE* 7:219), with boys focusing their interest on their penises and girls on their vaginas. At the same time, however, Freud emphasised a basic continuity between pre- and post-pubertal (or, child and adult) sexualities, in that sexuality after puberty was always to be an attempt to re-find the objects that gave satisfaction in infancy. The desire between mother and child is essentially the same as that between two adult lovers. We are all Oedipus, wanting to rekindle that bond with our mother: that is how Freud's Oedipus complex looked in 1905.

By 1909–12, Oedipus began to play an ever more significant role in Freud's writings. In Freud's 1910 biography of Leonardo da Vinci (to which we will return in more detail shortly), the drama clearly unfolds:

> A mother's love for the infant she suckles and cares for is something far more profound than her later affection for the growing child. It is in the nature of a completely satisfying love-relation, which not only fulfils every mental wish but also every physical need. [. . .] In the happiest young marriage the father is aware that the baby especially if he is a baby son, has become his rival, and this is the starting-point of an antagonism towards the favourite which is deeply rooted in the unconscious (*SE* 11:117).

Just as the father sees the boy as his rival, so the boy begins to view the father also as challenging his access to his mother. Indeed, his 'discovery' that the penis could be castrated makes him fear his father all the more, ensuring that the boy moves through his Oedipus complex to find a substitute for his mother, thereby not incurring the wrath of the father. The girl, on the other hand, resentful because of her sense of penile loss, seeks solace in desiring the father, hoping for a penis-substitute, a baby, thereby arousing the jealousy of her mother. Whereas, in 1905, Freud's *Three Essays* emphasised the 'polysexual' nature of our sexualities, by 1912 he came to see the successful resolution of the Oedipus complex as more and more important.

At the same time, however, Freud became very interested in another character from classical mythology: Narcissus. Freud's fascination with Leonardo da Vinci led him to think about homosexuality in more detail. In a footnote in *Three Essays*, he argued that homosexuals 'take *themselves* as their sexual object. That is to say, they proceed from a narcissistic basis and look for a young man who resembles themselves and whom *they* may love as their mother loved *them*' (*SE* 7:145). In 1914, Freud wrote his paper 'On Narcissism', where he theorised two principal types of love: 'anaclitic', 'leaning upon' (where the subject loves the person who protects him), or 'narcissistic' (whereby one loves an object modelled on the love of oneself) (*SE* 14:73–102). As Appignanesi and Forrester summarise, 'he may love, narcissistically, either what he himself is, what he himself was, what he himself would like to be, or someone who was once part of himself'.[10] And so it was not only the homosexual but also the heterosexual male who could attempt to hang on to the love of the mother. For heterosexual women, too, narcissism can be found to be the trigger of their sexual desires: 'in the child which they bear, a part of their own body confronts them like an extraneous object, to which, starting out from their narcissism, they can give complete object-love' (*SE* 14:89–90). Boys want to keep hold of what they fear losing and girls envy what they never had. As Appignanesi and Forrester explain, for Freud, 'the castration complex will come to mean that the subject is expelled from the narcissistic world precisely in order to preserve or acquire what comes to symbolize narcissism: the penis'.[11]

In a series of papers written between 1923 and 1925, Freud supplemented his theory of infantile sexuality. In *Three Essays*, in 1905, he had posited the oral and then the anal phases which were followed by latency: the sexual drives were to re-emerge at puberty with the genital phase, in which boys were to find sexual pleasure in the penis and girls were to transfer their concentration from the clitoris to the vagina. Freud had argued that at puberty the distinctiveness between maleness and femaleness finally issued, as girls focused their attentions on their vaginas because of societal pressures (that is, a societal horror of clitoridal sexuality) and women's 'natural' proneness to repressing their clitoridal pleasures. In these papers in the early 1920s, however, Freud moved the interest on the genitals back into infancy and called it the 'phallic phase'. Freud thereby brought together the Oedipus complex with the castration complex and penis envy. When children 'learn' that the world is made up of castrated and non-castrated beings, they resolve the Oedipus complex in order to hold on to their narcissism, which is the love of the penis. The boy turns his attentions away from the mother to find a substitute, whereas the girl's attentions on her father become a preoccupation with having a baby.

But Freud began to wonder whether there is ever anything after the phallic phase. As Rachel Bowlby succinctly puts it, 'Femininity *hopes* (to be masculine). Masculinity *is threatened* (with the loss of masculinity)'.[12] In Freud's own words:

> The girl's recognition of the fact of her being without a penis does not by any means imply that she submits to the fact easily. On the contrary, she continues to hold on for a long time to the wish to get something like it herself and she believes in that possibility for improbably long years'(*SE* 22:125).

Even though the girl should transfer her clitoridal sexuality to her vagina at puberty, her desire to receive the penis – her father's penis – remains, symbolically, as a desire to have a baby. Appignanesi and Forrester express the Freudian woman's problem eloquently: 'This woman does not desire a man *qua* man; she desires something else'.[13] Or, as Sarah Kofman has put it,

> what is most specifically feminine in woman is in fact her masculine desire to possess the penis, her penis envy. This desire thus becomes at once the vestige of woman's 'masculine' sexuality that *must* disappear in order to leave room for femininity and also what allows woman to bring her femininity to the best possible fruition – that is, in having a baby.[14]

The boy, similarly, is also jolted out of his primeval happiness at the realisation that there are castrated beings in the world – his mother being one of them. The threat of castration resolves the Oedipus complex for boys (whereas this possibility instigates the complex for girls, in their desire for their father's penis). The boy begins in 'hopeless longing' for his mother, which is supposedly dissolved. And yet there are many boys who never stop desiring the non-castrated, phallic mother.

By 1927, Freud was becoming very interested in sexual fetishism, where a fetish, according to Freud, was a substitute for the mother's penis. Just as the woman seemed stuck in the Oedipus complex, so Freud was certainly not confident of the boy's successful resolution of it either: the little boy's reaction to the 'lack' of his mother's genitals might haunt him ever after. Then, in 1931, in a paper called 'Feminine Sexuality', Freud began to wonder why the little girl did not cling to the mother after she 'discovered' she did not have a penis: apart from the fact that the father possessed the penis, what was it about the relationship between the mother and the daughter that turned the little girl away? Just as the bond between the pre-Oedipal phallic mother and the boy kept on returning in the man's psyche and in Freud's academic papers, so Freud couldn't help but continue to wonder about this stage of the girl's life as well:

> Our insight into this early, pre-Oedipus, phase in girls comes to us as a surprise, like the discovery, in another field, of the Minoan-Mycenaean civilization behind the civilization of Greece. Everything in the sphere of this first attachment to the mother seemed to me so difficult to grasp in analysis – so grey with age and shadowy and almost impossible to revivify – that it was as if it had succumbed to an especially inexorable repression (*SE* 21:226).

Freud was referring to the archaeologist Arthur Evans' sensational discoveries at Knossos in Crete, which had captured the imaginations of European historians, artists and writers. Freud was also alluding to a 13½-inch-tall ceramic faience figure, wearing a long, flounced skirt, baring her round breasts proudly, a sacred cat on her head, with two snakes writhing in her hands. The 'Minoan Snake Goddess', as Evans had called her, was interpreted as a matriarchal deity.[15] The Swiss antiquarian and Roman law professor Johann Jakob Bachofen had put forward the idea of an early pre-patriarchal matriarchal phase in cultural development back in 1861, and the idea offered a justification for Freud's theorisation of the all-powerful phallic mother.[16] Evans' bare-breasted 'Minoan Snake Goddess', grasping a pair of phallic snakes, offered archaeological proof of his psychoanalytic theory. Just as, back in the 1890s, archaeology offered an image of what prehistory might look like, so it continued to do so in the 1930s.

Despite the twists and turns in the history of Freud's writings on sexuality, then, his universalisation of the Oedipus complex – we are all Oedipus – saw to it that he consistently theorised that 'each individual is neither wholly a man nor wholly a woman, but rather both at once', as Appignanesi and Forrester have put it.[17] In fact, we might go so far as saying that Freud refused to theorise what masculinity and femininity actually are. In his last extended discussion of sexual difference, 'Analysis Terminable and Interminable', he ended up concluding:

> We often have the impression that with the wish for a penis and the masculine protest we have penetrated through all the psychological strata and have reached bedrock, and that thus our activities are at an end. This is probably true, since, for the psychical field, the biological field does in fact play the part of the underlying bedrock. The repudiation of femininity can be nothing else than a biological fact, a part of the great riddle of sex (*SE* 23:252).

Freud says that there is nothing more to be said about women than the biological fact of the repudiation of femininity, a denial which could also be imputed to men, who are also trapped in search for their phallic mother. And it is *the detachability of the penis* – the fear of its loss and the hope to (re)gain it – that triggers the sexual drives of the Freudian subject. The penis in Freudian psychoanalysis is not simply a signifier of masculinity. Rather, it is the penis' troublesome mobility as perceived by our unconscious that conditions human desires. Having 'penetrated through all the psychological strata and hav[ing] reached bedrock', there is nothing beyond the alarming truths of the fear of castration and penis envy.

By analysing himself in 1897, Freud had blurred the line between male doctor and female patient, between expert and layperson. This was to have huge consequences for his theorisation of sexuality. Freud viewed the history of our sexual self as an encounter, *for all of us* (whether 'women' or 'men'), as between Oedipus and the riddle of the Sphinx. As his career developed, Freud saw more and more that the relationship between the child and its (phallic) mother conditioned the possibilities and patterns of our sexual desires. And yet, despite Freud's hope that we might all be able to resolve our Oedipus complexes, his academic papers at the end of his career explore the difficulty of escaping the mother (the man's fetishism) and of truly understanding the hold the mother had over the girl (the pre-Oedipus phase). If, in *Three Essays*, back in 1905, Freud thought he could solve the riddle of the Theban Sphinx, in 1937 in 'Analysis Terminable and Interminable', he was less confident in his confrontation with this mythical monster. The knowledge of the psychoanalyst ended up becoming an encounter with the sexuality of the phallic mother. And just as we have seen men's knowledge continually pitted against women's wisdom about sex in this book, so construing the relationship between modern science and classical myth has also been crucial for knowing about sex. Indeed, however much modern medical science might know, Freud found it very hard to avoid the conclusion that we cannot escape the stories we tell ourselves – the classical myths of the past. Although modern *Wissenschaft* might claim to know all about sexuality, it is our formation recorded in the stories of ancient mythology which shapes who we are. Freudian scientific expertise had to confront the myths we enjoyed telling ourselves. There could be no straightforward historical account of sexual development. Like the sexology of the nineteenth century, Freudian psychoanalysis emerged out of a complicated intellectual history, informed by both scientific knowledges and the stories of the classical world.

Anthologies of desire: from the hermaphrodite to the phallic mother

So how were Freud's ideas about the detachability of the penis a product of this intellectual background? We have already seen how, during the Renaissance, the Greek nude male body offered a powerful symbol for modern masculinity. And yet, since then, this body has always been dangerously alluring as well as paradigmatically exemplary. Indeed, the modern reception of the ancient Greek nude has been conditioned by the precarious relationship between the body of the nude and its penis. Winckelmann's famous paean to the Apollo Belvedere, in his 1764 *History of the Art of Antiquity*, described in close detail the contours of the statue's form, without so much as mentioning Apollo's delicate little penis and testes.[18] Indeed, we should hardly be surprised, as the penis on many Greek statues – as on the Apollo – is so often absent or covered up. If Apollo's penis had indeed broken off by accident (that is to say, without the pressures of a modern censorious hand), then there has certainly been no rush to re-attach it, even though other parts of his body have been so carefully reconstructed.

Winckelmann was, of course, writing in the 1760s, at a time when the recently excavated sites of Herculaneum and Pompeii were radically changing modern perspectives of classical antiquity. The phallic artefacts unearthed at these sites were, as we have already discussed, very strange to behold. And, as we have examined, the craze for phallic collection soon took off and continued through the nineteenth and into the twentieth century. Following the model in Naples back in 1819, the British Museum founded its own 'Secretum' in 1865, when it acquired a collection of 'Symbols of the Early Worship of Mankind', owned by George Witt. By the end of the nineteenth century, a semi-clandestine publishing industry was booming with the publication of numerous titles on the subject of 'phallicism', or ancient phallic worship. At the same time, discoveries of phallic cults in the 'uncivilised' territories of Britain's ever expanding empire repeatedly made the news. In the 1890s, for instance, readers of *The Times* were told on more than one occasion of the phallic symbols uncovered in Mashonaland (northern Zimbabwe) by the well-known English explorer and archaeologist, James Theodore Bent.[19] And although they did not appear in the 1989 publication *Sigmund Freud and Art: His Personal Collections of Antiquities*, Freud also enjoyed collecting phallic amulets made of bronze, ivory and faience, very possibly acquired as early as 1902, during a trip to Pompeii.[20]

What is obvious, but should be noted, is that these phalli are detached from where we might expect to find a penis: on the male body. Just as the Greek body beautiful came to be viewed so often as bereft of a penis, so ancient phalloi, as they were excavated, were more often than not not connected to any male body. Whether the penis might even signify maleness in antiquity seemed to be at stake. However, at the same time, from the end of the seventeenth century modern medical science was gluing the penis back onto male anatomy. As Thomas Laqueur has argued in *Making Sex*, previous Renaissance anatomy had been influenced by various ancient medical theories that viewed the relationship between the male and the female body in hierarchical terms: a woman was a less developed, inverted version of a man, her vagina a phallic tube, her ovaries testes. During the course of the seventeenth and eighteenth centuries this picture changed, as men and women came to be viewed as opposite sexes, with anatomy peculiar to their own bodies. Women had a uterus; men a penis. The relationship between maleness and the penis was supposedly secured through scientific observation.[21]

When it came to thinking about sexual desire, Freud's interest in archaeology and his scientific professionalism produced a conflicted theorisation of the male member. Despite Freud's comparisons of psychoanalysis with archaeology, the archaeological study of the ancient phallic symbol and the medical study of the modern male body offered conflicting accounts of the significance of the penis for masculinity. Freud did, on the one hand, attempt to distinguish between masculinity and femininity. Whereas earlier theories of genital anatomy saw the vagina as an inverted penis, Freud's contention about the sexually mature female's pleasure from the vagina being an equivalent to the male orgasm made Freud a thoroughly 'modern' male scientist. It is hard to believe that Freud was unaware of the views of contemporary anatomists and physiologists that clearly demonstrated that the clitoris was the specific seat of female sexual pleasure. The Freudian girl nevertheless had to give up the phallic clitoris; she must differentiate herself from boys, to set herself on the path to sexual reproduction, thereby guaranteeing the modern, twentieth-century investment in the nuclear family. And yet, as we have seen and as Laqueur himself points out, 'Freud, more than any other thinker', 'also collapses the model. Libido knows no sex'.[22]

Freudian psychoanalysis, then, emerged out of a complex negotiation of modern scientific learning and the ancient archive unearthed by classical archaeologists. This is hardly surprising as Freud's own education ensured that he could never just be a scientist and never just a classical humanist. In 1865 Freud had entered the *Realgymnasium* in Leopoldstadt, Vienna, a bold new experiment in the history of Wilhelm von Humboldt's *Gymnasium*. Humboldt's reforms of the Prussian education system saw that the learning of languages was central to the pedagogic curriculum, through which one's character and personality were formed. Greek and Latin were the foundations of Humboldt's *Bildung*, which aimed to produce modern citizens for the modern civilised world. Austria, however, had not experienced the same history of educational reforms as Prussia. The important moment in Viennese educational history came in 1848–9 during the Revolution and counter-revolution when, under the neo-absolutist period, secondary and university education was widely reformed. In 1818 the curriculum was largely dominated by Latin; in 1849 the Latin element was reduced to a quarter of the student's time, and Greek and scientific subjects were introduced.[23] And so, under the influence of Humboldt's ideas, the Austrian *Gymnasium* contrived a 'reconciliation between "two cultures", one scientific, the other literary'. Jacques Le Rider has called the *Gymnasium*'s legacy 'this double debt', which Freud owed to his *alma mater*, placing in him 'an interest in languages and classical civilisation as well as a taste for science'. 'This double debt reflects the intellectual double identity' of Freud: humanist faithful to the grand tradition of the return to classical antiquity, *and* cautious and rigorous doctor, a professor of science.[24]

This does not fully explain, however, how Freud came to see a phallic mother as the ultimate source of all sexual pleasure. Rather, Freud was responding to a long history of discussion in German writing about the relationship between beauty and androgyny. Of course, Aristophanes' playful myth in Plato's *Symposium* about primordial physical union, which collapsed into fragmentation, offered an image for Freud's theory of sexual desire. More recently, though, Winckelmann, followed by Friedrich Schiller, Friedrich Schlegel and Wilhelm von Humboldt, was to argue that true beauty was neither wholly 'male' nor wholly 'female'. Their ideas were informed by the story about Zeuxis' principle of *ars combinatoria* (as told by Cicero and the Elder Pliny), in which Zeuxis the artist had combined the body parts of the five most beautiful virgins of Croton to produce the perfect likeness of Helen.[25] In his writings, Winckelmann went a step further, proposing that such a process of selection need not be limited to representing a beautiful woman. Rather, the Greek ideal of beauty 'comes from the fact that it incorporated into the manliness of a beautiful boy the forms of enduring feminine youth'. Winckelmann was thinking of ancient sculptures of divine hermaphrodites: 'this image was ideal [. . .] Hermaphrodites such as those produced by art have probably never been conceived in reality. All figures of this kind have, in addition to the reproductive organs of our sex, virginal breasts, and their bodies and facial appearance are generally feminine'. Winckelmann was describing figures such as the female-looking, penis-possessing hermaphrodite which can now be seen in the Louvre in Paris. The indeterminacy of sex reflected Winckelmann's interest in Greek sculpture's aesthetic indefinability - physical and spiritual, obviously stationary and seemingly moving, hard and soft, rigid and fluid. As well as the phallic woman, the pubescent boy, the 'Jüngling' represented true beauty:

> We receive the loftiest impression of youthful beauty in the figures of Apollo and Bacchus. These divinities reveal, in the depictions of them that come down to us, and due to the union of both sexes attributed to them by the poets, hybrid and ambiguous characteristics.

Such images seemed to Winckelmann to represent 'an already full-grown youth, who approaches the threshold of the springtime of life [. . .] between sleeping and walking'. Winckelmann's beautiful ancient adolescent looked like a perfect pupil beautifully poised for an aesthetic education, on the verge of enlightenment.[26]

The connections Winckelmann posited between beauty, androgyny and education informed Wilhelm von Humboldt's arguments about genius that contended that the artist (rather than the artwork) was constituted out of an androgynous personality. And yet, just as Winckelmann had emphasised the other-worldliness of the hermaphrodite, so Humboldt doubted that such an artist, other than Sophocles, might ever exist.[27] Nevertheless, the harmonising of binaries was a fundamental leitmotif for the philosophy of classical *Bildung*: an appreciation of the statue of Juno Ludovisi, a 'reconciliation' of masculine and feminine, of sensuality and rationality, stood at the centre of Schiller's *On the Aesthetic Education of Man*.[28] Furthermore, Schlegel's essay 'On Diotima' praised Socrates' female teacher, seeing her as 'a plenitude in free unity'.[29] And yet, as Catrina Macleod has made clear, there was a continual anxiety about female androgyny in this period of German writing: Winckelmann did not show much interest in educated women and Humboldt seemed altogether more interested in male geniuses, suggesting that 'the female sex, on the other hand, must take the utmost care to preserve precisely this feminine identity'.[30] In a letter to Goethe, Schiller worried 'at how our womenfolk are able now, in a purely dilettante fashion, to achieve a certain degree of talent in writing, that approaches art'.[31] And in Schiller's satirical poem 'Die Berühmte Frau' ('The Famous Wife'), one husband complains to another about his manly wife's writing career, a woman who is lambasted as a mere 'Zwitter' (hermaphrodite) and a 'Mittelding' (a 'middle creature').[32]

How seductive, how repulsive, how ideal and how real was androgyny to be? The re-publication of Beccadelli's *The Hermaphrodite* posed these questions yet again: his epigrams were both warts-and-all depictions and fantastical portraits, designed to blur the line between lust and digust, the beautiful and the grotesque. The figure of the hermaphrodite appeared to please everyone and no one. Only eight years after the re-issuing of Beccadelli along with Forberg's collecting together of sexual pleasures, the first (fairly) complete publication of the collection of the Neapolitan Secret Museum was printed, a clandestine affair organised by a French diplomat in Naples, Stanislas-Marie-César Famin (1799–1853). In 1839/40, Louis Barré was authorised by the museum to publish a properly complete edition of the collection. Together these catalogues quickly became collectors' items, anthologising an erotic typology like d'Hancarville's publications and Romano's Renaissance *I Modi*. In various images, hermaphrodites appeared in numerous different positions. The classic motif of the female, penis-possessing hermaphrodite being pursued by a satyr was interpreted by Famin as symbol of 'the taste of some old men for both sexes [which] is a consequence of the impotency of their resources'. In another image, a hermaphrodite was seen as 'full of grace, youth and beauty'. The same image for Barré represented an ideal combination of 'Galataea and Hylas'. In yet another image in Barré's book, we can see an ithyphallic female hermaphrodite intent on displaying 'herself' to a frightened satyr. As Whitney Davis puts it, 'Satyr and Hermaphrodite overtly performed a whole range of the [sexual] possibilities'. In these visual anthologies of sexual acts, the hermaphrodite offered the possibility of all sorts of sexual pleasure in one body. As Famin himself had written, 'the statuary who caused a beautiful hermaphrodite or ardent Satyr to stand forth from a formless block had no other object than to reproduce all kinds of beauty'.[33] Where, in Winckelmann, the hermaphrodite had provided a visual symbol for the concept of ideal beauty, by the 1830s the hermaphrodite catered for all sorts of sexual tastes.

Just as, with Winckelmann and his German readers, looking at hermaphroditic sculptures was a key part of an aesthetic education, and just as the beautiful pupil was 'himself' androgynously poised between femaleness and maleness, an effeminate boy and a virile youth, so the female, penis-possessing hermaphrodite subverted these claims to ideal beauty, inverting this idealism to suggest that 'she' catered for any type of sexual desire. The hermaphroditism of masculine aesthetic education and the polmorphous sexuality of the female hermaphrodite would become conjoined in Freud's theorising of the phallic mother, a figure of both knowledge *and* desire, whose influence over the pre-Oedipal 'boy' and 'girl' was to challenge the expertise of modern psychoanalytic science. And, just as the figure of androgyny oscillated between 'sleeping and walking' (as Winckelmann put it) – between an impossible fantasy and a worrying reality – so Freud's phallic mother is awkwardly positioned between the real and the fantastical, in dreams and in the unconscious. In his sexual biography of Leonard da Vinci, which appeared in 1910, we can see precisely how Freud's phallic mother emerged out of this intellectual history dating back to the decades around 1800. The collections of phallic artefacts produced the context for Forberg's, Rosenbaum's and Krafft-Ebing's efforts, and these collections also facilitated Freud's own rather different reception.

Just as Freud was not interested in reproducing the historicising autobiographical narratives of earlier medical research, so his biography of Leonardo would also look very different. Indeed, Freud based his analysis on a single memory Leonardo claims to have had of his early childhood:

> I recall as one of my very earliest memories that while I was in my cradle a vulture came down to me, and opened my mouth with its tail, and struck me many times with its tail against my lips (*SE* 11:82).

Crucially, Freud did not believe that this memory was even true: rather it was a fantasy-memory covering over a wish that Leonardo had about sucking on his mother's nipple. Freud supported his argument by referring to ancient Egyptian art, which presented their mother-goddess Mut with vulture's wings and sometimes a phallus. Freud refers his readers to an Italian Egyptology publication which depicts a phallic Mut (*SE* 11:93–4). Leonardo's fixation on his mother turned into a narcissism, which developed into homosexual desires. Because these could not be satisfied, Leonardo sublimated these desires into a seemingly unquenchable thirst for artistic production and scientific knowledge. His painting of beautiful women and his investigations into Mother Nature were nothing but attempts to return to the embrace of and to know (sexually) his own phallic mother – that is, to return to a time when he knew nothing about sexual difference. Just as the ancient Egyptians worshipped a phallic mother, so Leonardo's own life evidences his own unconscious wish to (re)attach the penis to his maternal parent.

Freud's argument about the survival of Leonardo's phallic worship into adulthood is supported by the apparent survival of 'primitive forms of genital worship in recent times'. At this point, Freud inserts a laconic footnote 'Cf. Knight' (*SE* 11:97), that is, *A Discourse on the Worship of Priapus and Its Connexion with the Mystic Religion of the Ancients*, by Richard Payne Knight. As explored in Chapter III, his history of religion had argued that a primordial worship of the 'Organ of Generation' represented man's original attempts to philosophise rationally and freely about the workings of nature. Payne Knight constructed an intricate account, which is important to examine for our reading of Freud: the earliest phallic objects did not simply represent the penis, but this abstract 'Organ of Generation'. As Whitney Davis, citing Knight, puts it, Knight theorised a '"first-begotten Love," an abstract if archaic principle of pansexual attraction and generativity'.[34] Throughout his treatise, Knight emphasised the 'double nature' of the Deity, 'possessing the general power of creation and generation, both active and passive, both male and female'.[35] Following d'Hancarville's thesis, Knight contended that ancient pictorial representations of the egg, the sun, the goat, the lamb and the bull were all more naturalistic representations of this original generative deity. But

> the grand and exalted system of a general First Cause, universally expanded, did not suit the gross conceptions of the multitude; who had no other way of conceiving the idea of an omnipotent God, but by forming an exaggerated image of their own Despot [penis], and supposing his power to consist in an unlimited gratification of his passions and appetites.[36]

According to Payne Knight, the religious arts of the ancient 'Hindoos', Egyptians, Greeks and Romans reflect this corruption of the original form of worship:

> Hence the many-shaped God, the Πολυμορφος [polumorphos], and Μυριομορφος [muriomorphos] of the ancient Theologists, became divided into many Gods and Goddesses, often described by the Poets as at variance with each other, and wrangling about the little intrigues and passions of men. Hence too, as the symbols were multiplied, particular ones lost their dignity; and that venerable one which is the subject of this Discourse, became degraded from the representative of the God of Nature to a subordinate rural Deity [...] standing among the Nymphs by a Fountain, and expressing the fertility of a

> Garden, instead of the general Creative power of the great Active Principle of the Universe.[37]

The Roman garden god Priapus was simply the surviving relic of a much more profound, more enlightened form of philosophical worship of the generative power of nature.

Just as, for Knight, the origins of artistic representation could be found in a double-natured Deity, both male and female, later in ancient culture to be 'represented by mixing the characters of the male and female bodies in every part, preserving still the distinctive organs of the male', so for Freud, behind all of Leonardo's art and scientific representations, can be found the very same anatomical figure: the phallic mother.[38] Even though Freud references Payne Knight in the briefest of notes, his study of Leonardo attends to the *Discourse on Priapus* very closely. The presence of Knight in Freud's text clearly comes through when Freud writes that

> Mythology can teach us that an androgynous structure, a combination of male and female sex characters, was an attribute not only of Mut, but also of other deities like Isis and Hathor [. . .] It teaches us further that other Egyptian deities like Neith of Sais – from whom the Greek Athene was later derived – were originally conceived of as androgynous [. . .] Mythology may then offer the explanation that the addition of a phallus to the female body is intended to denote the primal creative force of nature [. . .] that only a combination of male and female elements can give a worthy representation of divine perfection (*SE* 11:94).

Moreover, Payne Knight's model of historical change proved very useful for Freud's psychoanalytic model of history in *Leonardo*. For Payne Knight, ancient cultures such as those of the Greeks and the 'Hindoos' had 'buried the original principles of their Theology under a mass of poetical Mythology, so that few of them can give any more perfect account of their faith, than that they mean to worship one First Cause'.[39] Payne Knight's theory of the survival of original phallic worship, whose original significance is at the same time forgotten, provided a helpful framework for Freud's own arguments about the persistence of Leonardo's childhood love of the phallic mother in adulthood, whose original significance is also not consciously remembered.

As mentioned in Chapter III, one of the most provocative aspects of Payne Knight's history was the claim that Christianity itself could trace its roots to phallic worship, even though it does not remember such origins. Payne Knight's anti-clericalism was heard loud and clear in his own day, and just over 100 years later Freud was himself very attuned to the Enlightenment context of Payne Knight's history of the phallic symbol. Just as Payne Knight had argued that 'ancient Theologists' established phallic worship because of their enlightened ideas about the First Cause, so for Freud, children's 'infantile sexual theories provide the explanation' for the ancient worship of the phallus (*SE* 11:94).[40] Freud's actual German goes: 'Die Aufklärung kommt von seiten der infantilen Sexualtheorien': '*Enlightenment* comes from infantile sexual theories'. That is, before the male child learns of sexual difference, he imagines the phallic mother. But the term *Aufklärung* is used knowingly by Freud. As he reminded his readers in his biography of Leonardo, male children are captured by a 'curiosity' [*Wißbegierde*] that is manifested in their untiring love of asking questions [. . .] a curiosity (*Wißbegierde*)' which 'is aroused [. . .] by the actual birth of a little brother or sister, or by a fear of it based on external experiences – in which the child perceived a threat to his selfish interests' (*SE* 11:78). 'Enlightenment' for every male child comes in the form of sexual curiosity. Or, as Rachel Bowlby puts it, 'it is sexuality that precedes and engenders curiosity and knowledge, rather than the other way round'.[41] The drive for knowledge – Leonardo's drive for knowledge – began with infantile sexual theories. Not only are these theories about the phallic mother the source of *Aufklärung* for Freud's psychoanalytic biography of Leonardo, but they are also the very beginnings of *Aufklärung* for Leonardo himself.

Freud was particularly interested in the issue of Leonardo's knowledge about the Egyptian phallic vulture goddess Mut. Citing Aelian's *De Natura*

Animalium (2.46) and Horapollo's *Hieroglyphica* (1.11), Freud argued that the ancient Egyptians believed that only female, and no male, vultures existed (*SE* 11:88). The edition of Horapollo that Freud was using was that edited in 1835 by the Dutch Egyptologist Conrad Leemans (1809–93). Freud quotes a comment by Leemans that says that ancient Egyptian beliefs about vultures recorded by Greeks were 'eagerly taken up by the Fathers of the Church, in order to refute, by means of a proof drawn from the natural order [*ex rerum natura*], those who denied the Virgin Birth' (*SE* 11:90). Or, as Freud puts it, 'the Fathers of the Church' had 'at their disposal a proof drawn from natural history to confront those who doubted sacred history' (*SE* 11:90). Then, Freud hypothesises that Leonardo must have 'once happened to read in one of the Fathers or in a book on natural history' this argument, 'and at that point a memory sprang to his mind, which transformed into the phantasy that he also had been such a vulture-child – he had had a mother, but no father' (*SE* 11:90). Just like Payne Knight had done with the worship of the phallus, Freud traces out the worship of the phallic mother from ancient mythology, from the Egyptians and the Greeks, which was then taken up by Christian theologians, to be read by Leonardo in Renaissance modernity. The 'Naturgeschichte' of the ancient Egyptians asserted the truth of the Church Fathers' 'heilige Geschichte'. Freud was, of course, writing at a time when it was precisely the sciences of natural history (like geology) that were undermining sacred, biblical narratives. In Freud's highly provocative narrative, conversely, it was Leonardo's reading of 'heilige Geschichte', which created his 'Phantasie', which spurred his interest in Mother Nature, ultimately making him the great 'Naturforscher' – the great natural scientist – that he was.

From ancient mythology to modern science: Leonardo the Renaissance man, artist *and* scientist, offered Freud the opportunity to think about the relationship between *Wissenschaft* and the arts, between scientific and literary discourse, that is, his own intellectual self-positioning, both scientist and classicist. And similarly, out of eighteenth- and nineteenth-century classical–aesthetic debate about the ancient hermaphrodite emerges Freud's phallic mother. Payne Knight's '*polumorphos* and *muriomorphos*' deity becomes Freud's theory of polymorphous sexuality. The anthologising of sexual pleasures in one hermaphroditic body ends up as the endlessly flowing source of sexual stimulation and satisfaction of erogenous zones between the phallic mother and the child. Interestingly, ancient female mythological figures continued to appear in Freud's writing. In 1911, a year after he published his Leonardo biography, he penned a very short article entitled 'Great is Diana of the Ephesians'.[42] As Freud relates, despite different waves of invasion throughout history, Ephesus never gave up its worship of a mother-goddess. As Freud had learnt from Austrian archaeological reports, whose finds were collected in Félix Sartiaux's *Villes mortes d'Asie mineure*, the city's original Asiatic inhabitants worshipped a mother-goddess, whom they called Oupis. After the invasion of Ionian Greeks, this old deity survived under the name of Artemis. Even a disastrous fire that destroyed her temple in 356 BCE could not stop the Ephesians' veneration, as the temple was rebuilt more magnificently than ever. Only when Paul arrived to preach to the Ephesians was there an interruption in her worship. But later, John arrived at the city, the man who had supposedly written in his gospel that Jesus on the cross had 'called out to his favourite disciple, pointing to Mary: "Behold thy mother!"' 'And from that moment', so Freud continued, 'John took Mary to him. So when John went to Ephesus, Mary accompanied him. Accordingly, alongside the church of the apostle, the first basilica was built in honour of the new mother-goddess of the Christians'. And although 'the conquest of Islam' ruined the city, causing it to be abandoned, even now 'the great goddess of Ephesus had not abandoned her claims', as Freud notes, 'in our own days, she appeared as a saintly virgin to a pious German girl, Katharine Emmerich [...] and described to her her journey to Ephesus'. Just as Freud's child could not escape the figure of the all-powerful mother, so neither could the history of Western civilisation. Freudian psychoanalysis had emerged out of nineteenth-century historiographical debates about the relationship between ancient and modern, and now Freud was applying his theorisations back at the disciplines of history and classical archaeology. We have already seen how Krafft-Ebing had also learnt to apply historical scholarship to his own sexological work, only to re-apply the logic of the personal sexual narrative back onto the history of the West, more generally.

While much has been read here out of a tiny footnote ('Cf. Knight') in one text in a huge corpus of works by Freud, the figure of the phallic mother was to haunt Freud's career. His interest in female figures in classical Greek mythology was to continue alongside his theorisations of sexuality. In 1922, the year before Freud started publishing his papers on the phallic phase (between 1923 and 1925), he wrote a short interpretation of the figure of Medusa.[43] It seemed that Freud was almost drawn into staring into this face from antiquity. For Freud, 'Kopfabschneiden = Kastrieren', 'to decapitate = to castrate'. The horror of seeing Medusa's decapitated head was the horror of seeing castration. It was as if the little boy had caught sight of the mother's genitals, symbolised by Medusa's open mouth, surrounded by her wild hair. And yet, Freud noted, Medusa's serpentine hair served as 'a mitigation of the horror, because her hair replaces the penis'. For Freud, the sight of Medusa – which made the male viewer stiff as stone – was a symbol for the penile erection, and offered some 'consolation' to the viewer as he thinks that 'he is still in possession of a penis'. Whereas Perseus the hero managed to avoid looking at Medusa, the image of the phallic mother becomes so alluring and necessary for Freud that he cannot help but stare at her directly in the face.

Authority and desire

At the origins of civilisation, then, lay the truth of modern sexuality. The influence of the phallic mother, the castration complex and penis envy seemed to be the very 'bedrock' of identity. Freud had produced a human subject within whom a sexuality was lodged which served as the inner core of subjectivity, just as classical antiquity provided the modern West with its true sense of identity. It is in this way that the history of the reception of classical texts came to lie at heart of the invention of modern modes of knowing about sex. While Foucault's *Histoire de la sexualité* had triggered an important debate among classicists about the similarities and differences between ancient and modern sexuality, *Sex: Antiquity and its Legacy* has sought to demonstrate the centrality of Latin and Greek for the development of the modern languages of sexual pathology and psychoanalysis.

In his *Histoire* on the production of the sexual human subject, Foucault had emphasised that the history of modern sexuality should not been seen in terms of a repressive nineteenth century followed by an emancipatory period in the second half of the twentieth century. *Sex: Antiquity and its Legacy* has also shown that a straightforward distinction between restrictive authority and liberatory pleasure does not make sense. Foucault had argued that the possibilities of the sexual revolution of the 1960s had been mapped out by the scientific powers of the nineteenth century so that a polarisation of restrictive medico-legal discourse and rebellious sexual expressiveness is too simplistic. *Sex: Antiquity and its Legacy* began by outlining how the Roman conceptualisation of sex in terms of an opposition between active and passive participants was in itself an articulation of free-born male adult power over women, slaves and boys. But if the Roman language of sex was also an enunciation of a male citizen's authority, then this was not always clearly so, as Catullus' Poem 16 revealed. Beccadelli was to explore how using obscene and erotic Latin did or did not confer authority on the speaker. He wrote *The Hermaphrodite* in order to gain patronage with Cosimo de' Medici, thereby providing him with a status and position. His attempt, however, did not succeed but it did spark controversy, with some rushing to Beccadelli's defence and others burning his effigy. Beccadelli had, of course, anticipated such a conflicted response, as he explored the relationship between abusive invective and erotic chat-up, between lust and disgust, the beautiful and the grotesque. Beccadelli realised that censorious authorities appalled by erotic ancient texts were also capable of being aroused and titillated by such reading material. Indeed, those who had authority over Latin, those who knew how to use the language, could enjoy Beccadelli's mockery of the pederastic Latin teacher just as much as they might have enjoyed being implicated in Beccadelli's mockery: understanding the wit of Beccadelli's Latin suggested the possibility that one could have been once taught by such a teacher. But while Beccadelli enjoyed displaying his witty authority over the erotic and obscene language of Latin epigram, his poetry also voiced concerns that his control was not so complete, as Ursa had got hold of his obnoxious verses about her, and his 'domina', would only sleep with him if he delivered up to her a copy of Catullus' poems.

While Marsilio Ficino would argue that a chaste, intimate and intense friendship between men formed a bond that was superior to all other relationships, courtesan culture was also crucial to the formation and preservation of elite masculinity during the Italian Renaissance. Whereas Beccadelli had to contend with Ursa and his girlfriend, Renaissance humanists often enjoyed carousing and debating with female courtesans. The *Dialogo* of Tullia d'Aragona in the 1540s offered a more provocative challenge to Italian humanists, and she has taken her place in a canon of female writers and poets who contested male-authored stereotypes of women. So vexing was Tullia's voice that her name was used a century later in the 1660s for the knowledgeable cousin in Chorier's *Satyra Sotadica*, where sex becomes an eroticised battle for authority between husbands and wives. Ovid's playful amatory discourse, which questioned the possibility that one or the other sex might control the language of sexuality, lay behind Chorier's libertine text, which confounded the borders between serious seventeenth-century scientific writing and arousing pornographic literature.

Chapter III explored how the the professionalisation and institutionalisation of Classics provided a context for Forberg's research. But even if his scholarly Latin reflected the taxonomising discourses of biology and botany and of the collecting culture of the late eighteenth century, Forberg was also very aware that his Latin did not secure any authority for him over the reception of his work. He realised that some might be sexually titillated by what he had written. As he closes his book, he turns to write his own epigram advertising an accompanying booklet in which his readers can enjoy looking at pictures of the sexual positions he has described. Forberg knew that the line between scholarly and pornographic writing might be easily crossed. This, however, did not prevent one of his earliest readers, the doctor Rosenbaum, from appropriating Forberg's Latin as well as the

Latin of Roman epigram as a tool of control and authority over the modern *populus*.

Krafft-Ebing's sexual pathology utilised this Latin tradition to furnish his own scientific discourse with a terminology and a position of authority within a context of other medical professionals and an educated and respectable reading public. But Krafft-Ebing's Latin looked both technical and obscene, just as he depicted a world of people who appeared normal but also harboured all sorts of secret sexual identities that reminded the doctor of imperial Rome. The ambivalence of his Latin should, of course, not surprise us. Becccadelli's *Hermaphrodite* had positioned itself as both witty, sophisticated poetry to be enjoyed by the establishment, and obscene, unpleasant smut which could have no part in Renaissance humanist culture. Chorier's Latin also blurred the generic boundaries between materialist scientific writing and pornographic mockery of women. And Forberg was well aware that his Latin could have seemed both scholarly and arousing to his readers. The Latin vocabulary of sexual obscenity confusingly offered a language for the rebellious and for those in authority.

If the *Psychopathia Sexualis* reflected *fin-de-siècle* doubts about the relationship between the healthy and the sick, then Krafft-Ebing's Latin encapsulated his ambivalence. As we saw with the case study of the 'psychical hermaphrodite', Krafft-Ebing seemed torn between using Latin as a language to focus the scientific gaze on the perverted, and as a literary discourse, which gave a voice to the subject of the case study as he described his pleasure in kissing his soldier. But even if Symonds turned to ancient Greece to offer a corrective to late nineteenth-century sexual science, the second half of *Sex: Antiquity and its Legacy* has not depicted a straightforward story about the emancipatory turn to ancient Greek sexual mores in the face of the repressive authoritarianism of nineteenth-century science. Dichotomising the historical agents who have featured in Chapters IV through VI into heroes and villains should be avoided. Certain doctors and legal experts in the nineteenth century did sharply distinguish between the healthy and the pathological, the normal and the abnormal, in such a way that they contributed to a stigmatisation of people sexually attracted to members of their own sex. But we have seen with Krafft-Ebing that the situation could be much more complicated: this psychiatrist was very willing to provide 'perverts' with a platform to express their understanding of their sexuality, so much so that Krafft-Ebing began to sympathise with the disabling and often perilous position into which European legal frameworks placed homosexual people.

If Krafft-Ebing cannot be straightforwardly described as a villain, then those who critiqued sexual pathology and criminology should also not be uncritically lionised. While Symonds expressed himself with great eloquence on the subject of Greek love and its possible application to the nineteenth-century context, we have seen that he was rather less than compassionate about sexual relations between women. Some might even accuse him of hypocrisy in his admiration of Sappho's poetry written for another woman, while others might brand him as startlingly uncaring and uninterested in sexual love between women due to his readiness to dismember Sappho Fragment 31 to express his desire for Angelo Fusato and his jealousy of the woman next to him. Finally, it is also difficult to identify positively with the women who spoke up against male authority. Tullia d'Aragona's profession as a courtesan placed her in the company of male clients, but her conversational skills and wit for dialogue was part of a skill-set designed to arouse men sexually. The position from which this Renaissance woman could speak articulately was one which few today would want to share. Katherine Bradley and Edith Cooper were also complicated characters. Their Sappho provocatively challenged male-authored accounts of women's experiences of desire and sex, but their own relationship, one between an aunt and her niece, is not one to which many might aspire.

Freud's classical myths have also seemed restrictive and authoritarian, as well as subversive and emancipatory. His ideas about the phallic mother were often seen as especially negative: it seemed that it was she who was to blame for almost anything that went wrong in the sexual history of the child. Indeed, the overbearing mother who produced an emasculated, homosexual son became a particularly prevalent theme in debates about parenting in mainstream Western society, a view that ultimately emerged out of

Freud's biography of Leonard da Vinci. Freud was seen to be an architect of the modern family: his dramatic adaptation of the tragedy of Oedipus the King was viewed as an affirmation of the nuclear family – never had the steps to its creation been so minutely traced out. But perhaps more importantly, never had the dangers that attended young boys' and girls' maturation into a heterosexual dyad been so keenly described. And it was Freud's delineation of the perils that supposedly beset every child at every stage of their development that inspired other feminists and then gay and queer theorists. Whereas Freud's incapacity to come up with an actual theory of femininity had been a problem for some feminists, for others, Freud's seeming inability to distinguish firmly between maleness and femaleness at the level of the unconscious offered a liberating suggestion that perhaps there was no such thing as an instrinsic, essential masculinity or femininity. The drama of the Oedipus complex offered a theory for the social constructedness of sexuality: the subject's sexual desires and identities were not set at birth, but emerged gradually out of the complex interactions between the child and its carers. For many feminists, this proved an extremely valuable strategy in the campaign to break down Western hierarchies which naturalised the gendered distribution of characteristics (women are naturally primary carers, prone to want to reproduce, look after their nest and so on, whereas men are fundamentally acquisitive, competitive beings associated with the development of culture and intellectuality). That Freud thought so few managed to work through the Oedipus complex successfully (that for so many the phallic mother loomed so large), was a position that became an opportunity for anti-essentialist feminism which argued that our environments produced all sorts of subjectivities, which should not be hierarchised or demonised according to old-fashioned sex standards.

Similarly, Freud's arguments about the polymorphousness of sexuality have also provided food for thought for gay and queer theory: whereas sexological theory had once attempted to pathologise the homosexual (along with other types of same-sex desire), Freud has been seen to suggest that the distribution of the world's population in hetero- and homosexual groupings was a mistake. Rather than condemning gay and queer people to legal or medical mistreatment, Freud's texts perhaps emphasised the impossibility of living up to a heterosexual ideal. Whereas for some, Freud could be blamed for his misogynistic depiction of the all-controlling mother, who produced the weakly homosexual son, for others, Freudian texts could be appropriated to refuse the labels of sexual identity, which many queer theorists and activists have seen as repressive and normalising.[44]

Classical reception studies often emphasises how the ancient world was either used to supress and control modern subjects or to voice and activate radical and emancipatory ideals and programmes: 'discipline and revolution', as one classicist has memorably summed up the history of classical reception.[45] Classical texts have been used to justify modern European colonialism, but also to defend modern revolutionary causes against cruel political regimes, and to rationalise modern democratic foundations. But, rather than see the ancient world as alternatively providing either repressive or liberatory examples for modernity, *Sex: Antiquity and its Legacy* has shown the complexity of the intricate relationship between the exercise of authority and the pursuit of desire in the history of classical reception. Histories of sex and sexuality, Foucault reminded us, should move between the simple polarities of repression and freedom. *Sex: Antiquity and its Legacy* offers classical reception studies more generally an example of how the history of the reception of antiquity in modernity inhabits that space between discipline and revolution.

SOME SUGGESTIONS FOR FURTHER READING

INTRODUCTION

Michel Foucault's *Histoire de la sexualité* was very quickly translated into English: *The History of Sexuality,* vol. 1: *The Will to Knowledge,* trans. Robert Hurley (London: Penguin, 1998); *The History of Sexuality,* vol. 2: *The Use of Pleasure,* trans. Robert Hurley (London: Penguin, 1998); *and The History of Sexuality,* vol. 3: *The Care of the Self,* trans. Robert Hurley (London: Penguin, 1998). A couple of examples of the sort of history of sexuality published in the 1960s that succumbed to the 'repressive hypothesis', but which nevertheless remain an extremely enjoyable read, are Stephen Marcus, *The Other Victorians: A Study of Sexuality and Pornography in Mid-Nineteenth Century England* (London: Weidenfeld and Nicolson, 1967) and Ronald Pearsall, *The Worm in the Bud: The World of Victorian Sexuality* (London: Weidenfeld and Nicolson, 1969). An entertaining and interesting history of the 'sexual revolution' of the 1960s is David Allyn's *Make Love, Not War: The Sexual Revolution – An Unfettered History* (London: Little, Brown and Company, 2001). Lawrence Stone's *The Family, Sex and Marriage in England 1500–1800*, 2nd ed. (Penguin, London, 1990) is an influential and widely discussed work on the history of marriage. The pornographic autobiography discussed by Foucault is Anonymous, *My Secret Life* (New York: Grove Press, 1966). On the transformation from legal discussions of sodomy to medical accounts of the homosexual, see the very useful history presented in Christopher Craft, *Another Kind of Love: Male Homosexual Desire in English Discourse, 1850–1920* (Los Angeles: University of California Press, 1994). On Foucault's project, see David Halperin's account in *One Hundred Years of Homosexuality and Other Essays on Greek Love* (London: Routledge, 1990).

The important debate between David Halperin and Amy Richlin was played out in a series of publications. See Amy Richlin 'Not before homosexuality: the materiality of the *cinaedus* and the Roman law against love between men', *Journal of the History of Sexuality* 3:4 (1993), pp. 523–73; and David Halperin, *How to do the History of Homosexuality* (Chicago: University of Chicago Press, 2002). Halperin's extension, deployment and development of Foucault's arguments are shown to virtuosic effect in *One Hundred Years of Homosexuality: and Other Essays on Greek Love* (London: Routledge, 1990). Amy Richlin's significant *The Garden of Priapus: Sexuality and Aggression in Roman Humor* (Oxford: Oxford University Press, 1992) opened new possibilities for non-canonical Latin literary studies. Marilyn Skinner provides a vivid account of the debates in the 1990s in 'Zeus and Leda: the sexuality wars in contemporary classical scholarship', *Thamyris* 3:1 (1996), pp.103–23. Classicists' interest in Foucault continued: John Henderson's groundbreaking essay on Persius' *Satires* led the way for further engagement with Foucault's *Care of the Self*: 'Persius' Didactic Satire: The Teacher as Pupil', *Ramus* 20 (1993): pp. 123–48. Simon Goldhill's *Foucault's Virginity: Ancient Erotic Fiction and the History of Sexuality* (Cambridge: Cambridge University Press, 1995) extended and problematised Foucault's *Histoire* by turning to Greek literature produced in the Roman Empire. *Before Sexuality: The Construction of Erotic Experience in the Ancient Greek World*, ed. Froma I. Zeitlin, John J. Winkler and David M. Halperin (Princeton: Princeton University Press, 1991) is an important set of essays on ancient Greek erotics, emanating from Foucault's work. *Rethinking Sexuality: Foucault and Classical Antiquity*, ed. David H. J. Larmour, Paul Allen Miller and Charles Platter (Princeton: Princeton University Press, 1998) is a very interesting collection of essays, assessing the promise and limits of Foucault's *Histoire*. More recently still, Wolfgang Detel, *Foucault and Classical Antiquity: Power, Ethics and Knowledge*, trans. David Wigg-Wolf (Cambridge: Cambridge University Press, 2005). James Davidson's thought-provoking challenge to Foucault's work can be found in his volume *The Greeks and Greek Love: A Radical Reappraisal of Homosexuality in Ancient Greece* (London: Weidenfeld and Nicolson, 2007).

For readers who are interested in Foucault's reading of the ancient world more generally, Miriam Leonard's *Athens in Paris: Ancient Greece and the Political in Post-War French Thought* (Oxford: Oxford University Press, 2005) and Paul Allen Miller's *Postmodern Spiritual Practices: The Construction of the Subject and the Reception of Plato in Lacan, Derrida and Foucault* (Columbus: Ohio State University, 2007) are fascinating intellectual histories. On the history of the reception of ancient ideas about sex, which discusses many of the debates surveyed in my Introduction, see Alastair J. L. Blanshard's superb *Sex: Vice and Love from Antiquity to Modernity* (Chichester: Wiley-Blackwell, 2010). On Richard von Krafft-Ebing, see the excellent Harry Oosterhuis, *Stepchildren of Nature: Krafft-Ebing, Psychiatry and the Making of Sexual Identity* (Chicago: University of Chicago, 2000).

There are numerous accounts, since Foucault, which have attempted to identify the historical emergence of homosexuality. Two of the most widely read are Randolph Trumbach, *Sex and the Gender Revolution,* vol. 1: *Heterosexuality and the Third Gender in Enlightenment London* (Chicago: Chicago University Press, 1998); and Thomas King, *The Gendering of Men, 1600–1750: The English Phallus*, and *The Gendering of Men, 1600–1750: Queer Articulations* (Madison: University of Wisconsin Press, 2004; 2008). Readers will also enjoy Alan Bray's groundbreaking *Homosexuality in Renaissance England* (London: Gay Men's Press, 1982). A very readable account that brings together much of the scholarship of the last 30 years is Faramerz Dabhoiwala, *The Origins of Sex: A History of the First Sexual Revolution* (London: Penguin, 2012).

Eve Kosofsky Sedgwick has also made important contributions to the debates: *Epistemology of the Closet* (Berkeley/Los Angeles: University of Californa Press, 1990); *Between Men: English Literature and Male Homosocial Desire* (New York: Columbia University Press, 1985); and 'Gender criticism', in S. Greenblatt and G. Gunn (eds), *Redrawing the Boundaries: The*

Transformation of English and American Literary Studies (New York: Modern Language Association of America, 1992), pp. 271–301. Sedgwick's prose can sometimes be difficult for those less experienced with the technical terms used in literary and cultural theory. A very helpful, lively and enjoyable introduction to her work is *Eve Kosofsky Sedgwick*, by Jason Edwards (London/New York: Routledge, 2009).

On Roman male sexuality, see Jonathan Walters, 'Invading the Roman body: manliness and impenetrability in Roman thought', in Judith P. Hallett and Marilyn B. Skinner (eds), *Roman Sexualities* (Princeton: Princeton University Press, 1997), pp. 29–43. All the essays in this important collection are worth reading.

On the issue of sexual knowledge, see Simon Goldhill's intelligent and entertaining 'On knowingness', *Critical Inquiry* 32:4 (2006), pp. 708–23; on debates about the use of classical antiquity in debates about history in the nineteenth century, see Simon Goldhill's detailed discussion in *Victorian Culture and Classical Antiquity: Art, Opera, Fiction and the Proclamation of Modernity* (Princeton: Princeton University Press, 2011). On nineteenth-century homosexual codes in Greek, see Linda Dowling, 'Ruskin's pied beauty and the constitution of a "homosexual" code', *Victorian Newsletter* 75 (1989), pp.1–8.

CHAPTER I

Antonio Beccadelli's text has recently been republished, along with the letters and poems that comprised the debate around the circulation of his poetry: Antonio Beccadelli, *The Hermaphrodite*, ed. and trans. Holt Parker (Cambridge, MA: Harvard University Press, 2010). The Council of Trent decree on obscene reading material is quoted and discussed in Paula Findlen, 'Humanism, politics and pornography in Renaissance Italy', in Lynn Hunt (ed.), *The Invention of Pornography* (Cambridge, MA: Zone Books, 1993), pp. 49–108. There is an excellent survey of the Renaissance reception of Catullus by Julia Haig Gaissner, 'Catullus in the Renaissance', in Marilyn Skinner (ed.), *A Companion to Catullus* (Oxford: Blackwell, 2007), pp. 439–60; a more detailed account can be found in Julia Haig Gaissner, *Catullus and his Renaissance Readers* (Oxford: Oxford University Press, 1993). For Daniel Selden's careful reading of Catullus, see his '*Ceveat Lector*: Catullus and the rhetoric of performance', in Ralph Hexter and Daniel Selden (eds), *Innovations of Antiquity: The New Ancient World* (New York: Routledge, 1992), pp. 461–512; readers will also enjoy William Fitzgerald's *Catullan Provocations: Lyric and the Drama of Position* (Los Angeles: University of California Press, 1995). Those interested in reading about Martial should consult the following excellent books on this author: William Fitzgerald, *Martial: The World of Epigram* (Chicago: University of Chicago Press, 2007); and Victoria Rimell, *Martial's Rome: Empire and the Ideology of Epigram* (Cambridge: Cambridge University Press, 2008).

Beccadelli's poetry was not the only erotic and priapic verse circulating among Renaissance readers. As well as the other poetic productions reprinted in Holt Parker's edition, readers might also enjoy delving into: Girolamo Angeriano, *The Erotopaegnion: A Trifling Book of Love*, ed. and trans. with commentary by Allan M. Wilson (Nieuwkoop: De Graaf, 1995). On the homoerotics of Renaissance humanism, see Leonard Barkan's provocatively interesting *Transuming Passion: Ganymede and the Erotics of Humanism* (Stanford: Stanford University Press, 1991); on erotics and obscenity in neo-Latin literature, see the diverse collections of essays in Ingrid De Smet and Philip Ford (eds), *Eros et Priapus: Erotism et obscénité dans la littérature néo-latine* (Geneva: Librairie Droz, 1997). For more on the rich world of the neo-Latin epigram, see the essays in Susanna de Beer, Karl A. E. Enenkel and David Rijser (eds), *The Neo-Latin Epigram: A Learned and Witty Genre* (Leuven: Leuven University Press, 2009). On different areas of Renaissance sexuality, see Bette Talvacchia (ed.), *A Cultural History of Sexuality in the Renaissance* (London: Bloomsbury Academic, 2012).

CHAPTER II

For an excellent, advanced introduction to the intellectual environments of Beccadelli and Ficino, see Jill Kraye (ed.), *The Cambridge Companion to*

Renaissance Humanism (Cambridge: Cambridge University Press, 1996). On Marcilio Ficino, see M. J. B. Allen, *The Platonism of Marsilio: A Study of His Phaedrus Commentary its Sources and Genesis* (Berkeley: University of California Press, 1984); Michael Shepherd (ed.), *Friend to Mankind: Marsilio Ficino (1433–1499)* (London: Shepheard-Walwyn, 1999); Mikhail Oskar Kristeller, *The Philosophy of Marsilio Ficino,* trans. Virginia Conant (New York: Columbia University Press, 1943); and M. J. B. Allen, *Marcilio Ficino and the Phaedran Charioteer* (Berkeley: University of California Press, 1981). The edition of Ficino's commentary on Platonic love used here is Jayne Sears, *Marsilio Ficino: Commentary on Plato's Symposium* (Columbia: University of Missouri, 1944). This has more recently been published as Jayne Sears, *Marsilio Ficino: Commentary on Plato's Symposium on Love* (Dallas, Texas: Spring Publications, 1985) and is the standard translation of Ficino's *De Amore*. The study of Plato in the medieval period is discussed in Raymond Klibansky, *The Continuity of the Platonic Tradition during the Middle Ages* (London: The Warburg Institute, 1939). The revival of Greek learning in the West is mapped out in Rudolf Pfeiffer, *History of Classical Scholarship from 1300–1850* (Oxford: Oxford University Press, 1976) and James Hankins, *Humanism and Platonism in the Italian Renaissance* (Rome: Edizioni di storia e letteratura, 2003–4). The reception of Plato is examined in detail in James Hankins, *Plato in the Italian Renaissance*, 2 vols (Leiden: E.J. Brill, 1990). On Ficino on Plato's *Charmides*, see the detailed examination in Maude Vanhaelen, 'Marsile Ficin, traducteur et interprète du *Charmide* de Platon', *Accademia Revue de la Société Marsile Ficin* 3 (2001), pp. 23–52. The reference for Ficino's discussion of the *Charmides* can be found in Marsilio Ficino, 'Argumentum in Charmidem', in *Opera Omnia . . .* (Basileae: Ex Officina Henrici Petrina, 1576), p. 1304.

The Renaissance rediscovery of classical sculpture is lavishly recounted in Francis Haskell and Nicolas Penny, *Taste and the Antique: The Lure of Classical Sculpture 1500–1900* (New Haven: Yale University Press, 1981); Leonard Barkan, *Unearthing the Past: Archaeology and Aesthetics in the Making of Renaissance Culture* (New Haven: Yale University Press, 1999); and Kathleen Wren Christian, *Empire Without End: Antiquities Collections in Renaissance Rome, c. 1350–1527* (New Haven: Yale University Press, 2010). On Donatello and his *David*, see Horst Woldemar, *The Sculpture of Donatello* (Princeton: Princeton University Press, 1963) and L. Schneider, 'Donatello's bronze Davide', *The Art Bulletin* 55 (1973), pp. 213–16. On Michelangelo and the undressed male form, see Margaret Walters, *The Male Nude: A New Perspective* (London: Paddington Press, 1978).

The early sixteenth-century edition of Giulio Romano's images along with Pietro Aretino's poems has been reprinted, with introduction and notes: Lynne Lawner, *I Modi: The Sixteen Pleasures* (Evanston: Northwestern University Press, 1988). A detailed account of *I Modi* is offered by Bette Talvacchia, *Taking Positions: On the Erotic in Renaissance Culture* (Princeton: Princeton University Press, 1999). For those interested in Aretino, see Raymond Waddington, *Aretino's Satyr: Sexuality, Satire and Self-Projection in the Sixteenth Century Literature and Art* (Toronto: University of Toronto Press, 2003). On ancient sex manuals, see Holt Parker, 'Love's body anatomized: the ancient erotic handbooks and the rhetoric of sexuality', in Amy Richlin (ed.), *Pornography and Representation in Greece and Rome* (Oxford: Oxford University Press, 1992), pp. 90–111.

On Ovid's sexual teachings, there are many marvellous readings to enjoy: see Alison Sharrock, *Seduction and Repetition in Ovid's* Ars amatoria *2* (Oxford: Oxford University Press, 1994); Roy Gibson, Steven Green and Alison Sharrock (eds), *The Arts of Love: Bimillennial Essays on Ovid's* Ars amatoria *and* Remedia amoris (Oxford: Oxford University Press, 2006); and Victoria Rimell, *Ovid's Lovers: Desire, Difference and the Poetic Imagination* (Cambridge: Cambridge University Press, 2006), which expertly explores the mutual suspicion of men and women in love. On Roman love elegy, more generally, see Duncan Kennedy's now classic *The Arts of Love: Five Studies in the Discourse of Roman Love Elegy* (Cambridge: Cambridge University Press, 1993).

Christine de Pizan's famous work has most recently been published as *The Book of the City of Ladies*, trans. with introduction and notes by Rosalind Brown-Grant (London: Penguin, 1999). On de Pizan's book, see the interesting reading by Maureen Quilligan, *The Allegory of Female Authority:*

Christine de Pizan's Cité des Dames (Ithaca: Cornell University Press, 1991). Tullia d'Aragona's dialogue can be read in English: Tulla d'Aragona, *Dialogue on the Infinity of Love*, ed. and trans. Rinaldina Russell and Bruce Merry (Chicago: Chicago University Press, 1997). On Aragona's works, including the *Dialogo* and its interactions with Renaissance Platonism, see Elizabeth A. Pallitto, 'Laura's laurels: re-visioning Platonism and Petrarchism in the philosophy and poetry of Tullia d'Aragona', PhD dissertation, The City University of New York, 2002. A survey of women's Latin writings in the period can be found in: Laurie J. Churchill, Phyllis R. Brown and Jane E. Jeffrey (eds), *Women Writing Latin,* vol. 3: *Early Modern Women Writing Latin* (New York/London: Routledge, 2002). On the Latin and Greek poetry by other female Italian humanists, see Holt Parker's interesting essay, 'Latin and Greek poetry by five Renaissance Italian woman humanists', in Barbara K. Gold, Paul Allen Miller and Charles Platter (eds), *Sex and Gender in Medieval and Renaissance Texts: The Latin Tradition* (New York: State University of New York Press, 1997), pp. 247–85.

On women, and learned women in the Renaissance, see the following very interesting explorations: Jeanie R. Brink, *Female Scholars: A Tradition of Learned Women before 1800* (Montreal: Eden University Women's Publications, 1980); Joan Kelly, 'Did women have a Renaissance?', in *Women, History, and Theory: The Essays of Joan Kelly* (Chicago: Chicago University Press, 1984), pp. 19–50; Margaret King, *Women of the Renaissance* (Chicago: University of Chicago Press, 1991); Constance Jordan, 'Women defending women: arguments against patriarchy in Italian women writers', in Maria Ornella Marotti (ed.), *Italian Women Writers from the Renaissance to the Present: Revising the Canon* (University Park, PA: Pennsylvania State University Press, 1996), pp. 55–67; Merry E. Wiesner, *Women and Gender in Early Modern Europe* (Cambridge: Cambridge University Press, 2000); and Holly S. Hurlburt, 'A renaissance for Renaissance women?' *Journal of Women's History* 19:2 (2007), pp. 193–201. On the writerly courtesan, see Fiora A. Bassanese, 'Private lives and public lies: texts by courtesans of the Italian Renaissance', *Texas Studies in Literature and Language* 30:3, (1988), pp. 295–319. Details about Benedetto Varchi can be found in Louis

Crompton, *Homosexuality and Civilization* (Cambridge, MA: Harvard University Press, 2003). On the Renaissance courtesan more generally, see the excellent Tessa Storey, 'Courtesan culture: manhood, honour and sociability', in Sara F. Matthews-Grieco (ed.), *Erotic Cultures of Renaissance Italy* (Farnham: Ashgate, 2010), pp. 247–73.

On the Renaissance dialogue, one of the standard accounts is Virginia Cox, *The Renaissance Dialogue: Literary Dialogue in its Social and Political Contexts, Castiglione to Galileo* (Cambridge: Cambridge University Press, 1992). On women and this genre of writing, see Valeria Finucci, *The Lady Vanishes: Subjectivity and Representation in Ariosto and Castiglione* (Stanford: Stanford University Press, 1992), and Virginia Cox, 'Seen but not heard: the role of women speakers in the cinquecento literary dialogue', in Letizia Panizza (ed.), *Women in Italian Renaissance Culture and Society* (Oxford: Legenda European Humanities Research Centre, 2000), pp. 385–400.

Nicolas Chorier's *Satyra Sotadica* is an extremely rare collectors' item: seventeenth-century editions are highly scarce and, while eighteenth-century and nineteenth-century editions in Latin, French and English can be found with online booksellers, these are also expensive. The edition from which I have cited (and which can be accessed in several of the world's best resourced libraries) is by Bruno Lavagnini, *Aloisiae Sigeae Toletanae Satyra Sotadica de Arcanis Amoris et Veneris sive Joannis Meursii Elegantiae Latini Sermonis* (Catania: Romeo Prampolini, 1935). The French translation by Alcide Bonneau, *Les Dialogues de Luisa Sigea* (Paris: n.p., 1882) is mostly accurate. English translations, however, have been less good and also partial. Chorier's citation of Roman authors is discussed by Lise Leibacher-Ouvrard, 'Transtextualité et construction de la sexualité: la *Satyra sotadica* de Chorier', *L'Esprit Créateur* 35:2 (1995), pp. 51–66. The philosophical context of Chorier's work, the work itself and its influence on Western constructions of sexuality are masterfully and eruditely examined in James Grantham Turner, *Schooling Sex: Libertine Literature and Erotic Education in Italy, France and England 1534–1685* (Oxford: Oxford University Press, 2003). On the seventeenth-century context, see also the important book by Susan James, *Passion and Action: The Emotions in Seventeenth-Century Philosophy*

(Oxford: Oxford University Press, 1997). For those interested in reading Thomas Hobbes' fascinating work on the subject, see *Humane Nature, or The Fundamental Elements of Policie, Being a Discoverie of the Faculties, Acts, and Passions of the Soul of Man, from their Original Causes, according to such Philosophical Principles as Are not Commonly Known or Asserted* (London: Printed by T. Newcomb, for Fra: Bowman of Oxon, 1650).

Readers who would like to follow up Ovid's moralising receptions in the Middle Ages should consult the excellent essay by Jeremy Dimmick, 'Ovid in the Middle Ages: authority and poetry', in Philip Hardie (ed.), *The Cambridge Companion to Ovid* (Cambridge: Cambridge University Press, 2002), pp. 264–87, which also points to further bibliography. For those interested in Ovid's story about Byblis and Caunus, see Thomas E. Jenkins, 'The writing in (and of) Ovid's Byblis' episode', *Harvard Studies in Classical Philology* 100 (2000), pp. 439–51. On Ausonius' rewriting of Virgil, see Scott McGill, *Virgil Recomposed: The Mythological and Secular Centos in Antiquity* (New York/Oxford: Oxford University Press, 2005). On Horace's politics of friendship, see Kirk Freudenburg, *Satires of Rome: Threatening Poses from Lucilius to Juvenal* (Cambridge: Cambridge University Press, 2001). On Horace's reception in the Renaissance and beyond (with further bibliography), see Michael McGann, 'The reception of Horace in the Renaissance', and David Money, 'The reception of Horace in the seventeenth and eighteenth centuries', in Stephen Harrison (ed.), *The Cambridge Companion to Horace* (Cambridge: Cambridge University Press, 2007), pp. 305–17; 318–33.

CHAPTER III

On Enlightenment discussions about sex, consult the following important texts: Jacob Stockinger, 'Homosexuality and the French Enlightenment', in George Stambolian and Elaine Marks (eds), *Homosexualities and French Literature: Cultural Contexts/Critical Tests* (Ithaca: Cornell University Press, 1990), pp. 161–85; Robert Purks Maccubbin (ed.), *'Tis Nature's Fault: Unauthorized Sexuality during the Enlightenment* (Cambridge: Cambridge

University Press, 1987); and G. S. Rousseau and Roy Porter (eds), *Sexual Underworlds of the Enlightenment* (Manchester: Manchester University Press, 1987). On the eighteenth-century interest in nature and marriage, see A. E. Pilkington, '"Nature" as ethical norm in the Enlightenment', and Ludmilla Jordanova, 'Naturalising the family: literature and the bio-medical sciences in the late eighteenth century', in Ludmilla Jordanova (ed.), *Languages of Nature: Critical Essays on Science and Literature* (London: Free Association Books, 1986), pp. 51–85; 86–116. For Darwin's work, see Erasmus Darwin, *The Botanic Garden: A Poem in Two Parts: Part 1, containing The Economy of Vegetation; Part 2: The Loves of the Plants* (London: J. Johnson, 1791); and *The Temple of Nature; or, The Origin of Society: A Poem with Philosophical Notes* (London: J. Johnson, 1803). The contexts and works of Erasmus Darwin are fruitfully examined in Julie Peakman, *Mighty Lewd Books: The Development of Pornography in Eighteenth-Century England* (Basingstoke: Palgrave Macmillan, 2003). The discourse on nature in eighteenth- and early nineteenth-century debates about sex, gender and medicine are explored from various, very interesting angles in Ludmilla Jordanova, *Nature Displayed: Gender, Science and Medicine 1760–1820* (London: Longman, 1999). On *Aristotle's Masterpiece* and Nicolas Venette, readers will enjoy Roy Porter and Lesley Hall, *The Facts of Life: The Creation of Sexual Knowledge in Britain, 1650–1950* (New Haven/London: Yale University Press, 1995). On the cultural and intellectual contexts for the discovery of phallic objects in the eighteenth century, see Ian Jenkins and Kim Sloan, *Vases and Volcanoes: Sir William Hamilton and His Collection* (London: British Museum Press, 1996). Winckelmann's *Sendschreiben von den Herculanischen Entdeckungen* has recently been translated into English: Johann Joachim Winckelmann, *Letter and Report on the Discoveries at Herculaneum*, trans. Carol C. Mattusch (Los Angeles: Getty Publications, 2011). For those interested in taking in more, read the classic, Johann Joachim Winckelmann, *History of the Art of Antiquity*, trans. Harry Francis Mallgrave (Los Angeles: Getty Publications, 2006).

Baron d'Hancarville's eighteenth-century works are now extremely valuable collectors' items, but can be found in major library collections. The lavish images of his publication of William Hamilton's vases have been republished: Pierre-François Hugues d'Hancarville, *The Complete Collection of Antiquities from the Cabinet of Sir William Hamilton* (Cologne/Los Angeles: Taschen, 2004). D'Hancarville's exploration of his theories about the erotic origins of the arts can be read in the following reprint: Pierre d'Hancarville, *Recherches sur l'origine, l'esprit et les progrès des arts de la Grèce*, introduction by Burton Feldman (New York/London: Garland, 1984). On d'Hancarville himself, see Francis Haskell, 'The Baron d'Hancarville: an adventurer and art historian in eighteenth-century Europe', in Francis Haskell, *Past and Present in Art and Taste: Selected Essays* (New Haven: Yale University Press, 1987), pp. 30–45; P. Griener, *Le Antichità etrusche, greche e romane 1766–1776 di Pierre Hughes d'Hancarville* (Rome: Edizione dell'Elefante, 1992); F. Lissarrague and M. Reed, 'The collector's books', *Journal of the History of Collections* 9:2 (1997), pp. 275–94; James Moore, 'History as theoretical reconstruction? Baron d'Hancarville and the exploration of ancient mythology in the eighteenth century', in James Moore, Ian Macgregor Morris and Andrew J. Bayliss (eds), *Reinventing History: The Enlightenment Origins of Ancient History* (London: Centre for Metropolitan History, Institute of Historical Research, University of London, 2008), pp. 137–67; and Noah Heringman, *Sciences of Antiquity: Romantic Antiquarianism, Natural History, and Knowledge Work* (Oxford: Oxford University Press, 2013). D'Hancarville's *Monumens de la vie privée des XII Césars* (1780) and *Monumens du culte secret des dames romaines* (1784) were reprinted many times in the course of the 1780s, and editions were also produced in the early 1900s. Different versions can be found in the catalogues of online booksellers, although the prices are high since these rare tomes are also collectors' items.

William Hamilton's letter to Joseph Banks and Richard Payne Knight's treatise on phallic worship was published as: William Hamilton and Richard Payne Knight, *An Account of the Remains of the Worship of Priapus, Lately Existing at Isernia, in the Kingdom of Naples: In Two Letters; One from Sir William Hamilton, K.B. His Majesty's Minister at the Court to Naples, to Sir Joseph Banks, Bart. President of the Royal Society; and the other from a*

Person Residing at Isernia: To Which Is Added, A Discourse on the Worship of Priapus, and Its Connexion with the Mystic Religion of the Ancients, by R. P. Knight, esq. (London: T. Spilsbury, 1786). There were only some 200 copies printed of this first edition, which were distributed to members of the Society of Dilettanti and certain selected friends, making it an extremely scarce and collectible item. It was, however, reprinted in 1865, 1883 and 1895, and then numerous times in the twentieth century, and remains in print today. Alternatively, the original 1786 edition can be accessed on the online database Eighteenth Century Collections Online. On Payne Knight, see G. S. Rousseau, 'The sorrows of Priapus: anticlericalism, homosocial desire and Richard Payne Knight', in G. S. Rousseau and R. Porter, *Sexual Underworlds of the Enlightenment* (Manchester: Manchester University Press, 1987), pp. 101–53; and Giancarlo Carabelli, *In the Image of Priapus* (London: Duckworth, 1996); Andrew Ballantyne, *Architecture, Landscape and Liberty: Richard Payne Knight and the Picturesque* (Cambridge: Cambridge University Press, 1997); and Whitney Davis, *Queer Beauty: Sexuality and Aesthetics from Winckelmann to Freud and Beyond* (New York: Columbia University Press, 2010). On the history of the reception of ancient phallic artefacts in museum culture, see Walter Kendrick, *The Secret Museum* (New York: Viking Press, 1987), and Dominic Janus, 'The rites of man: the British Museum and the sexual imagination in Victorian Britain', *Journal of the History of Collections* 20:1 (2008), pp. 101–12. The title of Charles-François Dupuis's monumental seven-volume work is: *Origine de Tous les Cultes ou Religion universelle* (Paris: H. Agasse, An III, [1795]). This was rendered into English as Charles Francois Dupuis, *The Origin of All Religious Worship*, introduction by Robert D. Richardson, Jr (New York: Garland, 1984). See Frank Edward Manuel, *The Eighteenth Century Confronts the Gods* (Cambridge, MA: Harvard University Press, 1959). On the collecting of *phallica*, see the splendid Whitney Davis, 'Homoerotic Art Collections from 1750 to 1920', *Art History* 24:2 (2001), pp. 247–77. On the interest in phallic objects in the late nineteenth century, see the excellent Jennifer Ellen Grove, 'The collection and reception of sexual antiquities in the late nineteenth and early twentieth century', PhD dissertation, University of Exeter, 2013. Although the late eighteenth-century anthologies of priapic Latin verse discussed in this book remain out of print, they can be consulted in research libraries, or even acquired from antiquarian booksellers. Full bibliographical details: it apparently was first compiled in 1791, and yet the erotic French–Latin lexicon was only published in 1885: Nicolas Blondeau, *Carmina Ithyphallica: Dictionnaire érotique Latin–Français, précédé d'un essai sur la langue érotique par le traducteur de Manuel d'Erotologie de Forberg*, ed. François Noël (Paris: I. Liseaux, 1885); Barthélemy Mercier de Saint-Léger, *Quinque illustrium poetarum: Ant. Panormitae; Ramusii, Ariminensis; Pacifici Maximi, Asculani; Joan. Joviani Pontani; Joan. Secundi, Hagiensis. Lusus in Venerem* (Paris, 1791); François Noël, *Erotopaegnion, sive Priapeia Veterum et Recentiorum, Veneri jocosae sacrum* (Paris, 1798).

On *Altertumswissenschaft* and German historicism, see Anthony Grafton, 'Polyhistor into Philolog: Notes on the Transformation of German Classical Scholarship, 1780–1850', *History of Universities* 3 (1983), pp. 159–92; Suzanne Marchand, *Down from Olympus: Archaeology and Philhellenism in Germany, 1750–1970* (Princeton: Princeton University Press, 1996). On German historicism more generally, see Frederick C. Beiser, *The German Historicist Tradition* (Oxford: Oxford University Press, 2011). An excellent work on the history of scholarship is Anthony Grafton's *Defenders of the Text: The Traditions of Scholarship in an Age of Science, 1450–1800* (Cambridge, MA: Harvard University Press, 1994).

Full details of Forberg's edition of *The Hermaphrodite* are: *Antonii Panormitae Hermaphroditus: primus in Germania edidit et Apophoreta adjecit Frider. Carol. Forbergius* (Coburg: Meusel, 1824). This can most easily be accessed on Google Books. Forberg's appended essay, the 'Apophoreta', was translated into English: *Manual of Classical Erotology*, 2 vols published together (Manchester: Privately Printed for Viscount Julian Smithson, 1884). It was reprinted again in 1887, then in 1907 and, since then, several other reprints have appeared through the twentieth century. I have cited page numbers of the original 1824 edition and the 1966 Grove Press facsimile reprint of the 1884 edition. On Martial's *Apophoreta*, see Sarah Blake,

'Martial's natural history: the *Xenia* and *Apophoreta* and Pliny's encyclopedia', *Arethusa* 44:3 (2011), pp. 353–77. On Roman phallic sexuality, Amy Richlin (cited above) is a leading figure. Also very significant is Craig Williams, *Roman Homosexuality: Ideologies of Masculinity in Classical Antiquity*, 2nd ed. (Oxford: Oxford University Press, 2010). On Latin's intricate vocabulary of sex, see J. N. Adams, *The Latin Sexual Vocabulary* (London: Duckworth, 1982). On poetry written about Priapus in classical Latin, see Richard W. Hooper (ed.), *The Priapus Poems* (Urbana/Chicago: University of Illinois Press, 1999). The masculinist academic context in which Forberg worked is well analysed in Patricia Mazón, *Gender and the Modern Research University: The Admission of Women to German Higher Education, 1865–1914* (Stanford: Stanford University Press, 2003).

On Johann Eichhorn, see Grafton, *Defenders of the Text*. On the University of Göttingen, see the essays collected in Reinhard Lauer (ed.), *Philologie in Göttingen: Sprach und Literaturwissenschaft an der Georgia Augusta im 18. und beginnenden 19. Jahrhundert* (Göttingen: Vandehoeck and Ruprecht, 2001).

The first serious engagement with Forberg's work was by Julius Rosenbaum, *Geschichte der Lustseuche, erster Theil: die Lustseuche im Alterthume* (Halle: J. F. Lippert, 1839). This was later translated into English (by 'An Oxford M.A.') as *The Plague of Lust, Being a History of Venereal Disease in Classical Antiquity*, 2 vols (Paris: Charles Carrington, 1901). The preoccupation with venereal disease, prostitution and sexuality in the nineteenth century is now furnished with a massive bibliography. Here are some particularly interesting examples: Porter and Hall, *The Facts of Life* (op. cit.); Frances Finnegan, *Poverty and Prostitution: A Study of Victorian Prostitutes in York* (Cambridge: Cambridge University Press, 1979); Simon Szreter, *Fertility, Class and Gender in Britain, 1860–1940* (Cambridge: Cambridge University Press, 1996); Mary Spongberg, *Feminizing Venereal Disease: The Body of the Prostitute in Nineteenth-Century Medical Discourse* (Basingstoke: Palgrave Macmillan, 1997); Alison Bashford, *Purity and Pollution: Gender, Embodiment and Victorian Medicine* (Basingstoke: Palgrave Macmillan, 1998); Ian D. McCormick (ed.), *Sexual Outcasts, 1750–*

1850, vol. 1: *Sexual Anatomies;* vol. 2: *Sodomy;* vol. 3: *Prostitution;* vol. 4: *Onanism* (London: Routledge, 2000); Judith Walkowitz, *Prostitution and Victorian Society: Women, Class and the State* (Cambridge: Cambridge University Press, 1980), and *City of Dreadful Delight: Narratives of Sexual Danger in Late-Victorian London* (Chicago: University of Chicago Press, 1992).

Bibliographical details for the 'great' nineteenth-century works on prostitution, venereal disease and sexuality that are mentioned: Alexandre Parent-Duchâtelet, *De la prostitution dans la ville de Paris* (Bruxelles: Societe encyclopgraphique des sciences medicales, 1838); this has more recently been republished as Alexandre Parent-Duchâtelet, *La prostitution à Paris au XIXe siècle*, texte présenté et annoté par Alain Corbin (Paris: Seuil, 2008); Henry Mayhew, *London Labour and the London Poor; a cyclopædia of the condition and earnings of those that will work, those that cannot work, and those that will not work* (London: Office, 16 Upper Wellington St, Strand, 1851–2); a handy recent edition is Henry Mayhew, *London Labour and the London Poor: A Selected Edition*, ed. Robert Douglas-Fairhurst (Oxford: Oxford University Press, 2010); Cesare Lombroso, *L'uomo delinquente studiato in rapporto alla antropologia, alla medicina legale, ed alle discipline carcerarie . . . con incisioni* (Milano: Hoepli, 1876); a reasonably recent English translation is available (though now out of print): *Criminal Man, According to the Classification of Cesare Lombroso*, with an introduction by Cesare Lombroso, and a new introduction by Leonard D. Savitz (Princeton: Patterson Smith, 1972); Paul Moreau, *Des Aberrations du sens génésique* (Paris: Asselin, 1880). Paul Brandt's trilogy came out as: Hans Licht, *Sittengeschichte Griechenlands in zwei Bänden und einem Ergänzungsband. I: Die griechische Gesellschaft, II: Das Liebesleben der Griechen, III: Die Erotik in der griechischen Kunst* (Zurich: Paul Aretz Verlag, 1925). The pictorial encyclopaedia published by the Institut für Sexualforschung in Vienna is: Leo Schidrowitz et al. (eds), *Bilderlexikon der Erotik* (Vienna: Institut für Sexualforschung in Vienna, 1928–31). On Hirschfeld, see Ralf Dose, *Magnus Hirschfeld: Deutscher, Jude, Weltbürger* (Teetz: Hentrich und Hentrich, 2005); Manfred Herzer, *Magnus Hirschfeld: Leben und*

Werk eines jüdischen, schwulen und sozialistischen Sexologen (Hamburg: Männerschwarm, 2001). On Alfred Kinsey, see by Donna Drucker, *The Classification of Sex: Alfred Kinsey and the Organization of Knowledge* (Pittsburgh: University of Pittsburgh Press, 2014).

Richard von Krafft-Ebing's magnum opus was first published as Richard von Krafft-Ebing, *Psychopathia Sexualis: Eine klinisch-forensische Studie* (Stuttgart: Ferdinand Enke, 1886). On Krafft-Ebing, see the excellent Harry Oosterhuis, *Stepchildren of Nature: Krafft-Ebing, Psychiatry and the Making of Sexual Identity* (Chicago: University of Chicago, 2000) and Heinrich Ammerer, *Am Anfang war die Perversion: Richard von Krafft-Ebing, Psychiater und Pionier der modernen Sexualkunde* (Vienna: Styria, 2011). On sexology, psychoanalysis, and twentieth-century debates in sexuality studies, the reader should consult Arnold Davidson's *The Emergence of Sexuality: Historical Epistemology and the Formation of Concepts* (Cambridge, MA: Harvard University Press, 2001). On the culture of the *fin de siècle*, the following contain wonderful essays: Sally Ledger and Scott McCracken (eds), *Cultural Politics at the Fin de Siècle* (Cambridge: Cambridge University Press, 1995); and Gail Marshall (ed.), *The Cambridge Companion to the Fin de Siècle* (Cambridge: Cambridge University Press, 2007).

I have used and cited from the 1894 English translation by Charles Gilbert Chaddock of Krafft-Ebing's book, which can be easily consulted in good academic libraries: R. von Krafft-Ebing, *Psychopathia Sexualis, with Especial Reference to Contrary Sexual Instinct: A Medico-legal Study* (Philadelphia: F.A. Davis, 1894). Otherwise, the other most available English translation of Krafft-Ebing's book is *Psychopathia Sexualis, with Especial Reference to the Antipathic Sexual Instinct: A Medico-forensic Study*; translated from the twelfth German edition and with an introduction by Franklin S. Klaf; introduction by Joseph LoPiccolo; foreword by Daniel Blain (New York: Arcade, 1998). The social history of Rome that Krafft-Ebing read can also be enjoyed in English translation: Ludwig Friedländer, *Roman Life and Manners under the Early Empire*, 4 vols, trans. J. H. Freese (New York: Barnes and Noble, 1968). Friedrich Wiedemeister's book on the madness of the Caesars is: *Der Cäsarenwahnsinn der Julisch-Claudischen*

Imperatorenfamilie geschildert an den Kaisern Tiberius, Caligula, Claudius, Nero (Hannover: Carl Rümpler, 1875). Johannes Scherr's book on German history consulted by Krafft-Ebing: *Deutsche Kultur- und Sittengeschichte* (Leipzig: Otto Wigand, 1870). On Friedländer and the themes of luxury and debauchery more generally in Roman writing, see the important study by Catherine Edwards, *The Politics of Immorality in Ancient Rome* (Cambridge: Cambridge University Press, 1993). The madness of the Caesars was also the subject of an 1894 essay by a German historian called Ludwig Quidde, which was a camouflaged attack on Kaiser Wilhelm II: see Karl Holl, Hans Kloft and Gerd Fesser, *Caligula – Wilhelm II und der Caeserenwahnsinn: Antikenrezeption und wilhelminische Politik am Beispiel des 'Caligula' von Ludwig Quidde* (Bremen: Temmen, 2001).

This chapter examines the relationship between literature and the sciences, a relationship which is garnering growing attention from recent scholars: Laura Otis (ed.), *Literature and Science in the Nineteenth Century: An Anthology* (Oxford: Oxford University Press, 2002); Charlotte Sleigh, *Literature and Science* (Basingstoke: Palgrave Macmillan, 2010); Bruce Clarke and Manuela Rossini (eds), *The Routledge Companion to Literature and Science* (London/New York: Routledge, 2012).

CHAPTER IV

Winckelmann's first published essay can be found in: Johann Joachim Winckelmann, *Kleine Schriften, Vorreden, Entwürfe* (Berlin/New York: Walter de Gruyter, 2002). Several excerpts of Winckelmann's writings can be found translated into English in Johann Joachim Winckelmann, *Selected Writings on Art*, ed. David Irwin (London: Phaidon, 1972). On Winckelmann and his neo-classicist aesthetic, see Whitney Davis, 'Winckelmann divided: mourning the death of art history', in Whitney Davis (ed.), *Lesbian and Gay Studies in Art History* (New York: Haworth Press, 1994), pp. 141–60; Alex Potts, *Flesh and the Ideal: Winckelmann and the Origins of Art History* (New Haven: Yale University Press, 2000); Elizabeth Prettejohn, *Beauty and Art* (Oxford: Oxford University Press,

2005); Élisabeth Décultot, *Johann Joachim Winckelmann: enquête sur la genèse de l'histoire de l'art* (Paris: Presses Universitaires de France, 2000). On German philhellenism, the now classic study is E. A. Butler, *The Tyranny of Greece over Germany: A Study of the Influence Exercised by Greek Art and Poetry over the Great German Writers of the Eighteenth, Nineteenth and Twentieth Centuries* (Cambridge: Cambridge University Press, 2012 [1935]). See also Marchand, *Archaeology and Philhellenism in Germany, 1750–1970* (Princeton: Princeton University Press, 1996); and Miriam Leonard, *Socrates and the Jews: Hellenism and Hebraism from Moses Mendelssohn to Sigmund Freud* (Chicago: Chicago University Press, 2012), for excellent – and more recent – accounts of the German fascination with ancient Greece.

On the relationships between the scientific study of sex and literary writing in the decades around the year 1900, see the enlightening work by Heike Bauer, *English Literary Sexology: Translations of Inversion, 1860–1930* (Basingstoke: Palgrave Macmillan, 2009); and Anna Katharina Schaffner, *Modernism and Perversion: Sexual Deviance in Sexology and Literature, 1850–1930* (Basingstoke: Palgrave Macmillan, 2011).

On the history of encyclopaedias, which includes discussion of the *Allgemeine Encyclopädie*, see Robert Collison, *Encyclopaedias: Their History throughout the Ages: A Bibliographical Guide with Extensive Historical Notes to the General Encyclopaedias Issued throughout the World from 350 BC to the Present Day*, 2nd ed. (New York and London: Hafner Publishing Company, 1966). For those interested in reading Meier's article on Greek pederasty, here are the details: M. H. E. Meier, 'Päderastie', in J. S. Ersch and J. G. Gruber (eds), *Allgemeine Encyclopädie der Wissenschaften und Kunst in alphabetischer Folge von genannten Schriftstellern* (Leipzig: J. F. Gleditsch, 1837), vol. 9, sect. iii, pp. 149–89. It was also translated into French: M. H. E. Meier, *Histoire de l'amour grec dans l'antiquité*, trans. L. R. De Pogey Castries (Paris: Stendhal et Compagnie, 1930).

On nineteenth-century and early twentieth-century discussions and theorisations of same-sex desire, there is a wealth of material. See the following important studies: Eve Kosofsky Sedgwick, *Epistemology of the Closet*

(Berkeley/Los Angeles: University of Californa Press, 1990); Richard Dellamora, *Masculine Desire: The Sexual Politics of Victorian Aestheticism* (New York: Atlantic Books, 1990); Robert Aldrich, *The Seduction of the Mediterranean: Writing, Art and Homosexual Fantasy* (London: Routledge, 1993); Linda Dowling, 'Ruskin's pied beauty and the constitution of a "homosexual" code', *Victorian Newsletter* 75 (1989), pp. 1–8; Linda Dowling, *Hellenism and Homosexuality in Victorian Oxford* (Ithaca: Cornell University Press, 1994); Angus MacLaren, *The Trials of Masculinity: Policing Sexual Boundaries, 1870–1930* (Chicago: University of Chicago Press, 1997); Harry Cocks, *Nameless Offences: Homosexual Desire in the Nineteenth Century* (London: I.B.Tauris, 2003); Sean Brady, *Masculinity and Male Homosexuality in Britain, 1861–1913* (Basingstoke: Palgrave Macmillan, 2010); Matt Cook, *London and the Culture of Homosexuality, 1885–1914* (Cambridge: Cambridge University Press, 2003); Morris Kaplan, *Sodom on the Thames: Sex, Love, and Scandal in Wilde Times* (Ithaca: Cornell University Press, 2005); Daniel Orrells, *Classical Culture and Modern Masculinity* (Oxford: Oxford University Press, 2011).

On the so-called 'gay emancipation movement' in nineteenth-century Germany, see James D. Steakley, *The Homosexual Emancipation Movement in Germany* (New York: Arno, 1975). On Karl Heinrich Ulrichs, see Wolfram Setz (ed.), *Karl Heinrich Ulrichs zu Ehren: Materialen zu Leben und Werk* (Berlin: Rosa Winkel, 2000); Wolfram Setz, *Neue Finde und Studien zu Karl Heinrich Ulrichs* (Berlin: Rosa Winkel, 2004). The essay by Sebastian Matzner, 'From Uranians to homosexuals: Philhellenism, Greek homoeroticism and gay emancipation in Germany 1835–1915', *Classical Receptions Journal* 2:1 (2010), pp. 60–91, explores the issues well. Ulrichs' writings have been translated into English: Karl Heinrich Ulrichs, *The Riddle of 'Man-Manly' Love: The Pioneering Work on Male Homosexuality* (New York: Prometheus Books, 1994). On Karl-Maria Kertbeny, see Julia Takacs, 'The double life of Kertbeny', in Gert Hekma (ed.), *Past and Present of Radical Sexual Politics* (Amsterdam: Mosse Foundation, 2004), pp. 26–40. A collection of Kertbeny's writings has also been issued: Karl-Maria Kertbeny, *Schriften zur Homosexualitätsforschung*, ed. Manfred Herzer (Berlin: Rosa

Winkel, 2000). On the disagreements between Friedländer, Brandt and Hirschfeld, see Matzner, 'From Uranians to homosexuals'. On Hirschfeld, see Ralf Dose, *Magnus Hirschfeld: Deutscher, Jude, Weltbürger* (Teetz: Hentrich und Hentrich, 2005); Manfred Herzer, *Magnus Hirschfeld: Leben und Werk eines jüdischen, schwulen und sozialistischen Sexologen* (Hamburg: Männerschwarm, 2001).

On nineteenth- and early twentieth-century pederasty and Uranian poetry, see Timothy d'Arch Smith, *Love in Earnest: Some Notes on the Lives and Writings of English 'Uranian' Poets from 1889 to 1930* (London: Routledge, 1970), and Michael Matthew Kaylor, *Secreted Desires: The Major Uranians: Hopkins, Pater and Wilde* (Brno: Privately printed, 2006). William Johnson Cory's poetry books are now collectors' items: *Ionica* (London: Smith, Elder & Co., 1858); *Ionica II* (Cambridge: Cambridge University Press, 1877). Another edition of his poems was brought out at the end of his lifetime: *Ionica* (London: George Allen, 1891); finally, a collected edition appeared, *Ionica*, ed. A. C. Benson (London: George Allen, 1905). The longest treatment of his life is: Reginald Baliol Brett Esher, *Ionicus* (London: John Murray, 1923).

John Addington Symonds' writings on ancient Greek and on modern sexuality have been recently re-edited with excellent scholarly introductions and notes. *A Problem in Greek Ethics* and *A Problem in Modern Ethics* can be found in: Sean Brady, *John Addington Symonds (1840–1893) and Homosexuality: A Critical Edition of Sources* (Basingstoke: Palgrave Macmillan, 2012). Havelock Ellis' and Symonds' collaboration can be read in: Henry Havelock Ellis and John Addington Symonds, *Sexual Inversion: A Critical Edition*, ed. Ivan Crozier (Basingstoke: Palgrave Macmillan, 2008). Those interested in reading Symonds' autobiography should consult: John Addington Symonds, *The Memoirs of John Addington Symonds: The Secret Homosexual Life of a Leading Nineteenth-Century Man of Letters*, ed. Phyllis Grosskurth (London: Hutchinson, 1984). On Symonds' writings, his sexuality and his friendship with Benjamin Jowett, see Alastair Blanshard, 'Hellenic fantasies: aesthetics and desire in John Addington Symonds' *A Problem in Greek Ethics*', *Dialogos* 7 (2000), pp. 99–123; John Pemble (ed.),

John Addington Symonds: Culture and the Demon Desire (Basingstoke: Palgrave Macmillan, 2000); Stefano Evangelista, 'Platonic dons, adolescent bodies: Benjamin Jowett, John Addington Symonds, Walter Pater', in George Rousseau, *Children and Sexuality: From the Greeks to the Great War* (Basingstoke: Palgrave Macmillan, 2007), pp. 203–36; Orrells, *Classical Culture and Modern Masculinity*; Daniel Orrells, 'Greek love, orientalism and race: intersections in classical reception', *Cambridge Classical Journal* 58 (2012), pp. 194–230; Gideon Nisbet, *Greek Epigram in Reception: J.A. Symonds, Oscar Wilde and the Invention of Desire, 1805–1929* (Oxford: Oxford University Press, 2013). The political context is mapped out in Jeffrey Weeks, *Coming Out: Homosexual Politics from the Nineteenth Century to the Present* (London: Quartet Books, 1977, rev. ed. 1990). On M. H. E. Meier and Jowett, see Orrells, *Classical Culture and Modern Masculinity*. Benjamin Jowett published his translations of Plato in three editions during his lifetime. Bibliographical details on the third and last edition that Jowett personally worked on are as follows: Benjamin Jowett, *The Dialogues of Plato: Translated into English with Analyses and Introductions* (Oxford: Clarendon Press, 1892). On Jowett's Plato, see Lesley Higgins, 'Jowett and Pater: trafficking in Platonic wares', *Victorian Studies* 31:1 (1993), pp. 43–72. On the legal context, see the very informed H. Cocks, *Nameless Offences: Homosexual Desire in the Nineteenth Century* (London, I.B.Tauris, 2003).

On the poetry of Theocritus, see the sensitive study by Richard Hunter, *Theocritus and the Archaeology of Greek Poetry* (Cambridge: Cambridge University Press, 1996).

Symonds' interest in the past coincided with a Victorian fascination with history more generally, on which see Peter Allan Dale, *The Victorian Critic and the Idea of History: Carlyle, Arnold, Pater* (Cambridge, MA: Harvard University Press, 1977). On the Victorians and classical history, see Richard Jenkyns, *The Victorians and Ancient Greece* (Oxford: Basil Blackwell, 1980); and Simon Goldhill, *Victorian Culture and Classical Antiquity: Art, Opera, Fiction, and the Proclamation of Modernity* (Princeton: Princeton University Press, 2011). Of course, the Victorians were also very interested in ancient Rome (as Goldhill also excellently examines); regarding this issue, see also Norman Vance, *The Victorians and Ancient Rome* (Oxford: Wiley-Blackwell, 1997). On Victorian life-writing, see the excellent Marion Thain, *'Michael Field': Poetry, Aestheticism and the* Fin de Siècle (Cambridge University Press, 2007); and David Amigoni (ed.), *Life Writing and Victorian Culture* (Aldershot: Ashgate Publishing, 2006).

On Walt Whitman, see M. Jimmie Killingsworth, *Whitman's Poetry of the Body: Sexuality, Politics and the Text* (Chapel Hill: University of North Carolina Press, 1989); Michael Moon, *Disseminating Whitman: Revision and Corporeality in Leaves of Grass* (Cambridge, MA: Harvard University Press, 1991); and Bryne R. S. Fone, *Masculine Landscapes: Walt Whitman and the Homoerotic Text* (Carbondale: Southern Illinois University Press, 1992). On Edward Carpenter, see Sheila Rowbotham, *Edward Carpenter: A Life of Liberty and Love* (London/New York: Verso, 2009). On the collaboration between Henry Havelock Ellis and Symonds, see Henry Havelock Ellis and John Addington Symonds, *Sexual Inversion: A Critical Edition*, ed. Ivan Crozier (Basingstoke: Palgrave Macmillan, 2008). On Havelock Ellis himself: Phyllis Grosskurth, *Havelock Ellis: A Biography* (London: Allen Lane, 1980).

CHAPTER V

On female bodies in ancient Greek writing, consult the standard works by Lesley Dean-Jones, *Women's Bodies in Classical Greek Science* (Oxford: Oxford University Press, 1994); and Aline Rouselle, *Porneia: On Desire and the Body in Antiquity* (Oxford: Blackwell, 1993). On ancient female homoeroticism, see Judith P. Hallett, 'Female homoeroticism and the denial of Roman reality in Latin literature', *Yale Journal of Criticism* 3 (1989), pp. 209–27; Bernadette Brooten, *Love Between Women: Early Christian Responses to Female Homoeroticism* (Chicago: University of Chicago Press, 1996); and Sandra Boehringer, *L'homosexualité feminine dans l'antiquité grecque et romaine* (Paris: Belles lettres, 2007). Those keen to consult the sixteenth-century anatomical texts that discuss the female body can consult: Charles Estienne, *La Dissection des parties du corps humain* (Paris: S. de Colines, 1546); Gabriele Falloppio, *Observationes anatomicae* (Venice: M.A.

Ulmum, 1561); and Realdo Colombo, *De re anatomica* (Venice: Nicolò Bevilacqua, 1559). On the clitoris, see Thomas Laqueur, *Making Sex: Body and Gender from the Greeks to Freud* (Cambridge, MA: Harvard University Press, 1992); Katherine Park, 'The rediscovery of the clitoris: French medicine and the tribade, 1570–1620', in Carla Mazzio and David Hillman (eds), *The Body in Parts: Fantasies of Corporeality in Early Modern Europe* (New York: Routledge, 1997), pp. 171–93; and Lesley Hall's article on the clitoris in Colin Blakemore and Sheila Jennett (eds), *The Oxford Campanion to the Body* (Oxford: Oxford University Press, 2001). For critiques of Laqueur's narrative, see Katherine Park, 'Cadden, Laqueur and "The One-Sex Body"', *Medieval Feminist Forum* 46 (2010), pp. 96–100, and Helen King, *The One-Sex Body on Trial: The Classical and Early-Modern Evidence* (Farnham: Ashgate, 2013). On imperial Roman discussions about sexual relations with boys and women, see Simon Goldhill, *Foucault's Virginity: Ancient Erotic Fiction and the History of Sexuality* (Cambridge: Cambridge University Press, 1995). On the relationship between masculinity, the female body, female homoeroticism and transsexuality, see also the important queer theoretical perspective by Judith Halberstam, *Female Masculinity* (Durham, NC: Duke University Press, 1998).

The translation of Galen comes from: Tallmadge May, *Galen on the Usefulness of the Parts of the Body*, 2 vols (Ithaca: Cornell University Press, 1968).

On the debates about women's access to education – in particular a classical education – at the end of the nineteenth century, see Natalie Bluestone, *Women and the Ideal Society: Plato's Republic and Modern Myths of Gender* (Amhurst: University of Massachusetts Press, 1987); Christopher Stray (ed.), *Classics in Nineteenth- and Twentieth-Century Cambridge: Curriculum, Culture and Community*, Cambridge Philological Society, Supplement 24 (Cambridge: Cambridge Philological Society, 1999); Mary Beard, *The Invention of Jane Harrison* (Cambridge, MA: Harvard University Press, 2000); Isobel Hurst, *Victorian Women Writers and the Classics: The Feminine of Homer* (Oxford: Oxford University Press, 2006); Isobel Hurst, '"A fleet of . . . inexperienced Argonauts": Oxford women and the Classics, 1873–1920', in Christopher

Stray (ed.), *Oxford Classics: Teaching and Learning 1800–2000* (London: Duckworth, 2007), pp. 12–27; Yopie Prins, '"Lady's Greek" (with the accents): a metrical translation of Euripides by Mary F. Robinson', *Victorian Literature and Culture* 34:2 (2006), pp. 591–618; T. D. Olverson, *Women Writers and the Dark Side of Late-Victorian Hellenism* (Basingstoke: Palgrave Macmillan, 2010).

On the New Woman in the *fin-de-siècle* context, see the excellent: Elaine Showalter, *Daughters of Decadence: Women's Writers of the Fin-de-Siècle* (Princeton: Princeton University Press, 1993); Sally Ledger and Scott McCracken (eds), *Cultural Politics at the Fin de Siècle* (Cambridge: Cambridge University Press, 1995); Sally Ledger, *The New Woman: Fiction and Feminism at the Fin de Siècle* (Manchester: Manchester University Press, 1997); Sally Ledger and Roger Luckhurst (eds), *The Fin De Siècle: A Read in Cultural History, c. 1880–1900* (Oxford: Oxford University Press, 2000); Angelique Richardson and Chris Willis (eds), *The New Woman in Fiction and in Fact: Fin-de-Siècle Feminisms* (Basingstoke: Palgrave Macmillan, 2002); and Mary Louise Roberts, *Disruptive Acts: The New Woman in Fin-de-Siècle France* (Chicago: Chicago University Press, 2002). The following are also very enlightening: Angelique Richardson (ed.), *Women Who Did: Stories by Men and Women, 1890–1914* (London: Penguin Books, 2005), and Gail Marshall (ed.), *The Cambridge Companion to the Fin de Siècle* (Cambridge: Cambridge University Press, 2007).

The story of Anne Lister is recounted in Anna Clark, 'Anne Lister's construction of lesbian identity', *Journal of the History of Sexuality*, 7:1 (1996), pp. 23–50. Her diary has also been edited and published: Helen Whitbread, *I Know My Own Heart: The Diaries of Anne Lister 1791–1840* (London: Virago, 1988). Alison Oram, 'Sexuality in heterotopia: time, space and love between women in the historic house', *Women's History Review* 21:4 (2012), pp. 533–51, is a very interesting article which examines Lister's sense of the the past in the gothic and mock-Tudor 'home improvements' she made at her family seat in Yorkshire. Those interested in reading about Sappho in Pierre Bayle can consult: *Historical and Critical Dictionary*

. . . *The 2nd ed. . . . edited, revised and corrected and enlarged by Mr. Des Maizeaux*, 5 vols (London: J. J. and P. Knapton et al., 1734–8).

Many excellent histories of female same-sex desire and politics in the nineteenth and early twentieth century exist. Some of the most enjoyable and important include: Lillian Faderman, *Surpassing the Love of Men: Romantic Friendship and Love Between Women from the Renaissance to the Present* (London: The Women's Press, 1985); Terry Castle, *The Apparitional Lesbian: Female Homosexuality and Modern Culture* (New York: Columbia University Press, 1995); Laura Doan, *Fashioning Sapphism: The Origins of a Modern English Lesbian Culture* (New York: Columbia University Press, 2001); Alison Oram and Annemarie Turnbull, *The Lesbian History Sourcebook: Love and Sex between Women in Britain from 1780 to 1970* (London: Routledge, 2001); Martha Vicinus, *Intimate Friends: Women who Loved Women, 1728–1928* (Chicago: Chicago University Press, 2004); Sally Newman, 'The archival traces of desire: Vernon Lee's failed sexuality and the interpretation of letters in lesbian history', *Journal of the History of Sexuality* 14:1/2 (2005), pp. 51–75; and Sharon Marcus, *Between Women: Friendship, Desire, and Marriage in Victorian England* (Princeton: Princeton University Press, 2007).

Female same-sex sexuality in sexology has recently received some splendid scholarly analyses: Claudia Breger, 'Feminine masculinities: scientific and literary representations of "female inversion" at the turn of the twentieth century', *Journal of the History of Sexuality* 14:1/2 (2005), pp. 76–106; Heike Bauer, 'Theorizing female inversion: sexology, discipline, and gender at the fin de siècle', *Journal of the History of Sexuality* 18:1 (2009), pp. 84–102; Heike Bauer, *English Literary Sexology: Translations of Inversion, 1860–1930* (Basingstoke: Palgrave Macmillan, 2009); Chiara Beccalossi, 'The origin of Italian sexological studies: female sexual inversion ca. 1870–1900', *Journal of the History of Sexuality* 18:1 (2009), pp. 103–20; and Chiara Beccalossi, *Female Sexual Inversion: Same-Sex Desires in Italian and British Sexology, c. 1870–1920* (Basingstoke: Palgrave Macmillan, 2012).

Bibliographical details for Kenyon's *editio princeps* of Herodas are: Frederic Kenyon (ed.), *Classical Texts from Papyri in the British Museum*

Including the Newly Discovered Poems of Herodas (London: Oxford Clarendon Press, 1891). Headlam's edition of Herodas has been recently reprinted: Walter Headlam, *Herodas: The Mimes and Fragments*, ed. A. D. Knox (London: Bristol Classical Press, 2001). On Headlam and Herodas' dildo see Daniel Orrells, 'Headlam's Herodas: the art of suggestion', in Stephen Harrison and Christopher Stray (eds), *Expurgating the Classics: Editing Out in Latin and Greek* (London: Bristol Classical Press, 2012), pp. 53–72. On the colonial contexts for the discovery of papyri in 1880s British-occupied Egypt, see David Fearn, 'Imperialist fragmentation and the discovery of Bacchylides', in Mark Bradley (ed.), *Classics and Imperialism in the British Empire* (Oxford University Press: Oxford, 2010), pp. 158–85. On Walter Headlam and his scholarship, the following interesting studies can be consulted: Simon Goldhill, *Who Needs Greek? Contests in the Cultural History of Hellenism* (Cambridge University Press: Cambridge, 2002); and Michael Silk, 'Walter Headlam: scholarship, poetry, poetics', in Christopher Stray (ed.), *The Owl of Minerva: The Cambridge Praelections of 1906: Reassessments of Richard Jebb, James Adam, Walter Headlam, Henry Jackson, William Ridgeway and Arthur Verrall*, PCPS Supplementary Vol. 28 (Cambridge Faculty of Classics: Cambridge, 2005), pp. 69–86. On obscenity in Greek, see the standard work: Jeffrey Henderson, *The Maculate Muse: Obscene Language in Attic Comedy*, 2nd ed. (New York/London: Oxford University Press, 1991).

For those interested in following up the scholarship that Headlam examined: Jane Harrison, *Prolegomena to the Study of Greek Religion* (Cambridge: Cambridge University Press, 1903); and on Harrison, see Yopie Prins, 'Greek Maenads, Victorian Spinsters', in Richard Dellamora (ed.), *Victorian Sexual Dissidence* (Chicago/London: University of Chicago Press, 1999), pp. 43–82. Burton's infamous translation: Richard F. Burton, *A Plain and Literal Translation of the Arabian Nights' Entertainments, now Entitled: The Books of the Thousand Nights and a Night, with Introduction, Explanatory Notes on the Manners and Customs of Moslem Men and a Terminal Essay upon the History of The Nights*, 10 vols (Printed by the Burton Club for Private Subscribers Only, 1885–8).

One of my favourite modern renderings of Sappho is Anne Carson, *If Not, Winter: Fragments of Sappho* (New York/London: Virago Press, 2003). The history of Sappho's reception has received excellent treatment from Joan DeJean, *Fictions of Sappho, 1546–1937* (Chicago: Chicago University Press, 1989); Yopie Prins, *Victorian Sappho* (Princeton: Princeton University Press, 1999); and Simon Goldhill, *Victorian Culture and Classical Antiquity: Art, Opera, Fiction, and the Proclamation of Modernity* (Princeton: Princeton University Press, 2011). On the construction of Sappho as a schoolteacher, a characterisation which continued right into the end of the twentieth century, see the excellent survey by Holt Parker, 'Sappho Schoolmistress', *Transactions of the American Philological Association* 123 (1993), pp. 309–51. For Symonds' analysis of Sappho, see John Addington Symonds, *Studies of the Greek Poets* (London: Smith, Elder and Company, 1873). Full bibliographical details on Wharton's Sappho: Henry Thornton Wharton, *Sappho: Memoir, Text, Selected Renderings* (London: Stott, 1885).

On Michael Field, enjoy the following superb studies: Yopie Prins, 'Sappho Doubled: Michael Field', *Yale Journal of Criticism* 8 (1995), pp. 165–86; Christine White, 'The Tiresian Poet: Michael Field', in *Victorian Women Poets: A Critical Reader*, ed. Angela Leighton (Oxford: Blackwell, 1996), pp. 148–61; Christine White, '"Poets and lovers evermore": interpreting female love in the poetry and the journals of Michael Field', *Textual Practice* 4:2 (1990), pp. 197–212; Margaret D. Stetz and Cheryl A. Wilson (eds), *Michael Field and Their World* (High Wycombe: Rivendale Press, 2007); Marion Thain, *'Michael Field': Poetry, Aestheticism and the Fin de Siècle* (Cambridge: Cambridge University Press, 2007); Marion Thain and Ana Parejo Vadillo (eds), *Michael Field, the Poet: Published and Manuscript Materials* (Broadview Editions: Toronto, 2009); and Stefano Evangelista, *British Aestheticism and Ancient Greece: Hellenism, Reception, Gods in Exile* (Basingstoke: Palgrave Macmillan, 2009). Their love letters have been collected in: Sharon Bickle (ed.), *The Fowl and the Pussycat: Love Letters of Michael Field, 1876–1909* (Charlottesville: University of Virginia Press, 2008).

CHAPTER VI

On Havelock Ellis, see Phyllis Grosskurth, *Havelock Ellis: A Biography* (London: Allen Lane, 1980); Henry Havelock Ellis and John Addington Symonds, *Sexual Inversion: A Critical Edition*, ed. Ivan Crozier (Basingstoke: Palgrave Macmillan, 2008). On a comparison between Ellis' and Freud's methodologies, see Ivan Crozier, 'Taking prisoners: Havelock Ellis, Sigmund Freud, and the construction of homosexuality, 1897–1951', *Social History of Medicine* 13:3 (2000), pp. 447–66. On Krafft-Ebing and Freud, see also Heinrich Ammerer, *Krafft-Ebing, Freud und die Erfindung der Perversion: Versuch einer Einkreisung* (Tectum: Marburg, 2006).

Freud's first mention of his theory about Oedipus appeared in writing in a letter to Wilhelm Fliess: Jeffrey Moussaieff Masson (ed.), *The Complete Letters of Sigmund Freud to Wilhelm Fliess, 1977–1905* (Cambridge/London: Belknap Press of Harvard University Press, 1985).

Freud's works have been translated into English and published in a monumental edition: Sigmund Freud, *The Standard Edition of the Complete Psychological Works of Sigmund Freud*, 24 vols, ed. James Strachey in collaboration with Anna Freud, assisted by Alix Strachey and Alan Tyson (London: The Hogarth Press and the Institute of Psycho-analysis, 1953–74). The articles and books discussed in Chapter VI of this book come from the following: 'The Aetiology of Hysteria', 3, pp. 187–221; *Three Essays on Sexuality*, 7, pp. 123–243; *The Interpretation of Dreams*, 4–5; 'The Sexual Enlightenment of Children', 9, pp. 129–40; 'On the Sexual Theories of Children', 9, pp. 205–26; *Leonardo da Vinci and A Memory of His Childhood*, 11, pp. 59–138; 'Great is Diana of the Ephesians', 12, pp. 342–4; 'On Narcissism', 14, pp. 67–102; 'Contributions to the Psychology of Love 1: A Special Type of Choice Made by Men', 11, pp. 163–75; 'Medusa's Head', 18, pp. 273–4; 'The Infantile Genital Organisation: An Interpolation into the Theory of Sexuality, 19, pp. 141–8; 'The Dissolution of the Oedipus Complex', 19, pp. 173–82; 'Some Psychical Consequences of the Anatomical Distinction between the Sexes', 19, pp. 241–60, 'Fetishism', 21, pp. 147–58; 'Female Sexuality', 21, pp. 221–46; 'Femininity', 22, pp. 112–35; 'Analysis Terminable and Interminable', 23, pp. 209–54. Those interested in reading Freud's theorisations about sexuality in one handy volume might consult: Sigmund Freud, *The Psychology of Love* (London: Penguin, 2006), where some of the articles cited here are published in a new translation along with a scholarly introduction.

Among the numerous book on Freud, women and sexual desire, see the wonderful: Sarah Kofman, *The Enigma of Woman: Woman in Freud's Writings*, trans. Catherin Porter (Ithaca: Cornell University Press, 1985); and the superb: Lisa Appignanesi and John Forrester, *Freud's Woman* (London: Penguin, 2000).

On the sensational archaeology of the second half of the nineteenth century, especially that of Heinrich Schliemann, see the excellent account given in Cathy Gere, *The Tomb of Agamemnon: Mycenae and the Search for a Hero* (London: Profile, 2007).

On Freud and the ancient world from a range of very interesting perspectives, see: Peter Rudntysky, *Freud and Oedipus* (New York: Columbia University Press, 1987); G. Santas, *Plato and Freud: Two Theories of Love* (Oxford: Oxford University Press, 1988); Jacques Le Rider, *Freud, de l'Acropole au Sinaï: Le retour à l'antiquité des modernes viennois* (Paris: Presses universitaires de France, 2002); Richard Armstrong, *Freud and the Ancient World: A Compulsion for Antiquity* (Ithaca and London: Cornell University Press, 2005); Rachel Bowlby, *Freudian Mythologies: Greek Tragedy and Modern Identities* (Oxford: Oxford University Press, 2007); Daniel Orrells, 'Derrida's impression of Gradiva: *Mal d'archive* and antiquity', in Miriam Leonard (ed.), *Derrida and Antiquity* (Oxford: Oxford University Press, 2010), pp. 159–84; Daniel Orrells, *Classical Culture and Modern Masculinity* (Oxford: Oxford University Press, 2011); 'Ghosts, rocks and footprints: Freudian archaeology', in Shelley Hales and Joanna Paul (eds), *Pompeii in the Public Imagination from its Rediscovery to Today* (Oxford: Oxford University Press, 2011), pp. 185–98; 'Freud's phallic symbol', in Ellen O'Gorman and Vanda Zajko (eds), *Classical Myth and Psychoanalysis* (Oxford: Oxford University Press, 2013), pp. 39–57; Miriam Leonard, *Socrates and the Jews: Hellenism and Hebraism from Moses Mendelssohn to Sigmund Freud* (Chicago: Chicago University Press, 2012); Miriam Leonard, 'Freud and tragedy: Oedipus and the gender of the universal', *Classical Receptions Journal* 5:1 (2013), pp. 63–83. Freud's collection of antiquities can be viewed in Lynne Gamwell and Richard Wells, *Sigmund Freud and Art: His Personal Collections of Antiquities* (London: Freud Museum, in association with Abrams, New York, 1989). On the emergence of Freud from a history of aesthetic and art theory, see Whitney Davis, *Queer Beauty: Sexuality and Aesthetics from Winckelmann to Freud and Beyond* (New York: Columbia University Press, 2010).

For those interested in following up Niebuhr's scholarship, see Georg Barthold Niebuhr, *Römische Geschichte* (Berlin: G. Reimer, 1811–12). Richard Armstrong, *Freud and the Ancient World* analyses Freud's reading of Niebuhr. For those curious about Arthur Evans and the impact of ancient Crete on early twentieth-century cultural history, see Cathy Gere, *Knossos and the Prophets of Modernism* (Chicago: University of Chicago Press, 2009). On Johan Bachofen, see Lionel Gossman, 'Basle, Bachofen and the critique of modernity in the second half of the nineteenth century', *Journal of the Warburg and Courtauld Institutes* 47 (1984), pp. 136–85. The archaeological reports about Asia Minor which helped Freud to write 'Great is Diana of the Ephesians' were published as: Félix Sartiaux, *Villes mortes d'Asia mineure: Pergame, Éphèse, Priène, Milet, le Didymeion, Hiérapolis* (Paris: Librairie Hachette et Co., 1911).

Winckelmann's famous description of the Apollo Belvedere can be enjoyed in: Johann Joachim Winckelmann, *History of the Art of Antiquity*, trans. Harry Francis Mallgrave (Los Angeles: Getty Publications, 2006). An important reading of Winckelmann's work can be found in: Alex Potts, *Flesh and the Ideal: Winckelmann and the Origins of Art History* (New Haven/London: Yale University Press, 2000).

For those interested in the history of the science of sexual difference, see the important work of Thomas Laqueur, *Making Sex: Body and Gender from the Greeks to Freud* (Cambridge, MA: Harvard University Press, 1992). For critiques of Laqueur's narrative, see Katherine Park, 'Cadden, Laqueur and "The One-Sex Body"', *Medieval Feminist Forum* 46 (2010), pp. 96–100, and Helen King, *The One-Sex Body on Trial: The Classical and Early-Modern Evidence* (Farnham: Ashgate, 2013).

On the impact of Zeuxis' *ars combinatoria* on German thought, see Joel Black, 'The aesthetics of gender: Zeuxis' maidens and the hermaphroditic ideal', *New York Literary Forum* 8–9 (1981), pp. 189–209. On the history of German writing on hermaphroditism, see the excellent Catriona MacLeod, *Embodying Ambiguity: Androgyny and Aesthetics from Winckelmann to Keller* (Detroit: Wayne State University Press, 1998); and Eleanor Ter Horst, *Lessing, Goethe, Kleist, and the Transformation of Gender: From Hermaphrodite to Amazon* (New York: Peter Lang, 2003). Hermaphroditism was, of course, of great interest to sexology: see the very interesting and moving Alice Domurat Dreger, *Hermaphrodites and the Medical Invention of Sex* (Cambridge, MA: Harvard University Press, 1998); and Geertje Mak, *Doubting Sex: Inscriptions, Bodies and Selves in Nineteenth-Century Hermaphrodite Case Studies* (Manchester: Manchester University Press, 2012). Sexology inherited many ideas from classical antiquity via the Renaissance and the early-modern period: Lorraine Daston and Katharine Park, 'The hermaphrodite and the orders of nature: sexual ambiguity in early modern France', *GLQ* 1 (1995), pp. 419–38; and Ruth Gilbert, *Early Modern Hermaphrodites: Sex and Other Stories* (Basingstoke: Palgrave Macmillan, 2002).

The references for the art-historical works cited in this chapter are as follows: M[onsieur] C[ésar] F[amin], *Peintures, bronzes et statues érotiques, formant la collection du cabinet secret du Musée Royal de Naples* (Paris: Typographie Everat, 1832); Louis Barré et al., *Herculaneum et Pompéi: Récueil general des peintures, bronzes, mosaïques, etc . . . gravés au trait sur cuivre par M. Roux aîné* (Paris, 1839–40). These are discussed in Whitney Davis' interesting essay, 'Homoerotic art collection from 1750 to 1920', *Art History* 24:2 (2001), pp. 247–77.

Those interested in Conradus Leemans edition of Horapollo can enjoy reading: *Horapollinis . . . Hieroglyphica Edidit . . . versionem Latinam subjunxit, adnotationem, item hieroglyphicorum imagines et indices adjecit, C. Leemans. Gr. and Lat* (Amsterdam, 1835).

On the conflicted reception of psychoanalysis in queer theory, see the thought-provoking essays collected in Tim Dean and Christopher Lane (eds), *Homosexuality and Queer Theory* (Chicago: Chicago University Press, 2001).

NOTES

Introduction

1 See Stephen Marcus, *The Other Victorians: A Study of Sexuality and Pornography in Mid-Nineteenth Century England* (London: Weidenfeld and Nicolson, 1967) and Ronald Pearsall, *The Worm in the Bud: The World of Victorian Sexuality* (London: Weidenfeld and Nicolson, 1969).
2 For a history of the 'sexual revolution' of the 1960s, see David Allyn, *Make Love, Not War: The Sexual Revolution – An Unfettered History* (London: Little, Brown and Company, 2001).
3 Michel Foucault, *The History of Sexuality*, vol. 1*: The Will to Knowledge*, trans. Robert Hurley (London: Penguin, 1998), p. 43.
4 See Foucault, *History*, vol. 1, pp. 17–35, and also Lawrence Stone, *The Family, Sex and Marriage in England 1500–1800*, 2nd ed. (London: Penguin, 1990).
5 Foucault, *History*, vol. 1, p. 43.
6 Foucault, *History*, vol. 1, p. 22. Anonymous, *My Secret Life* (New York: Grove Press, 1966). See Stephen Marcus, *The Other Victorians*: *A Study of Sexuality and Pornography in Mid-Nineteenth Century England* (London: Weidenfeld and Nicolson, 1967) on *My Secret Life*.
7 Christopher Craft, *Another Kind of Love: Male Homosexual Desire in English Discourse, 1850–1920* (Los Angeles: University of California Press, 1994), offers a lucid account of the transformation of legal discussions of sodomy into medical analyses of the homosexual.
8 See the introduction in Michel Foucault, *The History of Sexuality*, vol. 2: *The Use of Pleasure* trans. Robert Hurley (London: Penguin, 1998). See also David Halperin, *One Hundred Years of Homosexuality and Other Essays on Greek Love* (New York/London: Routledge, 1990), on Foucault's change of focus from the modern to the ancient world.
9 Foucault, *History*, vol. 2, p. 44.
10 See Michel Foucault, *The History of Sexuality*, vol. 3: *The Care of the Self*, trans. Robert Hurley (London: Penguin, 1998).
11 See Foucault, *History*, vol. 2, pp. 194–5.

12 See the very interesting work collected in David H. J. Larmour, Paul Allen Miller and Charles Platter (eds), *Rethinking Sexuality: Foucault and Classical Antiquity* (Princeton: Princeton University Press, 1998). See also Wolfgang Detel, *Foucault and Classical Antiquity: Power, Ethics and Knowledge*, trans. David Wigg-Wolf (Cambridge: Cambridge University Press, 2005).

13 See important discussion in Simon Goldhill, *Foucault's Virginity: Ancient Erotic Fiction and the History of Sexuality* (Cambridge: Cambridge University Press, 1995).

14 See David M. Halperin, John J. Winkler and Froma I. Zeitlin (eds), *Before Sexuality: The Construction of Erotic Experience in the Ancient Greek World* (Princeton: Princeton University Press, 1991); Halperin, *One Hundred Years of Homosexuality*; David Halperin, *How to do the History of Homosexuality* (Chicago: University of Chicago Press, 2002); Amy Richlin, *The Garden of Priapus: Sexuality and Aggression in Roman Humor* (Oxford: Oxford University Press, 1992); and Amy Richlin, 'Not before homosexuality: the materiality of the Cinaedus and the Roman law against love between men', *Journal of the History of Sexuality* 3:4 (1993), pp. 523–73.

15 See James Davidson, *The Greeks and Greek Love: A Radical Reappraisal of Homosexuality in Ancient Greece* (London: Weidenfeld and Nicolson, 2007). See also Foucault, *History*, vol. 2, p. 194, for Foucault's comments on sexual relations between adult men in ancient Greece.

16 On Krafft-Ebing and his work, see Harry Oosterhuis, *Stepchildren of Nature: Krafft-Ebing, Psychiatry and the Making of Sexual Identity* (Chicago: University of Chicago, 2000).

17 R. von Krafft-Ebing, *Psychopathia Sexualis, with Especial Reference to Contrary Sexual Instinct: A Medico-legal Study* (Philadelphia: F.A. Davis, 1894), p. v.

18 See Jonathan Walters, 'Invading the Roman body: manliness and impenetrability in Roman thought', in Judith P. Hallett and Marilyn B. Skinner (eds), *Roman Sexualities* (Princeton: Princeton University Press, 1997) pp. 29–43, and Hallett and Skinner, *Roman Sexualities*, more generally.

19 Simon Goldhill, 'On knowingness', *Critical Inquiry* 32:4 (2006), p. 711.

20 Goldhill, 'On knowingness', p. 716.

21 Simon Goldhill, *Victorian Culture and Classical Antiquity: Art, Opera, Fiction, and the Proclamation of Modernity* (Princeton: Princeton University Press, 2011) is a very thorough examination of the role classical antiquity played in how history was defined in the nineteenth century.

22 On the idea that ancient Greece did provide nineteenth-century men with a code to express and name their desires, see Linda Dowling, 'Ruskin's pied beauty and the constitution of a "homosexual" code', *Victorian Newsletter* 75 (1989).

23 Foucault, *History*, vol. 1, p. 69.

Chapter I

1 See Antonio Beccadelli, *The Hermaphrodite*, ed. and trans. Holt Parker (Cambridge, MA: Harvard University Press, 2010), pp. viii–xiii on Beccadelli's life.

2 On the reception of Beccadelli's book, see Beccadelli, *The Hermaphrodite*, p. xiii–xvi.
3 Quoted in Paula Findlen, 'Humanism, politics and pornography in Renaissance Italy', in Lynn Hunt (ed.), *The Invention of Pornography* (Cambridge, MA: Zone Books, 1993), p. 55.
4 My discussion of Catullus here in the Renaissance relies on Julia Haig Gaissner, *Catullus and his Renaissance Readers* (Oxford: Oxford University Press, 1993); and Julia Haig Gaissner, 'Catullus in the Renaissance', in Marilyn Skinner (ed.), *A Companion to Catullus* (Oxford: Blackwell, 2007), pp. 439–460. On erotic and obscene poetry in neo-Latin, see the essays collected in Ingrid De Smet and Philip Ford (eds), *Eros et Priapus: Erotism et obscénité dans la littérature néo-latine* (Geneva: Librairie Droz, 1997). On Renaissance sexuality more generally, the essays collected in Bette Talvacchia (ed.), *A Cultural History of Sexuality in the Renaissance* (London: Bloomsbury Academic, 2012) make interesting reading and point to a huge bibliography.
5 Pontano's poem and Poliziano's scholarship are most recently discussed in Gaissner, 'Catullus in the Renaissance', pp. 441–5.
6 William Fitzgerald, *Catullan Provocations: Lyric and the Drama of Position* (Los Angeles: University of California Press, 1995), p. 63.
7 Ibid., p. 66.
8 See Jonathan Walters, 'Invading the Roman body: manliness and impenetrability in Roman thought', in Judith P. Hallett and Marilyn B. Skinner (eds), *Roman Sexualities* (Princeton: Princeton University Press, 1997) pp. 29–43.
9 Ralph Hexter and Daniel Selden (eds), *Innovations of Antiquity: The New Ancient World* (New York: Routledge, 1992), p. 478.
10 All translations of Beccadelli come from Holt Parker's edition of *The Hermaphrodite* (Cambridge, MA: Harvard University Press, 2010). Parker's introduction also lays out the book's possible links with contemporary Italian poetry (Beccadelli, 2010, pp. xxiv–xxvi). On neo-Latin epigram more generally, see the essays collected in Susanna de Beer, Karl A. E. Enenkel and David Rijser (eds), *The Neo-Latin Epigram: A Learned and Witty Genre* (Leuven: Leuven University Press, 2009).
11 Victoria Rimell, *Martial's Rome: Empire and the Ideology of Epigram* (Cambridge: Cambridge University Press, 2008), pp. 41–2. On Martial's epigrams, see also William Fitzgerald, *Martial: The World of Epigram* (Chicago: University of Chicago Press, 2007).
12 Rimell, *Martial's Rome,* p. 10.
13 Ibid., pp. 19–24, 52–93.
14 On the homoerotics of Renaissance humanism, see Leonard Barkan, *Transuming Passion: Ganymede and the Erotics of Humanism* (Stanford: Stanford University Press, 1991), especially pp. 48–59 and 66–74.
15 The debates are helpfully laid out in Beccadelli, *The Hermaphrodite*, pp. 128–203.
16 See Poggio's letter in ibid., pp. 130–9.
17 Ibid., pp. 150–1.
18 Ibid., pp. 176–7.
19 Ibid., pp. 184–5. See also Porcellio's other poem, pp. 178–85.

20 Porcellio himself penned pederastic verse and was denounced for it by other writers: see ibid., p. 256, n.93.

Chapter II

1 See also Leonard Barkan, *Transuming Passion: Ganymede and the Erotics of Humanism* (Stanford: Stanford University Press, 1991).
2 Antonio Beccadelli, *The Hermaphrodite*, ed. and trans. Holt Parker (Cambridge, MA: Harvard University Press, 2010), p. 115.
3 On Plato and the Italian Renaissance, see the important works of James Hankins: *Plato in the Italian Renaissance*, 2 vols (Leiden: E.J. Brill, 1990), and *Humanism and Platonism in the Italian Renaissance* (Rome: Edizioni di storia e letteratura, 2003–4), from which the account here draws.
4 Ibid.
5 These discussions about Platonic love in the Italian Renaissance are elegantly summarised in the excellent Alastair J. L. Blanshard, *Sex: Vice and Love from Antiquity to Modernity* (Chichester: Wiley-Blackwell, 2010), p. 124–35.
6 See Hankins, *Plato in the Italian Renaissance*, vol. 1, p. 313, and Maude Vanhaelen, 'Marsile Ficin, traducteur et interprète du *Charmide* de Platon', *Accademia Revue de la Société Marsile Ficin* 3 (2001) pp. 23–52.
7 Jayne Sears, *Marsilio Ficino: Commentary on Plato's Symposium* (Columbia: University of Missouri, 1944), pp. 117, 233. On Ficino more generally, see Mikhail Oskar Kristeller, *The Philosophy of Marsilio Ficino*, trans. Virginia Conant (New York: Columbia University Press, 1943), and Michael Shepherd (ed.), *Friend to Mankind: Marsilio Ficino (1433–1499)* (London: Shepheard-Walwyn, 1999).
8 On Renaissance sculpture, see Francis Haskell and Nicolas Penny, *Taste and the Antique: The Lure of Classical Sculpture 1500–1900* (New Haven: Yale University Press, 1981); Leonard Barkan, *Unearthing the Past: Archaeology and Aesthetics in the Making of Renaissance Culture* (New Haven: Yale University Press, 1999); and Kathleen Wren Christian, *Empire Without End: Antiquities Collections in Renaissance Rome, c. 1350-1527* (New Haven: Yale University Press, 2010). On Donatello's *David* see Horst Woldemar, *The Sculpture of Donatello* (Princeton: Princeton University Press, 1963). On Michelangelo and the nude male form, see Margaret Walters, *The Male Nude: A New Perspective* (London: Paddington Press, 1978).
9 See notes in Lynne Lawner, *I Modi: The Sixteen Pleasures* (Evanston: Northwestern University Press, 1988). On Romano's images, see Bette Talvacchia, *Taking Positions: On the Erotic in Renaissance Culture* (Princeton: Princeton University Press, 1999). And on Aretino, see Raymond Waddington, *Aretino's Satyr: Sexuality, Satire and Self-Projection in the Sixteenth Century Literature and Art* (Toronto: University of Toronto Press, 2003).
10 Holt Parker, 'Love's body anatomized: the ancient erotic handbooks and the rhetoric of sexuality', pp. 90–111, in Amy Richlin (ed.), *Pornography and Representation in Greece and Rome* (Oxford: Oxford University Press, 1992), p. 93.
11 Quoted in Parker, 'Love's body anatomized', p. 94.

12 Victoria Rimell, *Ovid's Lovers: Desire, Difference and the Poetic Imagination* (Cambridge: Cambridge University Press, 2006), p. 71. The discussion of Ovid's *Ars Amatoria* relies here on Rimell's excellent reading.

13 Ibid., p. 86.

14 Ibid., p. 92, whose translation I use here. See also the enjoyable discussion on pp. 89–94.

15 See Jonathan Walters, 'Invading the Roman body: manliness and impenetrability in Roman thought', pp. 29–43, in Judith P. Hallett and Marilyn B. Skinner (eds), *Roman Sexualities* (Princeton: Princeton University Press, 1997).

16 For a modern English translation of de Pizan, originally written in French, see Christine de Pizan, *The Book of the City of Ladies*, trans. and with an introduction and notes by Rosalind Brown-Grant (London: Penguin, 1999). On de Pizan's book, see Maureen Quilligan, *The Allegory of Female Authority: Christine de Pizan's* Cité des Dames (Ithaca: Cornell University Press, 1991).

17 On the Renaissance woman and education, see Joan Kelly, 'Did women have a Renaissance?', in *Women, History, and Theory: The Essays of Joan Kelly* (Chicago: Chicago University Press, 1984); Jeanie R. Brink, *Female Scholars: A Tradition of Learned Women before 1800* (Montreal: Eden University Women's Publications, 1980); Margaret King, *Women of the Renaissance* (Chicago: University of Chicago Press, 1991); Constance Jordan, 'Women defending women: arguments against patriarchy in Italian women writers', pp. 55–67, in Maria Ornella Marotti (ed.), *Italian Women Writers from the Renaissance to the Present: Revising the Canon* (University Park, Pennsylvania: Pennsylvania State University Press, 1996); Merry E. Wiesner, *Women and Gender in Early Modern Europe* (Cambridge: Cambridge University Press, 2000); and the review article by Holly S. Hurlburt, 'A Renaissance for Renaissance Women?', *Journal of Women's History* 19:2 (2007), pp. 193–201, which points to recent bibliography.

18 On Tullia's life as a courtesan and as a writer, see the introduction in Tulla d'Aragona, *Dialogue on the Infinity of Love*, ed. and trans. Rinaldina Russell and Bruce Merry (Chicago: Chicago University Press, 1997). On the writings of courtesans in the Italian Renaissance, see Fiora A. Bassanese, 'Private lives and public lies: texts by courtesans of the Italian Renaissance', *Texas Studies in Literature and Language* 30:3 (1988), pp. 295–319. On courtesan culture more generally, see Tessa Storey, 'Courtesan culture: manhood, honour and sociability', in Sara F. Matthews-Grieco (ed.), *Erotic Cultures of Renaissace Italy* (Farnham: Ashgate, 2010), pp. 247–73.

19 See Storey, 'Courtesan culture'.

20 See Valeria Finucci, *The Lady Vanishes: Subjectivity and Representation in Ariosto and Castiglione* (Stanford: Stanford University Press, 1992), pp. 29–45; and Virginia Cox, 'Seen but not heard: the role of women speakers in the Cinquecento literary dialogue', pp. 385–400, in Letizia Panizza (ed.), *Women in Italian Renaissance Culture and Society* (Oxford: Legenda European Humanities Research Centre, 2000).

21 On Tullia's *Dialogo*, see Elizabeth A. Pallitto, *Laura's Laurels: Re-Visioning Platonism and Petrarchism in the Philosophy and Poetry of Tullia d'Aragona*,

PhD dissertation, The City University of New York, 2002, and the introduction to d'Aragona, *Infinity of Love*. On the Latin and Greek poetry of other female Italian humanists, see Holt Parker, 'Latin and Greek poetry by five Renaissance Italian woman humanists', in Barbara K. Gold, Paul Allen Miller and Charles Platter (eds), *Sex and Gender in Medieval and Renaissance Texts: The Latin Tradition* (New York: State University of New York Press, 1997), pp. 247–85.

22 See d'Aragona, *Infinity of Love*, p. 90.

23 Pallitto, *Laura's Laurels*, p. 51.

24 On Varchi's erotic interests for boys and male pupils, see Pallitto, *Laura's Laurels*, p. 52, and Louis Crompton, *Homosexuality and Civilization* (Cambridge Massachusetts: Harvard University Press, 2003), pp. 276–7.

25 See d'Aragona, *Infinity of Love*, pp. 95–6. In the quotations from Tullia's dialogue, I have followed Pallitto's more precise translation: see Pallitto, *Laura's Laurels*, p. 54.

26 Varchi would indeed have reminded Tullia's readers of Ficino: in his defence of Plato and Socrates, he compares their love to that found in the Song of Solomon (d'Aragona, *Infinity of Love*, p. 96), just as Ficino had done in his commentary on his *Phaedrus* translation (see Hankins, *Plato in the Italian Renaissance*, vol. 1, p. 313, n. 130).

27 See Pallitto, *Laura's Laurels*, on Tullia's use of Italian intended for a wider readership.

28 Haskell and Penny, *Taste and the Antique*, pp. 37, 42.

29 Susan James, *Passion and Action: The Emotions in Seventeenth-Century Philosophy* (Oxford: Oxford University Press, 1997), p. 291.

30 See Thomas Hobbes, *Humane Nature, or The Fundamental Elements of Policie, Being a Discoverie of the Faculties, Acts, and Passions of the Soul of Man, from their Original Causes, according to such Philosophical Principles as are not Commonly Known or Asserted* (London: printed by T. Newcomb, for Fra: Bowman of Oxon, 1650), p. 107, which is also cited at James Grantham Turner, *Schooling Sex: Libertine Literature and Erotic Education in Italy, France and England 1534–1685* (Oxford: Oxford University Press, 2003), p. 19.

31 Turner, *Schooling Sex*, p. 16. Turner's excellent account underpins my account of seventeenth-century materialist thinking.

32 On Comenius, see ibid., pp. 47–8.

33 The edition from which I have cited is that by Bruno Lavagnini, *Aloisiae Sigeae Toletanae Satyra Sotadica de Arcanis Amoris et Veneris sive Joannis Meursii Elegantiae Latini Sermonis* (Catania: Romeo Prampolini, 1935). The first number in Roman numerals refers to the dialogue (the *Satyra Sotadica* comprises seven dialogues), and the second number refers to the page number of the 1935 edition.

34 On the engagement with classical texts in the *Satyra Sotadica*, see also Lise Leibacher-Ouvrard, 'Transtextualité et construction de la sexualité: la *Satyra Sotadica* de Chorier', *L'Esprit créateur* 35:2 (1995), pp. 51–66; and Turner, *Schooling Sex*, pp. 165–220.

35 See Jeremy Dimmick, 'Ovid in the Middle Ages: authority and poetry', in Philip Hardie (ed.), *The Cambridge Companion to Ovid* (Cambridge:

Cambridge University Press, 2002), pp. 264–87, which explores the medieval attempts to tame and moralise Ovid's ambivalent and often transgressive poetics, especially pp. 278–80.

36 See Thomas E. Jenkins, 'The writing in (and of) Ovid's Byblis episode', *Harvard Studies in Classical Philology* 100 (2000), pp. 439–51.

37 On Ausonius' re-writing of Virgil, see Scott McGill, *Virgil Recomposed: The Mythological and Secular Centos in Antiquity* (New York/Oxford: Oxford University Press, 2005), pp. 92–114.

38 See Sears, *Marsilio Ficino*, pp. 117, 233.

39 See Michael McGann, 'The reception of Horace in the Renaissance', in Stephen Harrison (ed.), *The Cambridge Companion to Horace* (Cambridge: Cambridge University Press, 2007), pp. 305–17.

40 On the wide reception of the *Satyra Sotadica*, see Turner, *Schooling Sex*.

Chapter III

1 See Robert Purks Maccubbin (ed.), *'Tis Nature's Fault: Unauthorized Sexuality during the Enlightenment* (Cambridge: Cambridge University Press, 1987); G. S. Rousseau and Roy Porter (eds), *Sexual Underworlds of the Enlightenment* (Manchester: Manchester University Press, 1987); and Jacob Stockinger, 'Homosexuality and the French Enlightenment', pp. 161–85, in George Stambolian and Elaine Marks (eds), *Homosexualities and French Literature: Cultural Contexts/Critical Tests* (Ithaca: Cornell University Press, 1990).

2 On marriage, see Ludmilla Jordanova, 'Naturalising the family: literature and the bio-medical sciences in the late eighteenth century', pp. 86–116, and A. E. Pilkington, '"Nature" as ethical norm in the Enlightenment', pp. 51–85, in Ludmilla Jordanova (ed.), *Languages of Nature: Critical Essays on Science and Literature* (London: Free Association Books, 1986). On the erotics of botany, see Julie Peakman, *Mighty Lewd Books: The Development of Pornography in Eighteenth-Century England* (Basingstoke: Palgrave Macmillan, 2003), pp. 67–86. On nature, sex and medicine, see Ludmilla Jordanova, *Nature Displayed: Gender, Science and Medicine 1760–1820* (London: Longman, 1999).

3 Roy Porter and Lesley Hall, *The Facts of Life: The Creation of Sexual Knowledge in Britain, 1650–1950* (New Haven/London: Yale University Press, 1995), p. 43.

4 Ibid., pp. 72–3.

5 Johann Joachim Winckelmann, *Letter and Report on the Discoveries at Herculaneum* trans. Carol C. Mattusch (Los Angeles: Getty Publications, 2011), p. 96.

6 On d'Hancarville, see Francis Haskell, 'The Baron d'Hancarville: an adventurer and art historian in eighteenth-century Europe', in Francis Haskell, *Past and Present in Art and Taste: Selected Essays* (New Haven: Yale University Press, 1987), pp. 30–45; F. Lissarrague and M. Reed, 'The Collector's Books', *Journal of the History of Collections* 9:2 (1997), pp. 275–94; James Moore, 'History as theoretical reconstruction? Baron d'Hancarville and the exploration of ancient mythology in the eighteenth century', in James Moore, Ian

Macgregor Morris and Andrew J. Bayliss (eds), *Reinventing History: The Enlightenment Origins of Ancient History* (London: Centre for Metropolitan History, Institute of Historical Research, University of London, 2008), pp. 137–67; and Noah Heringman, *Sciences of Antiquity: Romantic Antiquarianism, Natural History, and Knowledge Work* (Oxford: Oxford University Press, 2013), pp. 125–218.

7 On Hamilton, and his collaboration with d'Hancarville, see Ian Jenkins and Kim Sloan, *Vases and Volcanoes: Sir William Hamilton and His Collection* (London: British Museum Press, 1996); Lissarrague and Reed, 'The Collector's Books'; Whitney Davis, 'Homoerotic Art Collections from 1750 to 1920', *Art History* 24:2 (2001), pp. 247–77; and Heringman, *Sciences of Antiquity*, pp. 125–218.

8 William Hamilton and Richard Payne Knight, *An Account of the Remains of the Worship of Priapus, Lately Existing at Isernia, in the Kingdom of Naples: In Two Letters; One from Sir William Hamilton, K.B. His Majesty's Minister at the Court to Naples, to Sir Joseph Banks, Bart. President of the Royal Society; and the other from a Person Residing at Isernia: To Which Is Added, A Discourse on the Worship of Priapus, and Its Connexion with the Mystic Religion of the Ancients, by R. P. Knight, esq.* (London: T. Spilsbury, 1786), p. 11.

9 On Payne Knight, see Michael Clarke and Nicholas Penny (eds), *The Arrogant Connoisseur, Richard Payne Knight 1751–1824: Essays on Richard Payne Knight together with a catalogue of works exhibited at the Whitworth Art Gallery, 1982* (Manchester: Manchester University Press, 1982); G. S. Rousseau, 'The sorrows of Priapus: anticlericalism, homosocial desire and Richard Payne Knight', in G. S. Rousseau and R. Porter, *Sexual Underworlds of the Enlightenment* (Manchester: Manchester University Press, 1987), pp. 101–53; Giancarlo Carabelli, *In the Image of Priapus* (London: Duckworth, 1996); Andrew Ballantyne, *Architecture, Landscape and Liberty: Richard Payne Knight and the Picturesque* (Cambridge: Cambridge University Press, 1997); and Whitney Davis, *Queer Beauty: Sexuality and Aesthetics from Winckelmann to Freud and Beyond* (New York: Columbia University Press, 2010), pp. 51–81.

10 Hamilton and Payne Knight, *An Account*, p. 28.

11 Ibid., p. 41.

12 Ibid., p. 174.

13 Ibid., p. 48.

14 On secret museums, see Walter Kendrick, *The Secret Museum* (New York: Viking Press, 1987) and Dominic Janus, 'The rites of man: the British Museum and the sexual imagination in Victorian Britain', *Journal of the History of Collections* 20:1 (2008), pp. 101–12. On collections of phallic artefacts, see Davis, 'Homoerotic Art Collections', esp. pp. 264–6.

15 On the Victorian interest in the ancient phallus, especially within the museum context, see Jennifer Ellen Grove, 'The Collection and Reception of Sexual Antiquities in the Late Nineteenth and Early Twentieth Century', PhD dissertation, University of Exeter, 2013.

16 See Frank Edward Manuel, *The Eighteenth Century Confronts the Gods* (Cambridge, MA: Harvard University Press, 1959). pp. 259–70.

17 See Davis, 'Homoerotic Art Collections', pp. 263–4 on these late eighteenth-century publications.

18 See Hamilton and Payne Knight, *An Account*, p. 24.

19 See Anthony Grafton, 'Polyhistor into philolog: notes on the transformation of German classical scholarship, 1780–1850', *History of Universities* 3 (1983), pp. 159–92, on Heyne and Niebuhr; the quotation comes from p. 183. On the institutionalisation of German classical studies, see Suzanne Marchand, *Down from Olympus: Archaeology and Philhellenism in Germany, 1750–1970* (Princeton: Princeton University Press, 1996); on German historicism more generally, see Frederick C. Beiser, *The German Historicist Tradition* (Oxford: Oxford University Press, 2011). See Anthony Grafton, *Defenders of the Text: The Traditions of Scholarship in an Age of Science, 1450–1800* (Cambridge, MA: Harvard University Press, 1991) for a more general overview of the history of scholarship.

20 Antonio Beccadelli, *Hermaphroditus: primus in Germania edidit et Apophoreta adjecit Frider. Carol. Forbergius* (Coburg: Mensel, 1824), pp. iv–xiii.

21 Ibid., pp. x–xi, note d; xi–xii, note f. On Eichhorn, see Grafton, *Defenders of the Text*, pp. 234–41. On the University of Göttingen and its significance in the history of classical studies and textual criticism, see Reinhard Lauer (ed.), *Philologie in Göttingen: Sprach und Literaturwissenschaft an der Georgia Augusta im 18. und beginnenden 19. Jahrhundert* (Göttingen: Vandehoeck and Ruprecht, 2001).

22 See Ovid *Tristia* 1.1, as well as Horace *Epistles* 1.20. The trope appears several times in Martial's *Epigrams* (1.3, 1.70, 3.4, 3.5, 7.84, 7.97, 9.66, 10.20, 12.2 and 12.5), and was also used by Barthélemy Mercier de Saint-Léger, *Quinque Illustrium Poetarum: Ant. Panormitae; Ramusii, Ariminensis; Pacifici Maximi, Asculani; Joan. Joviani Pontani; Joan. Secundi, Hagiensis. Lusus in Venerem* (Paris, 1791), pp. 95–6, to introduce his collection of erotic Latin poetry. See also Holt Parker's notes on this poetic model at Beccadelli, *The Hermaphrodite* (2010), p. 240, nn. 158, 160.

23 Beccadelli, *Hermaphroditus* (1824), p. 3. See also William Fitzgerald, *Martial: The World of Epigram* (Chicago: University of Chicago Press, 2007), on Martial's relationship with his readers.

24 On the *Carmina Priapeia*, see Richard W. Hooper (ed.), *The Priapus Poems* (Urbana/Chicago: University of Illinois Press, 1999).

25 On Martial's Saturnalian poetics, see Victoria Rimell, *Martial's Rome: Empire and the Ideology of Epigram* (Cambridge: Cambridge University Press, 2008), pp. 140–80, and on the *Apopherata*, see Sarah Blake, 'Martial's Natural History: The Xenia and Apophoreta and Pliny's Encyclopedia', *Arethusa* 44:3 (2011), pp. 353–77.

26 See Beccadelli, *Hermaphroditus* (1824), pp. xiv–xv, on the activeness and passiveness of sexual activity.

27 Ibid., p. 234, and Frederick Charles Forberg, *Manual of Classical Erotology*, 2 vols (New York: Grove Press, [1824] 1966), I, p. 190.

28 Beccadelli, *Hermaphroditus* (1824), p. 213, and Forberg, *Manual*, 1, p. 24.

29 Beccadelli, *Hermaphroditus* (1824), p. 234 and Forberg, *Manual*, 1, p. 80.

30 Beccadelli, *Hermaphroditus* (1824), p. 277 and Forberg, *Manual*, 1, p. 190.

31 Beccadelli, *Hermaphroditus* (1824), p. 304 and Forberg, *Manual*, 2, p. 2.
32 See J. N. Adams, *The Latin Sexual Vocabulary* (London: Duckworth, 1982), p. 144 on *perficio* and *perago* as meaning 'ejaculate' or 'reach orgasm' in classical Latin.
33 Beccadelli, *Hermaphroditus* (1824), p. 348 and Forberg, *Manual*, 2, p. 114.
34 See Bruno Lavagnini, *Aloisiae Sigeae Toletanae* Satyra Sotadica *de Arcanis Amoris et Veneris sive Joannis Meursii Elegantiae Latini Sermonis* (Catania: Romeo Prampolini, 1935), III: 44.
35 Orgasms appear repeatedly in Forberg's essay: for instance, see Beccadelli *Hermaphroditus* (1824), pp. 214, 215, 219, 228, 229, 230, 233, 240 and Forberg, *Manual*, 1, pp. 26, 30, 40, 62, 64, 66, 68, 76, 92, 234, 236.
36 Beccadelli, *Hermaphroditus* (1824), pp. 294, 329–30 and Forberg, *Manual*, 1, pp. 234, 236; 2, pp. 66, 68, 70.
37 See also Jonathan Walters, 'Invading the Roman body: manliness and impenetrability in Roman thought', pp. 29–43 in Judith P. Hallett and Marilyn B. Skinner (eds), *Roman Sexualities* (Princeton: Princeton University Press, 1997); and Craig Williams, 'Roman homosexuality: ideologies of masculinity', in *Classical Antiquity*, 2nd ed. (Oxford: Oxford University Press, 2010).
38 Forberg makes very clear at the beginning of 'Apophoreta' that his book was written for men to read: see Beccadelli, *Hermaphroditus* (1824), p. 212 and Forberg, *Manual*, 1, p. 20.
39 Beccadelli, *Hermaphroditus* (1824), p. 384.
40 One of the two copies of Beccadelli's *The Hermaphrodite* (1824) held in the British Library, London, contains these plates. For the interested reader, the shelfmark of this copy is 'Cup.363.cc.30'.
41 Julius Rosenbaum, *Geschichte der Lustseuche, erster Theil: die Lustseuche im Alterthume* (Halle: J.F. Lippert, 1839), p. 117–18 and note 1, and Julius Rosenbaum, *The Plague of Lust, Being a History of Venereal Disease in Classical Antiquity*, 2 vols, trans. 'An Oxford M.A.' (Paris: Charles Carrington, 1901), 1, p. 110 with note 1.
42 See Rosenblaum, *Geschichte der Lustseuche*, pp. vii–xiv, 30–3, and Rosenbaum, *The Plague of Lust*, 1, pp. xiii–xx, xxxi–xxxiv.
43 On these nineteenth-century concerns, see Porter and Hall, *The Facts of Life* (1995); Francies Finnegan, *Poverty and Prostitution: A Study of Victorian Prostitutes in York* (Cambridge: Cambridge University Press, 1979); Simon Szreter, *Fertility, Class and Gender in Britain, 1860–1940* (Cambridge: Cambridge University Press, 1996); Mary Spongberg, *Feminizing Venereal Disease: The Body of the Prostitute in Nineteenth-Century Medical Discourse* (Basingstoke: Palgrave Macmillan, 1997); and Alison Bashford, *Purity and Pollution: Gender, Embodiment and Victorian Medicine* (Basingstoke: Palgrave Macmillan, 1998).
44 Quoted in Porter and Hall, *The Facts of Life*, p. 134.
45 Ibid., pp. 136–8.
46 See Rosenbaum, *Geschichte der Lustseuche*, pp. 219, 251, and Rosenbaum, *The Plague of Lust*, 2, pp. 3, 46. The explanation of *irrumare* is a direction quotation from Forberg (without, however, any acknowledgement). When Rosenbaum defines the *cunnilingus*, he takes Forberg's 'peragit opus ('accomplishes the

deed'), which Forberg had used to describe the penis' activity in anal sex ('pedicare'), and along with the gerund 'arrigendo' ('by erecting'), Rosenbaum explicitly makes the tongue look phallic. See Chapter III of this volume for Forberg's definitions.

47 Rosenbaum, *Geschichte der Lustseuche*, p. 263 and Rosenbaum, *The Plague of Lust*, 2, pp. 64–5. Rosenbaum is citing Martial *Epigram* 11.85. The translation used here comes from Rosenbaum, *The Plague of Lust* (1901).

48 See Rosenbaum, *Geschichte der Lustseuche*, p. 264 and Rosenbaum, *The Plague of Lust*, 2, p. 65.

49 Rosenbaum, *Geschichte der Lustseuche*, p. 242–3 and Rosenbaum, *The Plague of Lust*, 2, p. 35.

50 On Hirschfeld, see Manfred Herzer, *Magnus Hirschfeld: Leben und Werk eines jüdischen, schwulen und sozialistischen Sexologen* (Hamburg: Männerschwarm, 2001) and Ralf Dose, *Magnus Hirschfeld: Deutscher, Jude, Weltbürger* (Teetz: Hentrich und Hentrich, 2005). For the pictorial encyclopaedia, see Leo Schidrowitz et al. (eds), *Bilderlexikon der Erotik* (Vienna: Institut für Sexualforschung in Vienna, 1928–31).

51 On Alfred Kinsey, see Donna Drucker, *The Classification of Sex: Alfred Kinsey and the Organization of Knowledge* (Pittsburgh: University of Pittsburgh Press, 2014).

52 R. von Krafft-Ebing, *Psychopathia Sexualis, with Especial Reference to Contrary Sexual Instinct: A Medico-legal Study* (Philadelphia: F.A. Davis, 1894), p. 1.

53 On Krafft-Ebing and his work, see Harry Oosterhuis, *Stepchildren of Nature: Krafft-Ebing, Psychiatry and the Making of Sexual Identity* (Chicago: University of Chicago, 2000), and Heinrich Ammerer, *Am Anfang war die Perversion: Richard von Krafft-Ebing, Psychiater und Pionier der modernen Sexualkunde* (Styria: Vienna, 2011). On the development of nineteenth-century sexology – including Krafft-Ebing – into twentieth-century modes of thinking about sexuality, see also Arnold Davidson's *The Emergence of Sexuality: Historical Epistemology and the Formation of Concepts* (Cambridge, MA: Harvard University Press, 2001).

54 Krafft-Ebing, *Psychopathia Sexualis*, p. 378.

55 Ibid., p. 379.

56 On this distinction, see analysis in Oosterhuis, *Stepchildren of Nature*, pp. 39–62.

57 Ibid., pp. 51–3, 103–6.

58 On the culture of the *fin de siècle* at the end of the nineteenth century, see the essays collected in Sally Ledger and Scott McCracken (eds), *Cultural Politics at the Fin de Siècle* (Cambridge: Cambridge University Press, 1995) and Gail Marshall (ed.), *The Cambridge Companion to the Fin de Siècle* (Cambridge: Cambridge University Press, 2007).

59 Krafft-Ebing, *Psychopathia Sexualis*, p. 6.

60 Ibid., pp. 6–7.

61 Ibid., p. 5.

62 See Friedrich Wiedemeister, *Der Cäsarenwahnsinn der Julisch-Claudischen Imperatorenfamilie geschildert an den Kaisern Tiberius, Caligula, Claudius, Nero* (Hannover: Carl Rümpler, 1875), p. 306; see Krafft-Ebing, *Psychopathia*

Sexualis, p. 34, n. 1, where a bibliography of consulted literature is footnoted; and see Catherine Edwards, *The Politics of Immorality in Ancient Rome* (Cambridge: Cambridge University Press, 1993), pp. 6–7 on Friedländer. One other historical text in fact featured in Krafft-Ebing's bibliography, being Johannes Scherr's *Deutsche Kultur- und Sittengeschichte* (*German Cultural and Moral History*), a fairly widely read work, which first appeared in 1852, reaching a fourth edition by 1870. Scherr's book dated Germanic culture back to Roman colonialism, and so provided Krafft-Ebing with a concrete history of the link between ancient Roman and modern German life.

63 Krafft-Ebing, *Psychopathia Sexualis*, p. 30.
64 Ibid., p. 45.
65 Ibid., pp. 55, 88.
66 Ibid., p. 58.
67 Ibid., p. 76.
68 Ibid., p. 82.
69 Ibid., pp. 97, 98.
70 See Beccadelli, *Hermaphroditus* (1824), p. 335, note d, and Forberg, *Manual*, 1, p. 82.
71 Krafft-Ebing, *Psychopathia Sexualis*, p. v. This appears in the preface to the first edition.
72 Ibid., pp. 20, 22, 23, 30, 31, 42, 55, 62, 72, 76, 97–8, 133, 244, 247, 262, 269, 272–3, 296, 297, 299, 336, 382, 403.
73 On the politics of the institionalisation and professionalisation of psychiatry and psychology in the nineteenth century, see Oosterhuis, *Stepchildren of Nature*, pp. 77–99, 113–117.
74 On Krafft-Ebing's interest in sadism and masochism, see Oosterhuis, *Stepchildren of Nature*, pp. 49–50, 152–7, 174–9.
75 Krafft-Ebing, *Psychopathia Sexualis*, p. 297, emphases added.
76 See Chapter III of this volume.
77 Indeed it might be argued that *immitto* is hardly a neutral, scientific term, as it is often used in Latin literary texts in military settings, when authors talk of sending in or dispatching soldiers and cavalry or throwing in weapons – metaphors which might remind us of the belligerence of male–female relations in Latin poetry and in the *Satyra Sotadica*.
78 On Krafft-Ebing's bourgeois correspondents and readership, see Oosterhuis, *Stepchildren of Nature*, pp. 217–18, 237–8, 244–5, 248, 254.
79 See Krafft-Ebing, *Psychopathia Sexualis*, pp. 242–51.
80 Ibid., pp. 243, 248.
81 Oosterhuis, *Stepchildren of Nature*, p. 226, also observes how 'some autobiographical case histories resemble romances'.
82 Ibid., p. 186.
83 Quoted in ibid., p. 142.
84 Ibid., p. 201.

Chapter IV

1 See Harry Oosterhuis, *Stepchildren of Nature: Krafft-Ebing, Psychiatry and*

the Making of Sexual Identity (Chicago: University of Chicago, 2000), pp. 186–7.

2 Ibid., pp. 131–230.

3 See also Heike Bauer, *English Literary Sexology: Translations of Inversion, 1860–1930* (Basingstoke: Palgrave Macmillan, 2009), on the mutual impact of the sexual sciences and literature between 1860 and 1930.

4 This is my translation. For the original German, see Johann Joachim Winckelmann, *Kleine Schriften, Vorreden, Entwürfe* (Berlin/New York: Walter de Gruyter, 2002), p. 29. The call to German artists appeared in Winckelmann's first published work: 'Thoughts on the imitation of Greek works in painting and the art of sculpture', in Johann Joachim Winckelmann, *Johann Joachim Winckelmann on Art, Architecture, and Archaeology*, trans. David Carter (Rochester, NY: Camden House, 2013), pp. 31–56.

5 On German classical scholarship which emerged out of philhellenic tendencies, see Suzanne Marchand, *Down from Olympus: Archaeology and Philhellenism in Germany, 1750–1970* (Princeton: Princeton University Press, 1996).

6 Robert Collison, *Encyclopaedias: Their History throughout the Ages: A Bibliographical Guide with Extensive Historical Notes to the General Encyclopaedias Issued throughout the World from 350 BC to the Present Day*, 2nd ed. (New York and London: Hafner Publishing Company, 1966), p. 182.

7 M. H. E. Meier, 'Päderastie', in J. S. Ersch and J. G. Gruber (eds), *Allgemeine Encyclopädie der Wissenschaften und Kunst in alphabetischer Folge von genannten Schriftstellern* (Leipzig: J. F. Gleditsch, 1837), vol. 9, sect. iii, pp. 149, 155, 156. See also Daniel Orrells, *Classical Culture and Modern Masculinity* (Oxford: Oxford University Press, 2011), pp. 88–94.

8 See Linda Dowling, 'Ruskin's pied beauty and the constitution of a "homosexual" code', *Victorian Newsletter* 75 (1989), pp. 1–8; Linda Dowling, *Hellenism and Homosexuality in Victorian Oxford* (Ithaca: Cornell University Press, 1994) and Robert Aldrich, *The Seduction of the Mediterranean: Writing, Art and Homosexual Fantasy* (London: Routledge, 1993).

9 R. von Krafft-Ebing, *Psychopathia Sexualis, with Especial Reference to Contrary Sexual Instinct: A Medico-legal Study* (Philadelphia: F.A. Davis, 1894), p. 187.

10 On Ulrichs see Wolfram Setz (ed.), *Karl Heinrich Ulrichs zu Ehren: Materialen zu Leben und Werk* (Berlin: Rosa Winkel, 2000); Wolfram Setz, *Neue Finde und Studien zu Karl Heinrich Ulrichs* (Berlin: Rosa Winkel, 2004); and by Sebastian Matzner, 'From Uranians to homosexuals: philhellenism, Greek homoeroticism and gay emancipation in Germany 1835–1915', *Classical Receptions Journal* 2:1 (2010). On the context in which Ulrichs wrote, see James D. Steakley, *The Homosexual Emancipation Movement in Germany* (New York: Arno, 1975).

11 Quoted in Matzner, 'From Uranians to homosexuals', p. 80.

12 Ibid., pp. 81–2.

13 On Kertbeny, see Julia Takacs, 'The Double Life of Kertbeny', in Gert Hekma (ed.), *Past and Present of Radical Sexual Politics* (Amsterdam: Mosse Foundation, 2004) pp. 26–40. His writings on homosexuality have been collated in: Karl-Maria Kertbeny, *Schriften zur Homosexualitätsforschung*, ed. Manfred Herzer (Berlin: Rosa Winkel, 2000).

14 Quoted in Matzner, 'From Uranians to homosexuals', p. 87.
15 See Krafft-Ebing, *Psychopathia Sexualis,* pp. 414–20.
16 See the dedication in Reginald Baliol Brett Esher, *Ionicus* (London: John Murray, 1923). On the Uranian poets and Johnson Cory's place among them, see Timothy d'Arch Smith, *Love in Earnest: Some Notes on the Lives and Writings of English 'Uranian' Poets from 1889 to 1930* (London: Routledge, 1970), and Michael Matthew Kaylor, *Secreted Desires: The Major Uranians: Hopkins, Pater and Wilde* (Brno: Privately printed, 2006).
17 For Symonds' writings on sexuality, see John Addington Symonds, *The Memoirs of John Addington Symonds: The Secret Homosexual Life of a Leading Nineteenth–Century Man of Letters*, ed. Phyllis Grosskurth (London: Hutchinson, 1984); Henry Havelock Ellis and John Addington Symonds, *Sexual Inversion: A Critical Edition*, ed. Ivan Crozier (Basingstoke: Palgrave Macmillan, 2008); and Sean Brady, *John Addington Symonds (1840–1893) and Homosexuality: A Critical Edition of Sources* (Basingstoke: Palgrave Macmillan, 2012). On Symonds, see Jeffrey Weeks, *Coming Out: Homosexual Politics from the Nineteenth Century to the Present* (London: Quartet Books, 1977); Alastair Blanshard, 'Hellenic fantasies: aesthetics and desire in John Addington Symonds' 'A problem in Greek ethics', *Dialogos* 7 (2000), pp. 99–123; John Pemble (ed.), *John Addington Symonds: Culture and the Demon Desire* (Basingstoke: Palgrave Macmillan, 2000); Stefano Evangelista, 'Platonic dons, adolescent bodies: Benjamin Jowett, John Addington Symonds, Walter Pater', in George Rousseau, *Children and Sexuality: From the Greeks to the Great War* (Basingstoke: Palgrave Macmillan, 2007), pp. 203–36; Orrells, *Classical Culture and Modern Masculinity*; Daniel Orrells, 'Greek love, orientalism and race: intersections in Classical reception', *Cambridge Classical Journal* 58 (2012), pp. 194–230.
18 See Orrells, *Classical Culture*, p. 99.
19 Ibid., pp. 109–23, on Jowett's Plato, and sources of quotations here; see also Lesley Higgins, 'Jowett and Pater: trafficking in platonic wares', *Victorian Studies* 31:1 (1993), pp. 43–72. Those interested in Jowett's introductions to Plato's *Symposium* and *Phaedrus* will enjoy perusing Benjamin Jowett, *The Dialogues of Plato: Translated into English with Analyses and Introductions* (Oxford: Clarendon Press, 1892).
20 Symonds, in Brady, *Symonds and Homosexuality*, p. 43.
21 Ibid., p. 50.
22 Ibid., p. 59.
23 Ibid, pp. 44–5.
24 See Evangelista, 'Platonic Dons, Adolescent Bodies'.
25 Symonds, *Memoirs*, pp. 100–2.
26 See Harry Cocks, *Nameless Offences: Homosexual Desire in the Nineteenth Century* (London: I.B.Tauris, 2003), on the legalities of same-sex relations in nineteenth-century Britain.
27 Symonds, in Brady, *Symonds and Homosexuality,* p. 216, where in a letter he mentions his concern about 'Labby's inexpansible legislation'.
28 See Krafft-Ebing, *Psychopathia Sexualis,* p. 96, and Oosterhuis, *Stepchildren of Nature*, pp. 158, 188, 207, for instances of Krafft-Ebing's use of the phrase. See also Chapter IV of this volume.

29 Symonds, *Memoirs*, p. 64.
30 Ibid., p. 64.
31 Ibid., p. 64–5.
32 Ibid., p. 94.
33 Ibid., p. 97.
34 Ibid., p. 109.
35 Ibid., pp. 111–15.
36 Ibid., p. 99.
37 Ibid., p. 100.
38 Ibid., p. 99.
39 Ibid., p. 112.
40 Ibid., pp. 130–3.
41 Ibid., p. 18.
42 Ibid., p. 74.
43 Ibid., pp. 209–10.
44 See Michel Foucault, *The History of Sexuality*, vol. 2: *The Use of Pleasure*, trans. Robert Hurley (London: Penguin, 1998).
45 Symonds, *Memoirs*, p. 196.
46 Symonds also subtly explored his interest in Uranian themes in the Greek Anthology in his 1873 *Studies in Greek Poets*: see Gideon Nisbet, *Greek Epigram in Reception: J.A. Symonds, Oscar Wilde and the Invention of Desire, 1805–1929* (Oxford: Oxford University Press, 2013), pp. 116–69.
47 Johnson's book was discreetly circulated amongst like-minded men in the second half of the nineteenth century. Symonds' Oxford tutor Conington had given Symonds the undergraduate a copy of *Ionica* back in 1859, and the 'volume of verse [. . .] went straight to my heart and inflamed my imagination'. Symonds wrote to Johnson who replied with a 'long epistle on paiderastia in modern times, defending it' (Symonds, *Memoirs*, p. 109).
48 William Johnson Cory, *Ionica* (London: Smith, Elder & Co., 1858), p. 86.
49 Ibid., p. 116.
50 Ibid., p. 25.
51 Symonds, *Memoirs*, p. 105.
52 On Theocritus' poem and pederasty more generally as a poetics of a lost past in the *Idylls*, see Richard Hunter, *Theocritus and the Archaeology of Greek Poetry* (Cambridge: Cambridge University Press, 1996), pp. 167–95.
53 Symonds, *Memoirs*, pp. 253–4.
54 Symonds, *Memoirs*, pp. 271–3.
55 Symonds, in Brady, *Symonds and Homosexuality*, pp. 167, 210.
56 Ibid., p 134.
57 Ibid., pp. 205–8, on his comments on the law in *Modern Ethics*.
58 On Whitman's poetry, especially its erotic content, see M. Jimmie Killingsworth, *Whitman's Poetry of the Body: Sexuality, Politics and the Text* (Chapel Hill: University of North Carolina Press, 1989); Michael Moon, *Disseminating Whitman: Revision and Corporeality in Leaves of Grass* (Cambridge, MA: Harvard University Press, 1991); Bryne R. S. Fone, *Masculine Landscapes: Walt Whitman and the Homoerotic Text* (Carbondale: Southern Illinois University Press, 1992). On Edward Carpenter, see Sheila Rowbotham, *Edward*

Carpenter: A Life of Liberty and Love (London/New York: Verso, 2009).

59 Symonds, in Brady, *Symonds and Homosexuality*, p. 195.

60 Ibid., p. 200.

61 Ibid., pp. 200, 202. Symonds also reflects on Whitman and the erotics of democracy in his memoir: Symonds, *Memoirs*, pp. 189, 191.

62 See Phyllis Grosskurth, *Havelock Ellis: A Biography* (London: Allen Lane, 1980), p. 126.

63 Ibid., p. 122.

64 See Brady's introduction in Brady, *Symonds and Homosexuality*, pp. 25–32, especially p. 28.

65 Henry Havelock Ellis and John Addington Symonds, *Sexual Inversion: A Critical Edition*, ed. Ivan Crozier (Basingstoke: Palgrave Macmillan, 2008), p. 230. See also Symonds, in Brady, *Symonds and Homosexuality*, p 45.

66 See Symonds, *Sexual Inversion*, pp. 60–7.

67 Symonds, *Memoirs*, pp. 190.

Chapter V

1 Isobel Hurst, '"A fleet of . . . inexperienced Argonauts": Oxford women and the classics 1873–1920', in Christopher Stray (ed.), *Oxford Classics: Teaching and Learning 1800–2000* (London: Duckworth, 2007), p. 18.

2 See T. D. Olverson, *Women Writers and the Dark Side of Late-Victorian Hellenism* (Basingstoke: Palgrave Macmillan, 2010), p. 15. On the debates about women's access to university study, in particular to Classics, see Natalie Bluestone, *Women and the Ideal Society: Plato's Republic and Modern Myths of Gender* (Amhurst: University of Massachusetts Press, 1987); Christopher Stray (ed.), *Classics in Nineteenth- and Twentieth-Century Cambridge: Curriculum, Culture and Community*, Cambridge Philological Society, Supplement 24 (Cambridge: Cambridge Philological Society, 1999); Mary Beard, *The Invention of Jane Harrison* (Cambridge, MA: Harvard University Press, 2000); Isobel Hurst, *Victorian Women Writers and the Classics: The Feminine of Homer* (Oxford: Oxford University Press, 2006); Hurst, '"A fleet of . . . inexperienced Argonauts"'; and Yopie Prins, '"Lady's Greek" (with the accents): a metrical translation of Euripides by Mary F. Robinson', *Victorian Literature and Culture* 34:2 (2006), pp. 591–618.

3 On the 'New Woman', see Elaine Showalter, *Daughters of Decadence: Women Writers of the Fin-de-Siècle* (Princeton: Princeton University Press, 1993); Sally Ledger, *The New Woman: Fiction and Feminism at the Fin de Siècle* (Manchester: Manchester University Press, 1997); Angelique Richardson and Chris Willis (eds), *The New Woman in Fiction and in Fact: Fin-de-Siècle Feminisms* (Basingstoke: Palgrave Macmillan, 2002); and Mary Louise Roberts, *Disruptive Acts: The New Woman in Fin-de-Siècle France* (Chicago: Chicago University Press, 2002). On images of ancient women at the end of the nineteenth century, see Alastair J. L. Blanshard, *Sex: Vice and Love from Antiquity to Modernity* (Chichester: Wiley-Blackwell, 2010), p. 37–9.

4 Tallmadge May (trans.), *Galen on the Usefulness of the Parts of the Body*, 2 vols (Ithaca: Cornell University Press, 1968), 2, pp. 643–4.

5 On women's bodies in Greek medicine, see Lesley Dean-Jones, *Women's Bodies in Classical Greek Science* (Oxford: Oxford University Press, 1994).

6 See Judith P. Hallett, 'Female homoeroticism and the denial of Roman reality in Latin literature', *Yale Journal of Criticism* 3 (1989), pp. 209–27, and Sandra Boehringer, *L'homosexualité feminine dans l'antiquité grecque et romaine* (Paris: Belles lettres, 2007).

7 See Simon Goldhill, *Foucault's Virginity: Ancient Erotic Fiction and the History of Sexuality* (Cambridge: Cambridge University Press, 1995).

8 On the early-modern conceptualisation of the clitoris, see Katherine Park, 'The rediscovery of the clitoris: French medicine and the tribade, 1570–1620', in Carla Mazzio and David Hillman (eds), *The Body in Parts: Fantasies of Corporeality in Early Modern Europe* (New York: Routledge, 1997), pp. 171–93. See also Thomas Laquer, *Making Sex: Body and Gender from the Greeks to Freud* (Cambridge, MA: Harvard University Press, 1992). For critiques of Laqueur's narrative, see Katherine Park, 'Cadden, Laqueur and "The One-Sex Body"', *Medieval Feminist Forum* 46 (2010), pp. 96–100, and Helen King, *The One-Sex Body on Trial: The Classical and Early-Modern Evidence* (Farnham: Ashgate, 2013).

9 Antonio Beccadelli, *Hermaphroditus* (1824), pp. 345, 349, and Forberg, *Manual* (New York: Grove Press, [1824] 1966), 2, pp. 108, 118.

10 See Helen Whitbread, *I Know My Own Heart: The Diaries of Anne Lister 1791–1840* (London: Virago, 1988). On nineteenth-century social and sexual relations between women, see Martha Vicinus, *Intimate Friends: Women who Loved Women, 1728–1928* (Chicago: Chicago University Press, 2004), and Sharon Marcus, *Between Women: Friendship, Desire, and Marriage in Victorian England* (Princeton: Princeton University Press, 2007).

11 Pierre Bayle, *Historical and Critical Dictionary . . . The 2nd Ed. . . . Edited, Revised and Corrected and Enlarged by Mr. Des Maizeaux*, 5 vols (London J. J. and P. Knapton et al., 1734–8), 5, p.44.

12 See Anna Clark, 'Anne Lister's Construction of Lesbian Identity', *Journal of the History of Sexuality* 7:1 (1996), p. 34.

13 On Lister's philology, see Clark, 'Anne Lister's Construction of Lesbian Identity', pp. 32–5. See also Alison Oram, 'Sexuality in heterotopia: time, space and love between women in the historic house', *Women's History Review* 21:4 (2012).

14 On the lack of scientific discussion of sex between women, see Heike Bauer, *English Literary Sexology: Translations of Inversion, 1860–1930* (Basingstoke: Palgrave Macmillan, 2009), pp. 30–42, and further comments in Chiara Beccalossi, *Female Sexual Inversion: Same-Sex Desires in Italian and British Sexology, c. 1870–1920* (Basingstoke: Palgrave Macmillan, 2012), pp. 15–17. On French and Italian discussions, see Chiara Beccalossi, 'The origin of Italian sexological studies: female sexual inversion ca. 1870–1900', *Journal of the History of Sexuality* 18:1 (2009), pp. 103–120, and Beccalossi, *Female Sexual Inversion*. See also Claudia Breger, 'Feminine masculinities: scientific and literary representations of "female inversion" at the turn of the twentieth century', *Journal of the History of Sexuality* 14:1/2 (2005), pp. 76–106.

15 See James Grantham Turner, *Schooling Sex: Libertine Literature and Erotic Education in Italy, France and England 1534–1685* (Oxford: Oxford University Press, 2003) on the dissemination of the *Satyra Sotadica* and other seventeenth-century pornographic works, such as *L'Escole des filles*, into the nineteenth century. See also Marcus, *Between Women*, p. 140, on Victorian pornography set in girls' boarding schools. On the schoolgirl crush and female masturbation in boarding schools in nineteenth-century scientific writings, see Beccalossi, *Female Sexual Inversion*, pp. 73–8, 107–11.

16 Symonds certainly read Italian experts on sex, as he discusses the work of Cesare Lombroso and Paolo Mantegazza in *A Problem in Modern Ethics*, which can be found in Sean Brady, *John Addington Symonds (1840–1893) and Homosexuality: A Critical Edition of Sources* (Basingstoke: Palgrave Macmillan, 2012), pp. 162–6, 174–5. Both of these wrote about same-sex sexuality, including sex between women.

17 On nineteenth-century women studying Classics at university, see Bluestone, *Women and the Ideal Society*; Stray, *Classics in Nineteenth- and Twentieth-Century Cambridge*; Beard, *The Invention of Jane Harrison*; and Hurst, *Victorian Women Writers and the Classics* and '"A fleet of . . . inexperienced Argonauts"'.

18 See Daniel Orrells, *Classical Culture and Modern Masculinity* (Oxford: Oxford University Press, 2011), pp. 146–7.

19 Symonds, in Brady, *Symonds and Homosexuality*, p. 56.

20 Henry Havelock Ellis and John Addington Symonds, *Sexual Inversion: A Critical Edition*, ed. Ivan Crozier (Basingstoke: Palgrave Macmillan, 2008), pp. 292–4.

21 See Daniel Orrells, 'Hedlam's Herodas: the art of suggestion', in Stephen Harrison and Christopher Stray (eds), *Expurgating the Classics: Editing Out in Latin and Greek* (London: British Classical Press, 2012) pp. 53–72.

22 See David Fearn, 'Imperialist fragmentation and the discovery of Bacchylides', in Mark Bradley (ed.), *Classics and Imperialism in the British Empire* (Oxford University Press: Oxford, 2010), pp. 158–85.

23 Frederic Kenyon (ed.), *Classical Texts from Papyri in the British Museum Including the Newly Discovered Poems of Herodas* (London: Oxford Clarendon Press, 1891). p. 3.

24 See Orrells, 'Headlam's Herodas', p. 59.

25 On Headlam, his scholarship and Cambridge politics, see Simon Goldhill, *Who Needs Greek? Contests in the Cultural History of Hellenism* (Cambridge University Press: Cambridge, 2002), and Michael Silk, 'Walter Headlam: scholarship, poetry, poetics', in Christopher Stray (ed.), *The Owl of Minerva: the Cambridge Praelections of 1906: Reassessments of Richard Jebb, James Adam, Walter Headlam, Henry Jackson, William Ridgeway and Arthur Verrall, Proceedings of the Cambridge Philological Society,* Supplementary Volume 28 (Cambridge Faculty of Classics: Cambridge, 2005), pp. 69–86.

26 The verb *tribo*, with a variety of prefixes, including 'ek', is used in a sexual sense in earlier Greek texts, referring to the rubbing of an organ in preparation for sexual intercourse: see Jeffrey Henderson, *The Maculate Muse: Obscene Language in Attic Comedy*, 2nd ed. (New York/London: Oxford University

Press, 1991), p. 176. With the prefix 'epi' in Aristophanes' *Lysistrata*, it has a sense of sexual frustration (pp. 876, 952, 1090).

27 'Fig' in Greek could refer to male and female sexual organs: see Henderson, *The Maculate Muse*, pp. 117–18.

28 'Baubōn' appears in line 19 in Herodas' sixth poem, and Headlam's discussion can be found at the appropriate place in his commentary: see Walter Headlam, *Herodas: The Mimes and Fragments*, ed. A. D. Knox (Bristol Classical Press: London, 2001), p. 288.

29 Yopie Prins, 'Greek maenads, Victorian spinsters', in Richard Dellamora (ed.), *Victorian Sexual Dissidence* (Chicago/London: University of Chicago Press, 1999), p. 68. On the cultural context of Harrison's Dionysiac teaching, see pp. 43–82.

30 On Burton's 'Sotadic Love', see Orrells, 'Greek love, orientalism and race'.

31 Richard F. Burton, *A Plain and Literal Translation of the Arabian Nights' Entertainments, now Entitled: The Books of the Thousand Nights and a Night, with Introduction, Explanatory Notes on the Manners and Customs of Moslem Men and a Terminal Essay upon the History of The Nights*, 10 vols (printed by the Burton Club for private subscribers only, 1885–8), 10, pp. 208–9.

32 Ibid.,10, p. 208, note 1.

33 See Holt Parker, 'Sappho Schoolmistress', *Transactions of the American Philological Association* 123 (1993), p. 313.

34 John Addington Symonds, *Studies of the Greek Poets* (London: Smith, Elder and Company, 1873), p. 308.

35 Quoted in Prins, *Victorian Sappho* (Princeton: Princeton University Press, 1999) p. 60.

36 Yopie Prins, *Victorian Sappho*, p. 59.

37 Ibid., p. 52–73 for a superb analysis of Wharton's Sappho.

38 Quoted in Prins, *Victorian Sappho*, p. 63, note 20.

39 John Addington Symonds, *The Memoirs of John Addington Symonds: The Secret Homosexual Life of a Leading Nineteenth-Century Man of Letters*, ed. Phyllis Grosskurth (London: Hutchinson, 1984), p. 273. The translation is by Anne Carson: Anne Carson, *If Not, Winter: Fragments of Sappho* (New York/London: Virago Press, 2003), p. 63.

40 Symonds, *Memoirs*, p. 272.

41 See, for instance, Prins, *Victorian Sappho*, on Algernon Swinburne's decadent, sexually violent Lesbian Sappho and the example of Sappho for women's causes through the nineteenth century.

42 See Joan DeJean, *Fictions of Sappho, 1546–1937* (Chicago: Chicago University Press, 1989), p. 248, and Prins, *Victorian Sappho*, p. 59, note 19.

43 On the name, see Marion Thain and Ana Parejo Vadillo (eds), *Michael Field, the Poet: Published and Manuscript Materials* (Broadview Editions: Toronto, 2009), p. 28.

44 Marion Thain, *'Michael Field': Poetry, Aestheticism and the Fin de Siècle* (Cambridge: Cambridge University Press, 2007), p. 47.

45 Ibid., pp. 47–8.

46 Ibid., pp. 50, 62, 63.

47 Ibid., p. 53.
48 On 'Michael Field' as a Tiresian poet, see other readings in Yopie Prins, 'Sappho doubled: Michael Field', *Yale Journal of Criticism* 8, p.183; Christine White, 'The Tiresian poet: Michael Field', in *Victorian Women Poets: A Critical Reader*, ed. Angela Leighton (Oxford: Blackwell, 1996), pp. 148–61; and Thain, *Michael Field*, p. 60.
49 Prins, *Victorian Sappho*, pp. 74–80, characterises Bradley and Cooper as 'sly scholars'.
50 Thain, *Michael Field*, p. 41.

Chapter VI

1 From 'Three essays on sexuality', in Sigmund Freud, *The Standard Edition of the Complete Psychological Works of Sigmund Freud*, 24 vols, ed. James Strachey in collaboration with Anna Freud, assisted by Alix Strachey and Alan Tyson (London: The Hogarth Press and the Institute of Psycho-analysis, 1953–74), 7, pp. 190–1. Unless otherwise stated, all quotations from Freud will follow this edition (henceforth *SE*).
2 See Heinrich Ammerer, *Krafft-Ebing, Freud und die Erfindung der Perversion: Versuch einer Einkreisung* (Tectum: Marburg, 2006), for another account of the relationship between Krafft-Ebing and Freud. On Havelock Ellis and Freud, see Ivan Crozier, 'Taking prisoners: Havelock Ellis, Sigmund Freud, and the construction of homosexuality, 1897–1951', *Social History of Medicine* 13:3 (2000), pp. 447–66.
3 On Freud's engagement with Niebuhr, see Richard Armstrong, *Freud and the Ancient World: A Compulsion for Antiquity* (Ithaca and London: Cornell University Press, 2005), pp. 162–8.
4 See Cathy Gere, *The Tomb of Agamemnon: Mycenae and the Search for a Hero* (London: Profile, 2007), pp. 60–80.
5 Armstrong, *Freud and the Ancient World*, p. 118.
6 The letter is dated 15 October 1897: see Jeffrey Moussaieff Masson (ed.), *The Complete Letters of Sigmund Freud to Wilhelm Fliess, 1877–1905* (Cambridge/London: Belknap Press of Harvard University Press, 1985).
7 On the universalisation of Oedipus in the history of German thought, see Miriam Leonard, 'Freud and tragedy: Oedipus and the gender of the universal', *Classical Receptions Journal* 5:1 (2013), pp. 63–83. Hegel's words, which come from his *Philosophy of History*, are quoted in Leonard, p. 68.
8 Simon Goldhill, *Victorian Culture and Classical Antiquity: Art, Opera, Fiction, and the Proclamation of Modernity* (Princeton: Princeton University Press, 2011), p. 76.
9 Lisa Appignanesi and John Forrester, *Freud's Woman* (London: Penguin, 2000), p. 407. Pages 397–429 are an excellent account of Freud's theories of desire.
10 Ibid., p. 409.
11 Ibid., p. 411.
12 Rachel Bowlby, *Freudian Mythologies: Greek Tragedy and Modern Identities* (Oxford: Oxford University Press, 2007), pp. 146–7.
13 Appignanesi and Forrester, *Freud's Woman*, p. 419.

14 Sarah Kofman, *The Enigma of Woman: Woman in Freud's Writings*, trans. Catherine Porter (Ithaca: Cornell University Press, 1985), pp. 193–4.

15 Cathy Gere, *Knossos and the Prophets of Modernism* (Chicago: University of Chicago Press, 2009), pp. 153–60.

16 Bowlby, *Freudian Mythologies*, pp. 5–6.

17 Appignanesi and Forrester, *Freud's Woman*, p. 420.

18 See Johann Joachim Winckelmann, *History of the Art of Antiquity*, trans. Harry Francis Mallgrave (Los Angeles: Getty Publications, 2006), pp. 333–4.

19 Daniel Orrells, 'Freud's phallic symbol', in Ellen O'Gorman and Vanda Zajko (eds), *Classical Myth and Psychoanalysis* (Oxford: Oxford University Press, 2013), pp. 39–57.

20 See Lynne Gamwell and Richard Wells, *Sigmund Freud and Art: His Personal Collections of Antiquities* (London: Freud Museum, in association with Abrams, New York, 1989), and Whitney Davis, *Queer Beauty: Sexuality and Aesthetics from Winckelmann to Freud and Beyond* (New York: Columbia University Press, 2010), p. 51.

21 See Thomas Laqueur, *Making Sex: Body and Gender from the Greeks to Freud* (Cambridge, MA: Harvard University Press, 1992).

22 Ibid., p. 233. For other critiques of Laqueur's narrative, see Katherine Park, 'Cadden, Laqueur and "The One-Sex Body"', *Medieval Feminist Forum* 46 (2010), pp. 96–100, and Helen King, *The One-Sex Body on Trial: The Classical and Early-Modern Evidence* (Farnham: Ashgate, 2013).

23 See discussion in Jacques Le Rider, *Freud, de l'Acropole au Sinaï: Le retour à l'antiquité des modernes viennois* (Paris: Presses universitaires de France, 2002), p. 54.

24 Ibid., p. 63.

25 See Joel Black, 'The aesthetics of gender: Zeuxis' maidens and the hermaphroditic ideal', *New York Literary Forum* 8–9 (1981), pp. 189–209. See also Cicero, *De Inventione*, 2.1 and Pliny, *Natural History*, 35.64.

26 Winckelmann's words come from the second, posthumous edition of his *History* published in 1776 and his 1767 volume *Monumenti antici inediti* (*Unpublished Ancient Monuments*). Since the former has not been translated since the nineteenth century and the latter has never been fully translated into English, I have used Catriona MacLeod's clear and accurate renderings: see Catriona MacLeod, *Embodying Ambiguity: Androgyny and Aesthetics from Winckelmann to Keller* (Detroit: Wayne State University Press, 1998), pp. 30–1, 41, which underpins the account given here of androgyny in late eighteenth- and early nineteenth-century German writing. On Winckelmann's interest in hermaphroditism, see also Alex Potts, *Flesh and the Ideal: Winckelmann and the Origins of Art History* (New Haven/London: Yale University Press, 2000), p. 166.

27 MacLeod, *Embodying Ambiguity*, pp. 46–52.

28 Ibid., p. 54.

29 Ibid., p. 74.

30 Ibid., p. 51.

31 Ibid., p. 59.

32 Ibid., pp. 59–61.
33 Whitney Davis, 'Homoerotic art collections from 1750 to 1920', *Art History* 24:2 (2001), p. 270. Quotations from Famin and Barré are on pp. 269, 271.
34 Whitney Davis, *Queer Beauty*, p. 72. See William Hamilton and Richard Payne Knight, *An Account of the Remains of the Worship of Priapus, Lately Existing at Isernia, in the Kingdom of Naples: In Two Letters; One from Sir William Hamilton, K.B. His Majesty's Minister at the Court to Naples, to Sir Joseph Banks, Bart. President of the Royal Society; and the other from a Person Residing at Isernia: To Which Is Added, A Discourse on the Worship of Priapus, and Its Connexion with the Mystic Religion of the Ancients, by R. P. Knight, esq.* (London: T. Spilsbury, 1786), p. 26.
35 Hamilton and Payne Knight, *An Account*, p. 29.
36 Ibid., p. 174.
37 Ibid., p. 175. Payne Knight does not accent the Greek words here.
38 Ibid., p. 74.
39 Ibid., pp. 81–2.
40 Ibid., p. 74.
41 Bowlby, *Freudian Mythologies*, pp. 134.
42 Quotations given here come from *SE* 12, pp. 342–4.
43 References to Freud's Medusa paper can be found at *SE* 18, pp. 273–4.
44 For other comments on the hero/villain dichotomy in scholarly histories of sexology, see Chiara Beccalossi, *Female Sexual Inversion: Same-Sex Desires in Italian and British Sexology, c. 1870–1920* (Basingstoke: Palgrave Macmillan, 2012), pp. 14–15. On Freud's complicated reception, see Appignanesi and Forrester, *Freud's Woman*, pp. 455–74. On psychoanalysis and queer theory, see Tim Dean and Christopher Lane (eds), *Homosexuality and Queer Theory* (Chicago: Chicago University Press, 2001).
45 The title of the introduction of Simon Goldhill, *Victorian Culture and Classical Antiquity: Art, Opera, Fiction, and the Proclamation of Modernity* (Princeton: Princeton University Press, 2011), pp. 1–19.

INDEX

Milton Keynes UK
Ingram Content Group UK Ltd.
UKHW052325250324
439894UK00010B/248